Chasing Mallory's Dream

Chasing Mallory's Dream

The Race between Britain and Germany to Climb the Himalayan Peaks

EDWARD MORGAN

BODLEIAN
LIBRARY
PUBLISHING

First published in 2026 by Bodleian Library Publishing
Broad Street, Oxford OX1 3BG
www.bodleianshop.co.uk

ISBN 978 1 85124 661 8

PUBLISHER Samuel Fanous
MANAGING EDITOR Susie Foster
EDITOR Janet Phillips
PICTURE EDITOR Leanda Shrimpton
COVER DESIGN by Dot Little at the Bodleian Library
DESIGNED & TYPESET by Lucy Morton of illuminati in 10.2 on 14 Sabon
PRINTED & BOUND by Livonia Print, Latvia,
on 115 gsm Munken Print White paper

EU GPSR Authorised Representative Logos Europe,
9 rue Nicolas Poussin, 17000, La Rochelle, France Contact@logoseurope.eu

British Library Catalogue in Publishing Data
A CIP record of this publication is available from the British Library

Contents

PREFACE

Dreaming of high places

My home town Abingdon, on the meandering River Thames, is far from anything even the British would call a mountain. The French, Germans and Italians consider the whole of Britain fairly flat – 1,400-metre Ben Nevis would barely be a foothill in the Alps – but they admire the achievements of our climbers. In 1978, when I was 14, I came across Chris Bonington's *Everest the Hard Way* in a small bookshop in Abingdon. I devoured the story of the first ascent of Everest's hardest route, and an interest – almost an obsession – with Himalayan climbing was born. Soon I'd read the few mountaineering books in the local library, so I bought what I could afford in second-hand shops, including Blackwells bookshop in nearby Oxford, across the road from the historic Bodleian Library. I read about the early Everest expeditions and Maurice Herzog's *Annapurna*, telling of the epic first ascent of an 8,000-metre peak.

Then in a school jumble sale I found *Nanga Parbat Adventure* by Fritz Bechtold. I have no idea who donated it; perhaps some pupil's grandparents no longer wanted it. It tells the story of one of the most dramatic Himalayan expeditions, the 1934 German attempt on Nanga Parbat. It is a beautifully illustrated book with spectacular actions shots of climbers on broken glaciers and awe-inspiring ridges, but what struck me most was the swastika flag draped over a pile of equipment. I realized that Hitler had come to power the year before, and that the historic context can fundamentally shape an activity like mountaineering. I did not know it then, but there is much that is not told in Bechtold's book, which ignores the bitter conflicts within the team, the murky politics of German mountaineering and the reckless way the lives of Sherpas were put at risk. Nor did I realize the book's importance as a propaganda tool to promote a certain image of the nation's climbers to the German public.

I had already inherited a love of mountain walking from my parents, but after reading about Everest, Annapurna and Nanga Parbat I started to see British mountains in a new light, organizing trips with school friends and moving on to scrambling: the middle ground between walking and climbing and a great way of learning to safely navigate steep terrain. With Andrew Robson, later a world-class bridge player, I went to North Wales, staying in youth hostels and in a fortnight bagging every mountain in Snowdonia (Eryri), including classic scrambles like Crib Goch and Tryfan. The next winter, one of the coldest ever recorded, I was back in Snowdonia with another Andrew, Hooton. Whilst our parents worried whether the roads would be cleared in time for us to get back for the school term, we were using ice axes and crampons for the first time and experiencing fantastic snow conditions in the gullies. The summer after, I went to Scotland with both Robson and Hooton, collectively known as 'the Andes', and climbed in the Cuillins and Torridon: fantastic experiences which fermented my desire to explore higher and more distant peaks.

Proximity to places I could climb made me choose to study maths at Nottingham University. I learnt how to use ropes and joined the Mountaineering Club, spending most weekends in the nearby Peak District. I was not a natural technical climber, nor as courageous as some in a sometimes reckless group, but I enjoyed the small but challenging gritstone edges, leaving the hands scraped raw by the rough rock, before hitching back to Nottingham for student parties. But it wasn't quite the savage world of snow and ice that I had read about, and at the end of my first year I took the bus to Chamonix to explore the Alps. I gravitated to the Bar National where English-speaking climbers hang out, and teamed up with an American, whose name I've long forgotten, to attempt Mont Blanc. We were very fit, but very unprepared – we didn't have a rope or any climbing equipment. To save money, we walked all the way from the valley to the Refuge du Gouter, a vertical ascent of nearly 3,000 metres. The normal route crosses the stone-fall-threatened Grand Couloir, but this was dangerous without helmets, so we stayed on the more technical left-hand side. Slowed by long sections of rock climbing and the altitude, we were overtaken by nightfall on a final steep snow slope. I felt terrifyingly alone with a huge drop below, but suddenly we arrived at the hut, which was crowded with climbers planning to start the final ascent to Mont Blanc only a couple of hours later. There were no beds for us, so we squeezed into free spaces on the dining-room floor, where sleep was impossible. My companion didn't have crampons so couldn't go above the hut and I didn't have a head torch, but there was a full moon so I climbed on to the 4,300-metre Dôme du Goûter. In that magical moonlit glacial night I fell in love with alpine climbing. I started going every summer with friends like Charlie Stripp and Howard Lister. Hiring guides was far beyond our means, so we did what we could alone, learning from our mistakes and fellow climbers we met in the alpine huts. Less than ten years later I was looking down on the North Col of Everest from over 7,000 metres.

When I graduated, it was the mid-1980s; Margaret Thatcher's economic policies had driven up unemployment in Britain to the highest levels since the Second World War. Although working in an office felt like going to prison, I had to find a job and decided to apply my mathematical skills in the insurance industry, continuing to climb when I could. Life outside the mountains was very rewarding: I got married (twice) and had five wonderful children, with whom I shared some great mountain experiences. My interest in climbing's rich history never waned, and I realized there was plenty to discover beyond the existing literature. I first focused on the huge South Face of Lhotse, the world's fourth highest mountain, which resisted all attempts for twenty years before it was finally overcome in 1990. The story was tied to the death throes of the Communist regimes of Eastern Europe, and there was a bitter and still unresolved controversy about who actually first succeeded. I found it hard to believe that no one had written a history of this face, especially since those involved were growing older and had fantastic stories which would be lost if not recorded. Learning to write as I had learnt to climb, by a process of trial and error, and meeting some fantastic characters along the way, I wrote a book about the climb: *The Wall of Legends*. A rough self-published version in English led to translated versions by leading publishers in Italy, Ukraine and Russia.

Encouraged by the positive feedback on this book, I started to look into another period which fascinated me, the first serious attempts on the Himalayan peaks between the two world wars. The story is largely one of a competition between the British and the Germans, seen by some as a sporting continuation of the conflict in the trenches. Contemporary books like Bechtold's *Nanga Parbat Adventure*, which I had read enthusiastically forty years earlier, only told of the drama, heroism and tragedy, but not of all the political tensions that lay behind. Today, the account given in Bechtold's book, and many others, like Herzog's *Annapurna*, are open to challenge. I wanted to explore all available sources, including unpublished letters, notes and diaries, to understand not only the key events better, but also what drove these climbers, many of whom were veterans of the First World War, experiencing horrific fighting on opposite sides of the same battles. All combatant nations were traumatized by the horrors of the trenches, but at least the British came out as victors and still had their empire, which included many of the highest mountains in the world. The Germans, for their part, had lost their few overseas 'possessions' and faced anarchy and near civil war as well as hyperinflation and economic collapse. Even before the spectre of Nazi rule appeared, many saw climbing as a way of achieving national renewal. Some Britons also saw Himalayan climbing as a way to boost the country's morale, damaged despite victory in the war. 'Conquering' the summit of Everest could also be a way to make up for Britain's failure to be first to the North and South Poles. The most iconic early Everest pioneer, George Mallory, would perhaps not have fully shared this 'national mission' narrative, but he was happy to go along with it to satisfy his burning desire to succeed, as did others who followed him in chasing what I have called 'Mallory's dream'.

The importance attached to success in the Himalayas led to heavyweight 'siege style' expeditions, with big teams of local porters helping to construct a series of camps under the direction of autocratic leaders. When the Third Reich arrived it poisoned German climbing. The propagandists thought spectacular ascents showed supposedly heroic national characteristics, encouraging some to ever greater risks. Jack Longland, one of the leading British climbers between the wars, pointed out that mountaineering grew because it is 'a form of organized cowardice, an art of getting up ... dangerous terrain with the minimum risk',[1] and that 'alpine climbing ... developed as a decorous and gentlemanly sport, admittedly with the spice of risk'. Howard and I were not always decorous and gentlemanly, but we did graduate towards the organized cowardice model of climbing, accumulating a substantial haul of Alpine peaks and higher mountains further afield. Longland went on to contrast most mountaineering with climbing Everest, which he likened to fighting a war. For me, and many others like me, it is not too difficult to find reasons why we climb: the physical challenge, the spectacular scenery and the satisfaction of overcoming potentially dangerous situations without taking excessive risks. When, at the age of 59, I used the fixed ropes to climb two 6,000-metre peaks in Nepal, I looked across onto the giants of Everest and Lhotse. For the pioneering Himalayan climbers of the 1920s and 1930s the question we should be asking is not 'why did they climb?', but why were they drawn to this extremely risky form of climbing, spending months away from home and loved ones, with what leading 1930s climber Frank Smythe admitted was inevitable 'discomfort, doubt, anxiety and weariness'[2] and a significant chance of not returning. How much were their motivations driven by the troubled period they lived through, and their own experiences of war?

The 1920s and 1930s are one of the richest periods in mountaineering history, full of drama, tragedy and larger-than-life characters, but it is also a period when national rivalries and politics had an unhealthy impact on climbing. When I proposed exploring this theme to Bodleian Library Publishing, they were very enthusiastic. So I returned to my roots in Oxford to work in one of the oldest libraries in the world, using their fantastic archives to explore the unseen side of this period. Understanding this is particularly relevant in 2026, with nationalism on the rise in much of the world, threatening peace, stability and our ability to cooperate to overcome existential threats to our species and the planet on which we live.

ONE

Going strong

Knowing what we know now, Noel Odell's climb on Everest in 1924 was extraordinary: he went alone to Camp VI at 8,200 metres, and he did it twice within the space of three days with rudimentary equipment and hardly using oxygen. A climb like this is unusual even today: 8,000-metre peaks are climbed regularly, even by quite inexperienced mountaineers, but the vast majority of ascents benefit from artificial oxygen, Sherpa support, fixed ropes and one hundred years' experience of high-altitude climbing.

What continues to fascinate people today was what Odell saw during his first climb to Camp VI. The son of a vicar from the Isle of Wight and his Canadian wife, Odell was 33 at the time, having studied geology at Imperial College and Cambridge. Despite being close to gaining the highest altitude yet reached by man, his profession caused him to take a detour to study Everest's geology. The summit had been visible when he left Camp V, but then a bank of cloud rolled in, although brightness above made Odell think the summit might be clear. At close to 8,000 metres he reached a 30-metre-high cliff. It could have been circumvented, but Odell, a talented rock climber who had made solo first ascents in Snowdonia, decided to tackle it direct to test his condition. As he reached the top, a sudden clearing of the mists allowed him to see the summit pyramid of Everest, and on it two figures reaching the top of a rock step, 'going strong'. In the small window in the clouds, Odell was not able to determine which of the two steps on the North-East

Ridge they were on, but he had no doubt the figures were George Mallory and Sandy Irvine, making a final attempt to reach the summit. The clouds closed in again, and Odell lost sight of the pair, whom he was supporting by bringing a load of fresh provisions to Camp VI, from where Mallory and Irvine had left that morning. They seemed to be behind schedule, but when Odell saw them he considered they were moving upwards expeditiously.

Odell continued up to Camp VI, where he placed his load. Since it had started to snow, he took shelter in the tent, where he found pieces of oxygen apparatus lying around, suggesting that Irvine, much more of an engineer than the impractical Mallory, had been doing last-minute fixes before they set out. Odell continued a little further towards the summit, hoping to see his teammates, and whistling and yodelling, but there was no answer from the clouds above. Since there was only space for two people at Camp VI, Odell went all the way back down to Camp IV on the North Col, where he was greeted by John de Vars Hazard. That evening and the next morning Hazard and Odell scanned the upper part of the mountain in vain for signs of the summit pair. At midday Odell started back up again, accompanied by two Sherpas. After spending the night at Camp V, Odell couldn't rouse the Sherpas to continue upwards, so went alone, trying to use a spare oxygen set he had found, but finding it of so little benefit that he turned it off. Camp VI was unchanged from two days earlier, with no sign of Mallory and Irvine. Now very worried about their fate, Odell spent two hours looking for them on the upper part of Everest, which he called 'the remotest and least hospitable spot on earth'.[1] Realizing the chance of finding them was very small in the vast expanse of rock and snow, he returned to Camp VI. With great difficulty he dragged two sleeping bags out onto a patch of snow to make a 'T' to Hazard far below on the North Col: the agreed signal that his search had been fruitless. Before setting off back down, Odell looked up at the summit above, feeling it 'seemed to look down with cold indifference on me, mere puny man, and howl derision

Mallory and Irvine preparing to leave Camp IV on the North Col before their final attempt to reach the summit in 1924.

in wind-gusts at my petition to yield up its secret – this mystery of my friends'.[2] Mallory and Irvine never returned.

The death of friends was not a new experience for Noel Odell, like almost the whole team a veteran of the First World War, where 'death had been the backdrop of their lives'.[3] The impact of these horrific experiences varied: some suffered depression and the anxiety of what was called shell shock, but which today would be recognized as post-traumatic stress disorder (PTSD); others became battle-hardened and strangely insensitive to death. Not long after the loss of Mallory and Irvine was accepted, Odell's diary was referring to 'a lovely a.m.' and 'a glorious walk down good moraine track'.[4] The expedition leader, Edward Norton, wrote how 'from the first we accepted the loss of our comrades in that rational spirit which all of our generation had learnt in the Great War, and there was never any tendency to a morbid harping on the irrevocable.'[5]

Back in Britain, by contrast, there was an outpouring of grief: King George V sent condolences to the families, and at a memorial service in their home town of Birkenhead the Bishop of Chester spoke of how the climb would help men 'to enter more deeply, more reverently, into the spirit of the mountaineer'.[6] With their death, the greatest mystery in climbing was born: had Mallory and Irvine made it to the highest point on earth before perishing? The bishop spoke of how 'that last ascent, with the beautiful mystery of its great Enigma, stands for more than a heroic effort to climb a mountain'.[7] The public, in Britain and globally, was captivated by the story and there were countless theories about what had happened. The reaction of the British newspapers was often jingoistic: *The Smethwick Telephone* was 'thrilled at the noble death of Mr. Mallory and Mr. Irvine ... [who] had that unquenchable determination of the true Britisher'.[8] For climbers, particularly those of two competing nations, Britain and Germany, the problem of ascending Everest or one of the other Himalayan giants remained the holy grail for the next twenty-five years, and – as for Arthur and his knights – the quest was in some ways more important than its completion.

The third pole

Ever since the birth of mountaineering as a sport, people have aspired to reach the highest summits. Once it was identified as the tallest in the world in the mid-nineteenth century, the ultimate goal was naturally Everest, but other really high peaks had almost the same appeal. By the end of that century all Alpine peaks had been climbed, and prominent figures in British mountaineering were campaigning for an attempt on Everest. India was still part of the British Empire and contained a significant part of the Himalayas, but Everest lies on the border between Nepal and Tibet, meaning permission was required to approach it. Nepal had been completely closed to foreigners since the mid-nineteenth century, so the only realistic prospect was to pass through Tibet. Whilst there was a clear nationalistic undertone to many early expeditions, it was individuals, societies and clubs who organized them, rather than national governments. The first difficulty for climbers was persuading Britain's India Office to even ask the Tibetans for permission. Since the 1830s Britain had been involved in a diplomatic and military rivalry with the Russian Empire for influence in Central Asia, referred to as the

'Great Game', a term popularized in Rudyard Kipling's novel *Kim*. Tibet was a sensitive topic for the India Office because it served as a buffer between India and Russian Central Asia.

In 1893, on a polo field in Northwest India not far from the Khyber Pass, two young British Army officers, both highly colourful characters in different ways, conceived a plan to attempt Everest. Francis Younghusband, 30 at the time, was born to a military family in British India and had already carried out some daring exploratory voyages in Central Asia. He was a spiritual character, with esoteric religious beliefs, including that supernatural extraterrestrials lived on other planets. Charles Granville Bruce was three years younger and much more down to earth, with huge energy – he was an enthusiastic boxer and ran for England against France in an athletics meeting – and a love of practical jokes and bawdy humour. As the son of Baron Aberdare, Bruce had a privileged childhood – every Wednesday in London they had 'At Homes' with footmen in knee breeches – but he was more in his element at the family home in Wales, roaming the hills, hunting and chasing down poachers. At school Bruce read books about hunting in India and developed a passion for the country. It was natural that, after completing military college, he was posted to the Gurkha Rifles in India. The Gurkhas are Nepalese mercenary soldiers in the British Army. Bruce learnt Nepalese and took a profound interest in their welfare. Bruce had already climbed in the Alps and took his love of mountains to India, introducing the sport of hill running, at which the Gurkhas excelled. His rapport with the locals was to prove invaluable in early Himalayan expeditions.

Both Bruce and Younghusband played important parts in the Everest story, but it was nearly thirty years before their idea could be put into action. Bruce was involved in many early Himalayan expeditions, but it was Younghusband who made the first step forward in the Everest project, via a military operation in the Great Game. Lord Curzon, the Viceroy of India, suspected the Russians of influencing the Tibetan government, and when they showed unwillingness to conduct trade negotiations he sent a mission to

Lhasa led by Younghusband. His force included 3,000 well-armed soldiers, and it was inevitable that casualties were high among the opposing Tibetans, mainly poorly trained and ill-equipped peasants, many wearing amulets which they believed would protect them in battle. Younghusband's mission reached Lhasa in 1904 and imposed a treaty on the Tibetans. Following this, Cecil Rawling and another officer surveyed large parts of Tibet and observed Everest from a long distance. Rawling wrote of 'a glittering pyramid of snow ... remarkable not only on account of its height, but for its perfect form'.[9] An expedition was proposed for 1907, to commemorate the fiftieth anniversary of the Alpine Club, but was blocked by the Secretary of State for India, who believed that going into Tibet might upset the balance of the Great Game. In 1908 Bruce's proposal of an expedition through Nepal was also thwarted by political objections, and in 1913 Rawling's plans for an expedition through Tibet came to nothing because of the outbreak of the First World War.

Only a month after the Armistice, the president of the Royal Geographical Society wrote to the Secretary of State for India, requesting permission to attempt Everest. By then Cecil Rawling was dead, killed by German shellfire during the Battle of Passchendaele. Initially there was no reply, and it took a lecture at the Society by a member of Rawling's proposed team, John Noel, to generate momentum for the idea. Whilst serving in the British Army in India, Noel had made a clandestine journey into Tibet with the hope of approaching Everest. The maps he used turned out to be hopelessly wrong and he faced opposition from hostile Tibetan officials, but he still arrived closer than any westerner previously. Noel had been part of the British Expeditionary Force that had retreated towards the sea in the face of a much larger German army in August 1914. He had been taken prisoner and managed to escape, but not before being reported 'believed killed' in *The Times*. Despite suffering shell shock, he returned to serve throughout the war. When Noel spoke to the Society of honouring Rawling's 'lamented death' by climbing Everest, which 'now that the poles have been reached ... is generally felt ...

[to be] the next and equally important task',[10] his call was taken up by those attending. Francis Younghusband declared that 'we are all determined that it shall be a British expedition'.

It took a great deal of lobbying and persuasion before permission was received from the Tibetans in late 1920. Everest was seen as both a mountaineering and an exploratory goal; so two venerable British institutions, the Royal Geographical Society (RGS) and the Alpine Club, formed an uneasy partnership to organize expeditions via a joint Mount Everest Committee, with Younghusband as president. There were disagreements from the beginning. Percy Farrar of the Alpine Club thought an expedition should include Marcel Kurz, a talented Swiss climber, but he soon understood that 'the Geographical people are very intent ... [on it] being purely British'.[11] The first resolution of the Committee stated that the personnel 'be British subjects, and that no applications ... of non-British subjects'[12] should be entertained, although in the days of the Empire that did not exclude Australians, Canadians and New Zealanders from participating. The belief that Himalayan climbing was a national activity endured for many years, with regrettable consequences.

Rongbuk

Two expeditions were planned: a reconnaissance in 1921 and then a full attempt the following year. The reconnaissance was led by Charles Howard-Bury, who was not an active climber but had done a lot to lobby for permission from the Tibetans, had travelled extensively in India and, importantly for the Committee, which was perennially short of funds, had enough private wealth to meet his own expenses. His team only had four climbers; two of these, Alexander Kellas and Harold Raeburn, were well over 50. Kellas, a Scottish chemist, was one of the most experienced Himalayan climbers of the day, having made seven independent expeditions, climbing a number of high peaks and being the first to recognize the potential of the Sherpa people as mountain porters. However, he was ill before they set out, and died of heart failure during the march across Tibet towards Everest. He was buried on a hillside with views of three peaks which he had been the first to climb.

Raeburn was also unwell, and it was decided he should return to Sikkim, the Indian state from where they had entered Tibet. This left only two dedicated climbers, but crucially one of these was George Mallory, an inspirational figure, forever associated with Everest. The son of a vicar, Mallory was born in 1886 and had a comfortable upper-middle-class upbringing, winning a scholarship to Winchester College, where he was introduced to climbing by one of the masters. He studied history at Cambridge and became friends with intellectuals and writers like poet Rupert Brooke and economist John Maynard Keynes. Good looking, charming and with an artistic sensibility, Mallory was nicknamed Galahad by influential mountaineer Geoffrey Winthrop Young. After finishing his studies, Mallory drifted for a year, unsure of what career to follow, before taking a job as a teacher at Charterhouse. He continued to climb and was elected to the Alpine Club. He got married just before the outbreak of the First World War. Teaching was a protected occupation, so Mallory did not need to fight, but this made him feel guilty, especially after the death of friends like Brooke. Eventually he persuaded his headmaster to let him enlist, was commissioned as an officer and fought in the Battle of the Somme. As for so many others, the experience deeply marked him and he returned restless and dissatisfied, interested in liberal politics, education theory and the League of Nations and wanting to do something more meaningful with his life than teaching at a traditional public school. The chance to go to Everest filled a gap created by the trauma of the trenches.

The only other dedicated climber in the 1921 team was Guy Bullock, a schoolfriend and climbing partner of Mallory, but fortunately the professional surveyors in the team were also very competent climbers. One of them, Henry Morshead, had been to over 7,000 metres on an expedition with Kellas the previous year. After a long arduous voyage across the windswept and cold plateau of Tibet, they arrived close to Everest and divided up to explore and survey the largely unknown area. Mallory and Bullock headed into the

Camp IV on the North Col and the view to the North-East Shoulder of Everest in 1922.

Rongbuk Valley, which contains an important Buddhist monastery and leads up to the North Face of Everest. Some way beyond the monastery they set up a base camp. The Rongbuk is not a classic high mountain valley with dramatic peaks visible all around, nor with the graceful lines of a Matterhorn or an Ama Dablam, but it does have Everest filling the end of the valley, massive and solid like a Romanesque cathedral. It is a place I know well: in 1990 I spent three weeks there as part of an expedition attempting the 7,500-metre north peak of Everest, Changtse. When the sun is out and the wind is low, Base Camp is a pleasant place, but it can also feel bleak, windy and cold, particularly before the body has adapted to being at 5,000 metres.

The 1921 team explored the eastern and northern approaches to Everest, but nearly missed the route which was later used for almost all attempts from Tibet. Mallory had quickly evaluated that the North Face as too difficult, but saw that if the 7,000-metre high North Col on its left-hand side could be reached, then there was a viable route up the North Ridge to its junction with the North-East Ridge, which could be followed to the summit. The western side of the North Col looked tricky, but Mallory suspected the eastern side could be easier angled and a viable route. Despite being given a map made by one of the surveyors, correctly showing that the east side rose from a tributary valley of the Rongbuk, Mallory was convinced it drained into the Kharta Valley, to the east of Everest. The error is understandable: the side valley of the East Rongbuk Glacier leading up to the North Col contains only a modest stream, seemingly too small to drain a large glacier, but this is because Tibet is extremely dry and most snow evaporates directly rather than melting and flowing down in streams. Mallory only understood his error late in the expedition, but by then he had already reached the North Col following a longer route from the Kharta Valley.

The first attempt on Everest

Mallory held a vague ambition to attempt the summit in 1921 and wanted to continue above the North Col, but his companions were cold and eager to get down. The 1921 expedition was successful in identifying a viable route and was always intended to be followed by a full attempt in 1922. Fatigued by the months of travelling and discomfort, and missing his adored wife Ruth and his children, Mallory was initially uncertain about his participation in the full expedition, but a burning ambition to climb Everest had been born in him, and inevitably he agreed to join the 1922 attempt. The only other person returning was the surveyor Henry Morshead, who was now selected as a climber. The first action of the Committee was to replace Howard-Bury with Charles Bruce, always viewed as the natural leader for a full attempt. Bruce finally got the chance to try to realize the plan he had conceived on that polo field nearly thirty years earlier. Now in his mid-fifties, Bruce had risen to the rank of brigadier general; in the First World War he had commanded a

Gurkha battalion at Gallipoli, where he had been severely wounded. He had put on weight and chose to walk a lot in the warm valleys of Sikkim at the start of the approach march, 'expressing the probable advantage to his figure of profuse perspiration'.[13] Even sweating off a bit of weight, General Bruce was unlikely to go high on Everest, but he remained an inspirational and very experienced leader.

Arguably the strongest 'British' climber of the day was not of British origin, although he spent most of his life there. George Finch was born in Australia to second-generation immigrants, before coming to Europe with his family when he was 14. He went to university at the prestigious ETH in Zurich and climbed incessantly in the Alps. Some of the Alpine Club members of the Mount Everest Committee, particularly Percy Farrar, saw Finch as one of Europe's best snow and ice climbers and an obvious choice for Everest. However, he was unpopular with others, particularly the pushy secretary Arthur Hinks of the RGS. Finch had been rejected from the 1921 team following a medical exam, a decision which many felt was suspicious, but in 1922 he passed. There were others who would prove to be very strong additions to the team, such as Howard Somervell and Edward Norton, very tough men, hardened by the horrific experience of the war. Somervell was a medical student when the war started and signed up in 1915, spending the rest of the war operating on 'a constant stream of dying and mutilated men'.[14]

Deputy leader Edward Strutt had plenty of experience, but usually climbed in a traditional style and with local alpine guides. The Committee's requirement for all members to be 'British subjects' meant that alpine guides could not be brought to Everest, although this, of course, did not apply to the Nepalese and Tibetan porters, without whom it would have been impossible to transport all the equipment considered necessary to attempt the mountain. From an aristocratic background, Strutt had studied at Innsbruck University, where he started climbing with his Austrian governess. Considered a hero for rescuing the Austrian Emperor Charles from a revolutionary mob at the end of the First World War, he was a pompous and opinionated man: when he left the expedition before its third and

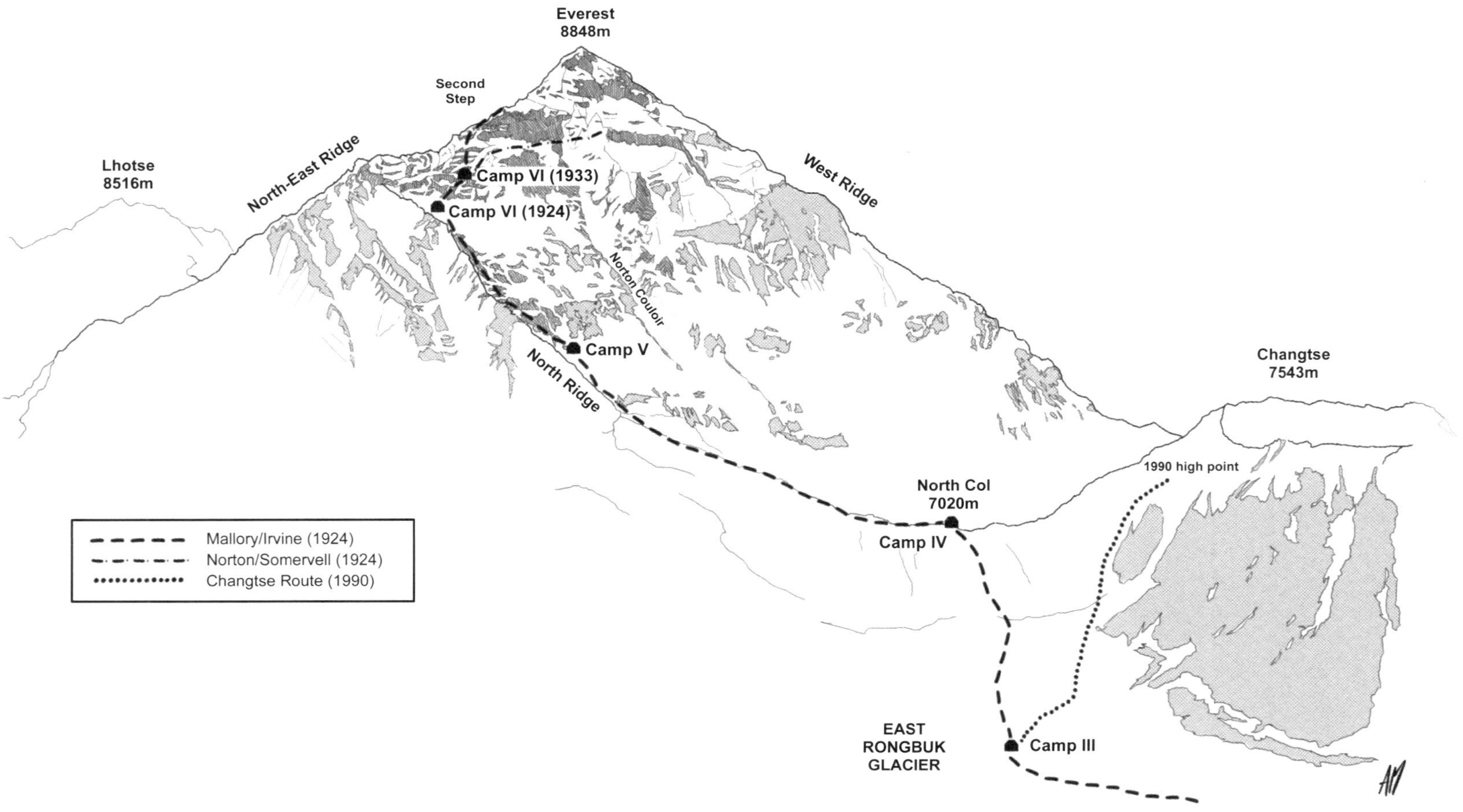
Everest
8848m
Second
Step
Lhotse
8516m
North-East Ridge
Camp VI (1933)
Camp VI (1924)
West Ridge
Norton Couloir
Camp V
North Ridge
Changtse
7543m
1990 high point
North Col
7020m
Camp IV
EAST
RONGBUK
GLACIER
Camp III
Mallory/Irvine (1924)
Norton/Somervell (1924)
Changtse Route (1990)

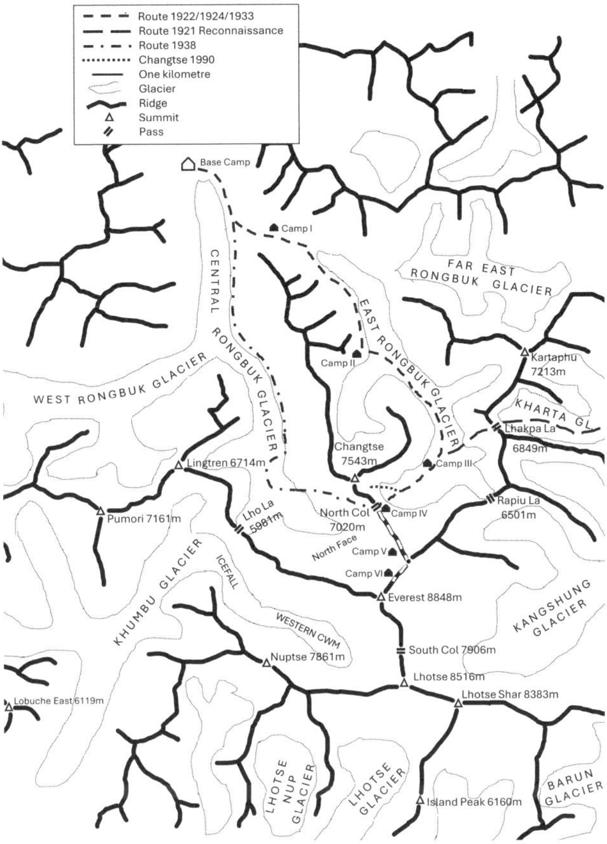

Everest North Face route.

Everest map.

final summit attempt, Bruce was glad to be rid of him. Strutt later came to exemplify the stubborn resistance to change of the Alpine Club establishment, something which hampered the development of British mountaineering in the 1930s. The much more forward-looking Tom Longstaff was the expedition's official medic, even though there were two other doctors in the team. After qualifying, Longstaff had never practised, and told the team they should not seek or rely on his professional advice, but that he would be 'willing, if necessary, to sign a certificate of death'.[15]

There was much discussion about whether to use artificial oxygen high on the mountain. Alexander Kellas had wanted to test its use

George Mallory and Edward Norton approach their highest point of 8,120 metres on Everest in 1922.

in 1921, but after his death these experiments were never carried out. Finch was a professional scientist, something which set Strutt against him: after seeing a photo of Finch repairing his own boots, Strutt remarked, 'I always knew the fellow was a shit.'[16] Whatever the snobbish Strutt may have thought, Finch's skills were very useful, and he was put in charge of the oxygen equipment in 1922. The question of whether to use it became very divisive within the Mount Everest Committee and the team. Some, including Mallory, saw oxygen as unsporting and even un-British, and their cause was taken up by the anti-Finch Hinks, who took a very strong anti-oxygen position, even publishing a long article on its faults in the *Geographical Journal* whilst the expedition was in Tibet.

From Base Camp, the team went up the East Rongbuk Glacier to the foot of the North Col, from where the more serious climbing started. They were using what Tom Longstaff called 'the polar method', where camps were set quite short stages apart, reflecting the distance that could be comfortably walked by heavily laden porters. The polar reference was to Scott's doomed Antarctic expedition, but, as Isserman and Weaver pointed out in their history of Himalayan climbing, it was much more an 'articulation of the Great War mentality; in laying siege to Everest in this way, the expedition established a military model for Himalayan mountaineering that lasted half a century'.[17] To simplify logistical planning, the camps were numbered Camp I, Camp II and so on, a system universally used to this day. Three camps were made up to the foot of the North Col. Our team went the same way in 1990. We had the advantage of having yaks rather than porters to carry our equipment, allowing us to move all we needed in a single trip; the 1922 team had to work with a large team of porters over several weeks to stock their camps. Although the height gain is only gradual to the foot of the North Col, it was hard work for us on the rough, stony and undulating glacier, especially since we weren't full acclimatized. I was initially going well after leaving Base Camp, but we had studied the classic accounts of the 1920s expeditions and were heading up the left-hand side of the glacier. By 1990 the commonly followed route was on the right side and after a few hours we saw the yaks, which were carrying our sleeping bags and tents, on the other side. I was suffering from the altitude and found it a terrible struggle to cross the glacier to reach our camp. I doubted I could go much further, but the next day I felt much better, and progress was faster thanks to the flatter central moraine, which forms a trough-like pathway through the huge ice towers of the glacier.

The site of the British Camp III, our Advanced Base Camp in 1990, is spectacular: after the mainly stone-coloured vistas of the East Rongbuk Glacier, whiteness dominates in the glacier bowl formed by Changtse and Everest. The route to Everest heads to the North Col, the pass between these two peaks, whereas our intended route up Changtse was on the right. In 1922 Mallory and Somervell made the route up to the North Col, where a large team of porters carried loads to establish Camp IV. Up to this point the

British had been able to rely on the experience of previous ascents of 7,000-metre peaks, but from the North Col onwards they were on completely new ground, both literally and physiologically. They did not appreciate the scale of the challenge: Mallory believed that the summit could be climbed with only one intermediate camp, which vastly overestimated the speed at which they could gain height at very high altitudes.

The 8,000-metre barrier is breached

Above the North Col the route up the North Ridge towards its junction with the North-East Ridge is initially straightforward climbing, but as Mallory, Norton, Somervell and Morshead headed up with a group of porters to place Camp V they were fully exposed to a bitter wind blowing across the North Face. Suffering from the cold and thin air, they could only find an unsatisfactory place to camp on a series of ledges, other options being even steeper and rockier. They sent the porters back down and spent the night at 7,600 metres, higher than any human had been before: indeed, Camp IV on the North Col at 7,000 metres was already higher than anyone had camped before. The four men were already tired, did not sleep much and had some frostbite. Before setting off in the morning, a rucksack was dropped down the slope below. Morshead descended 30 metres to retrieve it, and by the time he returned he was too tired to go on. Mallory, Norton and Somervell left him at the camp and continued. They were initially able to gain 130 metres an hour, but slowed as they got higher, with tempers fraying and all three feeling edgy. Around midday they became the first people in history to cross the 8,000-metre contour, passing into what has subsequently been named the 'Death Zone'. They climbed on for another couple of hours, but all then agreed on the need to turn around. They stopped in the shelter of a rock, had something to eat, made a sketch and took some photos.

They were far from being within reach of the summit, but it was a fantastic achievement to reach 8,120 metres, breaking the altitude record by more than 700 metres. They returned to Camp V, picked up Morshead and continued the descent, feeling desperately tired. Mallory accidently took a different line than on the way up, forcing them to cross the top of a steep couloir which swept 1,000 metres down to the glacier below. Norton slipped and pulled the anchorman Somervell off his feet. Morshead managed to hold the rope for a moment and then fell too, but fortunately Mallory had time to dig his axe into the hard snow and held all three men. Much more focused, they continued the descent. The climb had taken a lot out of them and they all had frostbite, the worst affected being Morshead, an extremely tough man with behaviour verging on the masochistic, such as not putting on all his available clothing, despite the extreme cold.

A second attempt was made by George Finch, who had missed out on the first try due to dysentery. Doubting the fitness of the remaining climbers, Finch decided to make his attempt with one of the transport officers, Geoffrey Bruce, a cousin (once removed) of expedition leader Charles. Bruce had no mountaineering experience, but was extremely fit, resourceful and brave. Tejbir Bura, one of several Gurkha non-commissioned officers participating in the expedition, carried a load as far as the North-East shoulder, before descending. Using oxygen, which brought an advantage despite the heavy apparatus, Finch and Bruce passed the height reached by Mallory's team, but at 8,380 metres Bruce suddenly stopped because his set was malfunctioning. It seemed he would fall, but Finch managed to reach and support him, and then made a temporary repair to his equipment. They were still far from the summit when they turned back, but were getting closer. As he descended, Geoffrey Bruce looked back up at Everest and said, 'Just you wait, old thing, you'll be for it soon!'[18]

Climbing on Everest is constrained by the summer monsoon season, which typically arrives around the end of May, bringing storms and making climbing difficult and dangerous. Despite the apparent onset of the monsoon and with half a metre of new snow at Camp III, the obsessively determined Mallory led a new attempt. There was pressure from the Committee back in London, particularly the pushy Hinks, who kept writing letters encouraging further attempts. Mallory headed up to the North Col with Somervell, Colin Crawford and thirteen porters. When conditions are unfavourable, there is a high risk of avalanches on the slope below the North Col. When we arrived at Base Camp in 1990 we learnt that a Spanish expedition had been overwhelmed by an avalanche there a couple of weeks earlier, with two Sherpas and a Spaniard killed. We took grim note: our planned route on Changtse was up an adjacent and similar slope. In 1922 they had to plough a waist-deep trench through the snow, but none of the three British climbers 'had an inkling of danger or thought of an avalanche on such easy slopes'.[19] Some 200 metres below the top there was a sound 'not unlike an explosion of untampered gunpowder',[20] and a large section of the slope avalanched. They were climbing as four separate ropes; the last two of these, comprising nine porters, were swept over an ice cliff and into a crevasse. Despite desperate efforts to dig them out, seven of the porters were killed. The expedition was of course terminated.

The accident illustrated the danger of the North Col. It left the climbers wracked with guilt. Mallory asked his friend Geoffrey Winthrop Young, 'Do you know that sickening feeling that you can't go back and have it undone and nothing will make it good?'[21] Somervell wrote that he would 'gladly at that moment have been lying dead in the snow, if only to give those fine chaps who had survived the feeling that we shared their loss'.[22] Tom Longstaff blamed Bruce for not preventing the third attempt, Hinks and Younghusband for pressing too hard for a summit success, and above all Mallory and Somervell for an 'absence of knowledge of snowcraft'. Longstaff considered the attempt 'idiotic', and asked, 'what the hell did they think they would do on Everest in such conditions even if they did get up to the North Col?' In his view Mallory was 'a stout-hearted baby ... quite unfit to be placed in charge of anything, including himself'.[23]

The invisible engines

The British press did not share Somervell's view on the relative value of European and indigenous life, and there was nothing like the outpouring of grief which would later be seen for Mallory and

Irvine. 'Avalanche kills six coolies. Explorers safe'[24] was a typical headline reporting on the 'lucky' escape of the Europeans, and using the pejorative term for lowly paid Indian labourers. When telling the story of Himalayan climbing, the huge contribution of local porters, who all too often paid with their lives, should never be forgotten. Appendix III illustrates how many of the early climbs to high altitudes were made by porters. Some explanation is needed to understand the origin and role of these brave people, but it would need a whole book to deal properly with this dimension.[25]

There were two different roles, which became more distinct as Himalayan climbing developed. The first was simply porters who carried the equipment of an expedition from the last point that could be reached by mechanized transport to Base Camp, from where the climbing started. Portering is a well-established form of casual labour in mountainous regions, where humans are often the most efficient way to move goods. Men, and sometimes women, could be hired for several weeks, but they might also be local to the area the expedition was moving through, and would only work for a few days. The early Everest expeditions sometimes employed local farmers, but on occasion they simply returned to their farms if conditions became too extreme. The second role was high-altitude porters, who were employed to carry loads to camps on the mountain itself. This meant working in dangerous places, like crevassed glaciers and steep slopes requiring mountaineering ability. They needed to be equipped appropriately, as did all porters when crossing high passes: a number of expeditions overlooked the importance of this or tried to avoid the costs of it. Only in the mid-1930s did British climbers reach the conclusion that 'porters who go high should have just as good equipment as the climbers. Expense should not be spared.'[26] European attitudes towards the local employees often distinguished between the high-altitude workers, who were generally viewed positively and sometimes named in accounts, and the general porters, who were 'often depicted as weak, lazy and craven'.[27]

Many of the expeditions described in this book took place in the north-east of the Indian subcontinent, so it was natural to use

Everest taken by Sandy Irvine from Pang La on 28 April 1924.

porters from this region. The first Everest climbers distinguished between two main groups, Sherpas and Bhotias; but this can be confusing because the Bhotias – which is actually the Chinese word for Tibetan – are a wider ethnic group that includes the Sherpas. Sherpas have been so strongly identified with the work of high-altitude porters that it is a common misunderstanding that being a Sherpa is a profession. The Sherpas are in fact a people, who moved several centuries ago from Tibet to some mountainous areas of Nepal, including the Solu Khumbu, on the south side of Everest. There is also an important Sherpa community in Darjeeling in India, where the first Sherpa porters were recruited. Increasingly, many Sherpas came from their home villages in the Solu Khumbu to work on expeditions, and there arose a distinction between 'Solu Khumbu men' and the Darjeeling Sherpas. However, because Nepal did not allow Europeans to visit, as late as the 1930s climbers still did not know exactly where or what Solu Khumbu was. For expeditions in the central and western parts of the Himalayas, local porters were usually employed to go to Base Camp, and sometimes for work above. The Sherpas gained such a strong reputation on Everest that expeditions to other areas started employing them too.

Contemporary accounts tend to grate for the twenty-first-century reader, with their flagrant unconscious colonialist bias, such as reference to the 'simple, childlike psychology of the primitive hill people'.[28] Take, for example, books such as Bruce's *The Assault of Mount Everest 1922*, which doesn't even give the names of the local porters who died, and where 'the notion of the superior white man [is] openly on display, along with the mistaken belief that Asians valued life less than Westerners'.[29] Although there is often crude racial stereotyping, it is clear that many of the climbers felt affection for the porters with whom they spent months, often in difficult and dangerous conditions. Indeed, some climbers took considerable interest in the personality and background of their high-altitude porters. Neverthless they always remained to some extent the invisible engines behind expeditions. In a letter to his wife, Francis Younghusband described the 1922 tragedy as 'particularly bad luck', and added 'thank goodness no European life was lost'.[30]

Norton's fantastic climb

Despite the deaths, enthusiasm for the Everest project remained undimmed, with public interest high, boosted by a book, a film and a lecture tour. A new attempt was planned for 1924. Charles Bruce was again the leader and most of the 1922 team returned, but not George Finch, who was already unpopular with some on the Committee. When Finch gave lectures in Germany in 1923, the Committee felt this breached their exclusivity on publicizing the Everest expeditions and demanded a share of his fees. When Finch refused, they sent a solicitor's letter and he became *persona non grata*. Strutt and Longstaff, for their part, had found the 1922 expedition hard and were also not returning. One new team member was Noel Odell, who also recommended the strangest addition to the team – and the one who would become most famous. Andrew ('Sandy') Irvine was a 22-year-old Oxford University student with an incredible physique; a rowing star who was a member of the winning 1923 Boat Race crew. He performed well on an exploratory expedition to Spitsbergen, but had limited mountaineering experience. His inclusion illustrates the shallowness of the pool of candidates considered; social class being more important than climbing credentials.

Before the expedition General Bruce had gone tiger hunting. He 'bagged his tiger, but also picked up malaria';[31] it was soon clear that he was too unwell to continue to Base Camp. Although he was a charismatic and inspirational figure, his replacement by his deputy Norton did not weaken the team. Norton was universally liked and had a way of obtaining sensible consensus decisions, which over time came to be seen as a key attribute for expedition leaders. Hinks had written after the fatal accident in 1922 that 'Mallory's judgement in purely alpine matters was bad and inferior to Norton of whom everyone speaks very highly.'[32] The process by which Norton was selected for the 1922 expedition is not entirely clear, but he was known for his keenness for adventure, having applied to join Shackleton's Polar Expedition in 1914. His grandfather, Alfred Wills, the third president of the Alpine Club, had built a chalet in the French Alps, where Norton and his brothers frequently spent holidays. Norton had not made notable first ascents in the Alps but had often climbed on the mountains near the chalet, where the loose shaly rock was an excellent training ground for the higher slopes of Everest. In his late thirties by the time of the expedition, Norton was a career soldier, with many postings in India and medals for bravery in the First World War.

Learning their lessons from 1922, Norton's team realized that at least two, if not three, camps were needed above the North Col, but bad weather and logistical problems slowed progress. The team found itself strung out over the camps on the East Rongbuk Glacier,

The porters who took loads to Camp VI (8,170 metres) on Everest in 1924. From left to right: Bom, Narbu Yishe, Semchumbi, Lobsang, Lhakpa Chedi, Ang Tenjin.

with the North Col not yet reached. The porters were underequipped and some were seriously ill, which eventually led to the death of one porter and a Gurkha NCO. As in 1922, they did not seem too disturbed by the deaths of the local people, but Norton realized a reset was necessary and ordered the whole team to descend to Base Camp, where they arrived 'a very dirty and bedraggled party'.[33] Before returning up the mountain, the climbers and porters visited the Rongbuk Monastery to be blessed by the head lama, which Norton felt greatly restored the porters' morale. But there was a cost for the team: Irvine noted in his diary that they had eaten meat and macaroni with chopsticks with 'well chewed ends', which led to 'a touch of dysentery ... for sixteen days'.[34]

Worried that the monsoon might start, Norton sent Somervell, Hazard and Irvine to establish Camp IV on the North Col, leaving Hazard there with twelve porters. When the weather turned bad and they were forced to retreat, Hazard arrived back at Camp III with only eight men; the other four were too frightened to follow him down the dangerous slopes of the Col. With little food, the four porters were in a very precarious position and Norton went to the rescue with his two strongest climbers, Somervell and Mallory. Near the top, a delicate traverse led to a ledge, where the porters were waiting. With the avalanche risk high and the fatal accident of 1922 in their minds, Somervell insisted on going ahead. Belayed by Norton and Mallory, he got to within 10 metres of the porters, before running out of rope, meaning the porters had to cross the first tricky section unaided. The first two moved at the same time, and their weight triggered an avalanche, which seemed certain to carry the men to their deaths, but the snow balled up around them and they stopped after 10 metres. Somervell untied himself, reached the porters and dragged them to safety.

The descent to Camp III was difficult and the team was again in a state of disarray, with many climbers and porters exhausted or sick. Then the weather started to improve, allowing attempts on the summit. The first to try were Mallory and Geoffrey Bruce, who made Camp V at a similar height to 1922 and slept there with a team of porters. The next morning there was a strong wind, and they were unable to persuade the porters to climb higher. As they descended, they met Norton and Somervell with another team of porters, going up to make the next attempt.

Given Mallory and Bruce's failure to persuade the four porters to carry to Camp VI, Norton and Somervell knew the importance of motivating the men at Camp V, and in the morning Norton 'turned on his eloquence for a good long time'. It did not help that the afternoon before Norton and Somervell had dislodged stones onto the porters' tent, causing a cut to Lobsang Tashi's head and injuring Semchumbi's knee. Whether it was because of Norton's pep talk or the lead of Lhakpa Chedi, according to Somervell 'a real sportsman with guts',[35] he, Semchumbi and Narbu Yishe agreed to climb to Camp VI with heavy loads. Norton and Somervell's climb is a notable event in climbing history, but it would not have happened without the contribution of these three porters, the first locals to go above 8,000 metres. The terrain was fairly easy, but thin air

Edward Norton climbing along towards his high point of nearly 8,600 metres on Everest in 1924.

made it very hard work, especially for Somervell, who was greatly troubled by his throat. They camped at 8,170 metres, and Norton and Somervell sent the porters down, extremely grateful for their fantastic work. Somervell slept soundly, but woke with his throat worse than ever. He and Norton set out, carrying little apart from a flask of coffee, a pocket camera, ice axes and a rope. At first it was quite easy, the weather sunny and nearly windless. An hour beyond the camp they reached the lower edge of a band of sandstone which runs across the whole North Face, the 'Yellow Band', which allowed them to progress more easily on broad ledges. Norton was not wearing goggles because they interfered with his vision and most of the climbing was on rocks, but with the extremely bright high-altitude light this was a mistake and he started to have trouble with his eyes, sometimes seeing double.

Norton found their pace 'wretchedly' slow: he tried to make twenty steps before resting, but never managed more than about thirteen. Somervell was coughing badly and eventually told Norton that his only chance of the summit was to go on alone. Leaving Somervell on rocks, Norton headed for the big couloir, which crosses the face and now bears his name. It was filled with powdery snow, Norton sinking in up to his knees or even his waist, but not having a secure footing and very aware of the huge drop below. After the couloir, things became worse, and Norton had to depend on the friction of his boot nails on sloping rocks. Having gained 30 metres in height and 100 metres in distance from the point he left Somervell, Norton decided to turn back. The top was only 270 metres higher, but there was no chance of making it and returning safely before nightfall. It was the second time that Norton had turned back very high on Everest, but he did not feel great disappointment, his senses dulled by the altitude, leaving him with little other than relief that he no longer had to struggle uphill. Somervell considered that they were 'beaten in a fair fight'.

Norton's eye problems were getting worse and Somervell dropped his axe. As they continued to descend towards the North Col in the gathering darkness, Somervell had a particularly bad coughing fit, which dislodged something in his throat and prevented him from breathing. They had taken the rope off and Norton was ahead, so Somervell had no chance to make a sign to him and was sure he would die, before managing to remove the obstacle by pushing on his chest with both hands. He felt intense pain and coughed up blood, but could breathe and continue his descent. The pair reached Camp IV, where Odell, Mallory and Irvine welcomed them with oxygen and hot drinks.

Galahad and Percival of Everest

In their shared tent, Mallory explained to Norton that he wanted to make a final attempt, this time with oxygen. Mallory had been part of the anti-oxygen, anti-Finch faction in 1922, but was now willing to use it to realize his obsessive dream. Mallory was poor

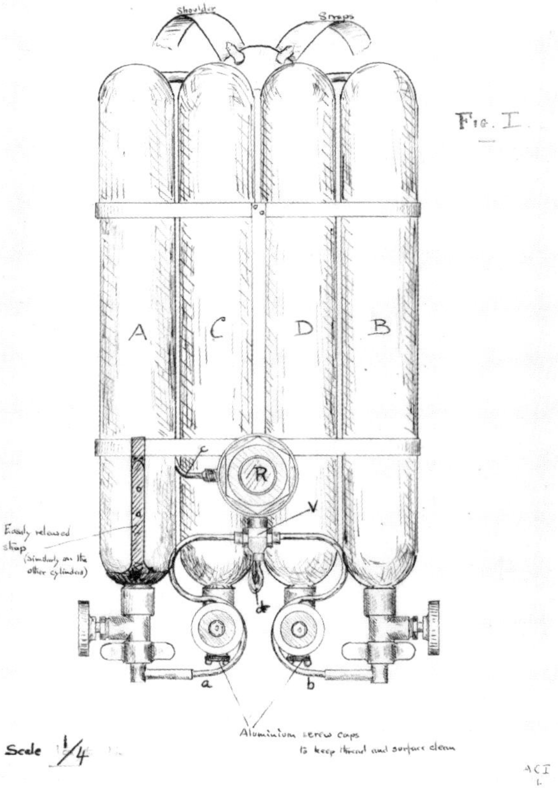

Diagram of oxygen cylinder by Sandy Irvine.

with technology and needed to partner with someone familiar with the equipment, which meant either Noel Odell or Sandy Irvine. Why he chose Irvine over the much more experienced Odell has been analysed repeatedly, with theories even including a romantic attraction on the part of Mallory to the handsome young Irvine. That the two became friendly is clear: Irvine's diary initially refers to everyone by their surnames, then at a certain point starts referring to Mallory as George. But there seems to be no evidence for anything more between them, and whilst Mallory had had homosexual experiences as a student at Cambridge before later marrying, Irvine seemed to be unquestionably heterosexual. The truth is that the choice was not that surprising: they had discussed a number of different permutations of summit teams during the expedition and Irvine's name had often been included. In his last letter to his mother, Irvine had reported that he was considered the second fittest climber after Geoffrey Bruce, and was a natural choice to accompany an experienced climber.

Irvine was born in 1902 and of a different generation to all the other climbers. The closest in age was Geoffrey Bruce, born in 1896; none of the others were born later than 1890. Significantly, this meant that Irvine was the only one who had not fought in the war. In the extensive literature about the 1924 Everest expedition Sandy Irvine tends to be presented as a rather one-dimensional figure, 'an uncomplicated young man of almost unshakable good humour',[36] in contrast to Mallory's far more complex character. He is painted as the stereotypical British public schoolboy who is 'good at games', resilient, optimistic and physically strong, but lacking in depth and intellect. Such a view seems largely based on his expedition diary, which does not demonstrate a lot of introspection and uses a somewhat hackneyed vocabulary, describing walks as 'very delightful' and views as 'very pleasant'. When Irvine writes 'I wish I was in the first party instead of a bloody reserve' or 'by God I should like to have a whack at it myself',[37] he sounds like a public-school boy talking about being in a sports team. But a diary is not intended to be a work of literature, and Irvine was recording the events of the voyage often late at night in his tent after a tiring day. By contrast, his letters to his mother, including small pencil illustrations, show curiosity about Tibet and its people.

One of the first comments Mallory made about Irvine on the boat to India was that he would be 'one to depend on, for everything perhaps except conversation'.[38] Mallory was more cultured and articulate, but Irvine's reticence on the boat could have been largely down to shyness, as he seems to have opened up and become friendly with the team in Tibet. Certainly, they were very different: Mallory was a dreamer with literary ambitions, compared to the very practical Irvine, who was by nature an engineer, forever tinkering with the oxygen equipment to improve it and offering to repair everything from ice axes and crampons to stoves and cameras for his teammates.

With this rather one-dimensional portrayal of Irvine's character, historians have focused less on his feelings and motivations and more on how the other climbers saw him. Historian Wade Davis suggests that the older climbers were powerfully drawn to Irvine because 'in some small way he embodied, with his vitality, innocence and limitless possibilities, the reason they had all fought and the future for which so many of their friends had died'.[39] It is also interesting to consider how, even without fighting, Irvine's experience growing up during the war shaped his character. He was attending Shrewsbury, a prestigious public school, on which the war had 'a dislocating effect ... in that boys left at odd times to join up and the casualty lists marked the end of many promising lives'.[40] The Irvine family were hit hard by the death of a favourite cousin, Edward, a 20-year-old medical student, killed at Arras in 1918; and Irvine's elder brother Hugh, having enlisted in 1917, was the following year splattered with mustard gas from a German shell. His wounds, which never properly healed, had to be dressed twice a day for the rest of his life. Despite the disruptions of war, Irvine had a positive experience at Shrewsbury, helped by the presence of Monsignor Ronald Knox, a priest, author and broadcaster, who felt it was his duty to entertain as well as educate the boys. According to Irvine's great niece and biographer Julie Summers, Knox engaged with the younger boys, who he reasoned 'would be going up to university after the war. The older boys he left pretty much to their own devices, reasoning that their next, and probably last, step would be the trenches.'[41]

Young men of Irvine's generation were inevitably affected by the war, but in a different way to those who had fought. The author Christopher Isherwood, who was a couple of years younger than Irvine, wrote that at the end of the war the sixth form 'was still composed of boys who had only just missed being conscripted, potential infantry officers trained to expect the brief violent career of the trenches: they had outgrown their school life long before they left it. And now, suddenly, the universal profession of soldiering was closed to them; and the alternatives seemed vague and dull.'[42] Some found an escape in the hedonism of the Roaring Twenties, but Irvine found a purpose in adventure. Julie Summers thinks he 'felt an obligation not to waste his life and to make the most of any opportunity that was offered him. Hence his enthusiasm for the Spitsbergen expedition of July/August 1923, his passionate embrace of skiing in December/January 1923–4 and of course his thrill at being invited to the Everest Expedition.'[43] The skiing trip to Mürren in Switzerland had been made at Odell's suggestion to gain more experience on snow and ice prior to Everest. There Irvine made a ski tour with a group including Tony Knebworth, the son of the Earl of Lytton and a slight acquaintance from Oxford. Knebworth was a 'a representative figure of ... the generation ... just too young to serve in the war'; he had written to his father that 'my goodness, the war must have brought things really down to bed-rock – but then afterwards the world spends its time in rebuilding all the artificialities'. This feeling of having missed out drove Knebworth to cram as much as he could into a short life: he was a competitive skier and became an MP before he was 30, but was killed in an aviation accident after joining the Royal Auxiliary Air Force. Many in this generation shared Knebworth's desire to make the most of life, but Irvine's determination to seize opportunities went beyond mere enthusiasm: when he was leaving Liverpool he told a journalist that 'it is the duty of the Alpine Club to climb as near as it can to heaven'.[44]

War veterans suffered from a persistent feeling that the country was divided into two distinct Britains: those who had fought and the rest, who did not remotely understand the trauma of what the soldiers had been through. This created a chasm which 'would be a defining reality of British life in the immediate years after the war, a current of memory and distinction flowing beneath the survivors, never spoken about and never forgotten'.[45] But the resentment against what D.H. Lawrence called 'the middle-aged jackals feeding on our death' would not have applied to the generation too young to fight – how could they be blamed for a war which had taken place when they were only children? – and this explains the appeal of Irvine to the rest of the team. His enthusiasm and sense of duty to make the most of opportunities perfectly matched their expectations. If Mallory was Galahad, then Irvine can be seen as Percival, who aged 15 saw Arthur's knights pass through the forest where he lived and, struck by their heroic bearing, begged to join them. Although the youngest of the knights, Percival is one of the last to stay with Galahad in the quest for the Grail.

Norton did not agree with Mallory's choice of Irvine as summit partner, but, exhausted and in pain from the onset of snow blindness, did not attempt to make him change his mind. Mallory and Irvine set off the next day with eight porters, four of whom returned the same evening, reporting that the others were safely ensconced in Camp V. Mallory sent a note for Odell saying 'there is no wind here and things look hopeful'. In the morning they went up to Camp VI and the remaining four porters descended, bringing another note from Mallory, saying he and Irvine would start early for the summit the next day and that Odell should start looking for them 'going up the skyline at 8 p.m.' This was presumably an error and Mallory meant 8 a.m., but it was much later when Odell saw them cresting one of the two rock steps. Mallory was in favour of the ridge route, rather than going across the North Face below the ridge, as Norton and Somervell had done, and it is usually assumed he went this way; however, we now know that the Second Step is a formidable rock-climbing challenge. It became the normal way on the north side of Everest only after the Chinese placed a ladder up it in 1975. Did Mallory overcome it, was he turned back from it, or did he try another way?

In the century since Mallory and Irvine's disappearance, their story has lost none of its allure. Several expeditions have visited the North Face to look for evidence of what happened. In 1999 Mallory's body was found at 8,160 metres. Some have pointed to circumstantial evidence that they might have made it to the summit and fallen on the descent. Despite all the investigations, the mystery of whether they made it to the summit remains unsolved, and the chances are it always will be, for the following reason: it is hard to conceive of any proof that could be found that they turned back before the summit. They would not have written a note on a scrap of paper saying they were turning back, and if a camera was found the absence of summit photographs would not be conclusive – it could have been dark or the weather too bad to take photographs when they were on top. Definitive proof that they summitted could theoretically be found, most obviously via the missing camera, but with the passage of time that gets less and less likely. In 2024 the dramatic discovery was reported of part of Sandy Irvine's body by Jimmy Chin and a *National Geographic* team on the Central Rongbuk Glacier below the North Face. Before the news broke, Chin contacted Irvine's great niece Julie Summers. Her biography and work on the Sandy Irvine Archive at Merton, his old Oxford college, have done much to let the world know about Irvine as a person in his own right, rather than just a foil for Mallory. I had a very interesting chat with Julie in Oxford after visiting the archive: her knowledge of Sandy Irvine through research and passed-down family stories felt as though she knew him personally, whereas of course she was born long after his death. Chin's find inevitably raises the possibility of gaining further clues regarding the fate of Mallory and Irvine, and whether they made it to the summit. Initial reports, though, suggest we are unlikely to gain further knowledge of what came to pass that day a hundred years ago. Be that as it may, it can only be positive that once again the story of the two intrepid climbers, and the enduring mystery of what happened to them on Everest, should return to fire public imagination.

TWO

A very British activity?

For Mallory, there had never been any doubt that the British would continue to respond to the challenge of Everest until they succeeded. A factor behind his final attempt with Irvine was that, 'if he returned to England with Everest unclimbed, he would have to face once again the decision as to whether to put himself forward for a further attempt, thus inflicting another separation on Ruth and the children.'[1] For the others, the obsession with Everest was not quite as burning. When asked whether it was mere luck that his father survived and Mallory died, Edward Norton's son replied, 'No, I think there was one difference: My father ... didn't need the mountain.'[2]

In the months following the 1924 expedition the British remained very focused on Everest. In December, Norton read a severely practical paper to the Alpine Club on 'The Problem of Mount Everest', discussing the issues of route selection, camp placement and oxygen. Over three expeditions the British had learnt an awful lot about Himalayan climbing: Norton had understood the 'climb high, sleep low' acclimatization approach that is still conventional today. There was also a core of climbers with invaluable high-altitude experience. It looked as though another expedition would soon solve the problem of Everest once and for all. However, the mountain was to become inaccessible for unexpected reasons.

Permission from the Tibetans was requested by the Political Officer for Sikkim and Tibet, Frederick Bailey, himself an intrepid explorer but not keen on Everest expeditions. He proved to be a significant obstacle. Already in 1921, Bailey had noted various breaches of the Tibetan permit by Howard-Bury's team, and in 1924 he raised further concerns. These included an unauthorized visit to the Rongshar Valley by a team of climbers to recuperate at the end of the expedition. Norton was able to provide satisfactory explanations for this. However, the 'affair of the dancing Lamas' proved thornier.

The financing of the 1924 expedition depended on a film made by John Noel, who, with an eye for attention-catching publicity stunts, brought a group of Tibetan monks to Britain to promote the film. The Dalai Lama and the Tibetan government felt that the film and the pseudo-religious performances required of the monks ridiculed Tibetan culture. Noel originally said that he had official permission to bring the monks to the UK, but it was later found out that shortcuts had been taken. The Mount Everest Committee tried to argue that Noel, who had formed a company and had his own porters, was independent of the expedition, but the India Office and Bailey found this unconvincing, especially since Francis Younghusband was a director of Noel's company. Noel had bet heavily on the 1924 expedition reaching the summit, which he believed would make his film a big success. When they did not, his company went bust and he could not afford to pay for what the Mount Everest Committee's secretary Arthur Hinks called 'those infernal Lamas' to return, leaving them stuck in Ceylon (Sri Lanka) for some time.

The Committee was forced to apologize; the prime minister of Tibet demanded the monks' return and said that permission could no longer be given for expeditions. Hinks blamed Bailey for 'an exaggerated deference to the more reactionary side of Tibetan feeling',[3] a view Noel encouraged since it shifted blame away from him. He told Hinks that Bailey had said he did not like the expeditions 'because of the trouble and work they gave him'. In early 1926 General Bruce went to India to see if he could iron out the difficulties, but the visit suggested there were real obstacles from the murky world of Tibetan politics. Tsarong, a modernizing general and 'friend of Britain', had lost influence to those who were opposed to expeditions and wanted to maintain a closed society. Bruce was told that there was no chance of permission until Tsarong's party returned to power. On receiving Bruce's report, the exasperated Hinks replied that 'Noel has much to answer for, but I am afraid he will never realize it.'[4] Everest historian Walt Unsworth, who uncovered the previously hushed-up 'affair of the dancing Lamas' in the 1980s, concluded that Bailey 'fixed the whole affair from start to finish',[5] but this overstates the impact of Bailey's obstructiveness and ignores the real anger and political barriers in Tibet. In the mid-1930s the Committee still did not understand 'what are the real reasons and what merely excuses'[6] for being refused permission to enter Tibet.

The Committee never gave up trying, but the 1920s passed without any real hope that the Tibetans would change their minds. Whilst trying to overcome the obstacles of the Tibetan government, Hinks had to fend off requests from climbers around the world wanting to join future expeditions or organize their own. He discouraged all such requests, using a range of justifications, including that Tibetan permission was only for British subjects, and simply that the Committee was 'not disposed'[7] to international parties. When Anne Bernard, a 22-year-old French woman, who admitted to never having made particularly high or dangerous excursions but did claim great endurance, asked to be selected, Hinks replied that it would be 'quite impossible ... to contemplate the appointment of a lady of whatever nationality', concluding with a condescending 'the difficulties would be too great. Believe me.'[8] Women were quite active in alpine climbing, but their involvement in the Himalayas, although not unheard of, was much rarer, with some modern scholars arguing that men wanted to maintain 'the high Himalaya as spaces for manly experience'.[9]

German mountaineer and publisher Rudolf Rother wrote, perhaps naively, to the Committee that, whereas people in Germany to whom he mentioned his plans for an expedition told him the 'English Government would never allow a group of German mountaineers to cross the frontier', he was 'certain that you do not take up the stand that only Englishmen may be the first to reach the summit of the world highest mountain, and that you would welcome honourable competition'.[10] Nothing could be further from the truth: the Committee was intent on keeping Everest to themselves if at all possible. Concerned that they might not be able to stop someone else trying, they had fretted over rumours of foreign attempts from the very beginning. When Howard-Bury suggested deferring the first full attempt from 1922 to 1923 to give more time to prepare, Hinks rejected the idea because delaying would 'not impossibly let in other people'.[11]

In autumn 1924 there were press rumours of an expedition by Swiss guides, which the Committee did not take seriously, and of one by the German team, which they were not sure about. Hoping that the threat of foreign competition would incentivize them to lean on the Tibetans, Hinks reminded the India Office that 'the Committee have not relinquished their attempt to conquer the mountain, but are fully determined to organize a Fourth Expedition ... and would be very sorry to see any other party take advantage of the preliminary spade work ... to snatch the final victory.'[12] The problem was that Everest was not in their empire and anyone could get permission from the Tibetans, although it would be complicated to get to Tibet without passing through British India. Following further rumours about American and German expeditions, Hinks wrote to *The Times* in late 1924 that it is 'extremely unlikely Americans would invade what is still regarded as British field enterprise', and that the Germans would find it difficult to get to Tibet unless they went 'a long way through Soviet country'.[13] At least the India Office was able to reassure the Committee in 1925 of the 'Tibetan Government's decision to refuse [permission] to any foreign expedition',[14] including the German, Swiss and American ones rumoured in the press.

The potential competition was not only from abroad. The Committee's expeditions were not government-backed, although the Royal Geographical Society and the Alpine Club were prestigious establishment bodies. When the India Office received an enquiry from the Scottish desert explorer Angus Buchanan, who wanted to lead his own expedition, they tipped off Hinks. He replied reiterating that he considered the Committee to have 'priority' and pointing out Buchanan's lack of mountaineering experience. Buchanan gave up, but plenty of others were interested. Most infuriating for Hinks was the fear of 'inside men' wanting to break away from the Committee and organize their own attempts. In 1925 Hinks wrote to John Noel that he had 'heard a curious yarn that you are projecting an expedition to the Himalaya ... with those Germans who were immediately turned down by us when they ... asked us to help them in obtaining leave ... to climb in Sikkim'. Hinks saw no need to help the Germans, 'because we felt pretty sure they would play false'. He informed Noel that he had 'no sympathy whatever with your going in with Germans into any enterprise in the Himalaya',[15] and told him there was no chance he would receive permission from the Indian government, because he was 'very much in their bad books for the Lamas'. When the *New York Times* reported that in a lecture Noel Odell had expressed hope of making another attempt, Hinks was paranoically concerned that it implied Odell rather than the Committee would be running the expedition and pressed Odell to confirm this wasn't the case.

Where have all the climbers gone?

With Everest beyond their reach, there were plenty of other huge mountains to which the top British climbers could have turned their attention. Although six of the world's fourteen 8,000-metre peaks were within or on the borders of the British Empire, none of these were attempted by the British; hence in the second half of the 1920s very little climbing took place in the Himalayas. The expeditions that were undertaken, often by climbers resident in British India, did not tackle the high peaks and tended to be exploratory in nature. When distinguished veteran Douglas Freshfield suggested to the Committee that spare funds might be used to explore other areas of the Himalayas, including Kangchenjunga, they made clear their lack of interest in his ideas whilst remaining intent on obtaining permission for Everest.

With the exception of Noel Odell, none of the 1920s 'Everesters' would engage in significant further Himalayan climbing. Geoffrey Bruce and Edward Norton were pursuing successful military careers and were too busy for expeditions. Norton never really saw himself as a dedicated climber, referring to his two Everest expeditions as 'a funny little slice out of my life',[16] although he remained very interested in later attempts to climb Everest and was frequently consulted. Howard Somervell, a deeply principled man with a very strong Christian faith, had toured India after the 1922 expedition. On seeing 'unhealed disease and unrelieved suffering [at a missionary hospital] ... so colossal as to defy imagination',[17] he decided that this should be his life's work.

It required a new generation to take up the challenge of Everest, but the pipeline of young British climbers was not yielding much more than a trickle. The terrible human cost of the Great War, with close to 900,000 British military deaths and an even higher number of wounded, removed a large swathe of a generation. In the Alps, relatively few new routes or important ascents were undertaken by British climbers, who, as Percy Farrar reported in the *Alpine Journal* were 'unfortunately, seldom in evidence. One sorely misses the young English climbers of old days. There are still to be seen men in the thirties or early forties, usually with competent guides ... the young French, Swiss, Italians, even Germans are more numerous than formerly in the Western Alps, while the Italians, Austrians and Germans are in an overwhelming majority in the Eastern Alps.'[18]

The narrow class constraints of the Alpine Club did not help; although there were other clubs with a broader social composition, these were not usually sources for Everest expedition members. Alpine climbing was the way to get experience for the Himalayas, but for Britons even getting to the Alps was expensive and not always an option for middle-class climbers in the straitened financial conditions of the 1920s. The Germans were much closer to the Alps and so travel was much less of a barrier: when the Schmid brothers made the first ascent of the North Face of the Matterhorn in 1931 they cycled from Munich and back to make the climb. They were part of a group in Germany referred to as 'mountain vagabonds': generally from a modest social background, often unemployed and spending as much time as possible in the mountains, getting casual work and scraping a living. They accepted death rather casually and were willing to take risks to achieve spectacular climbing exploits; one of the brothers, Toni, was killed in a fall the following year.

The invention of climbing

The British tend to feel, with some justification, that they invented climbing. In reality, the earliest climbs in the Alps were made by other nations: Mont Blanc in 1786 by two Frenchmen, the Jungfrau by the Swiss in 1811, and so on, but these climbs were generally made in a spirit of exploration and scientific research. What the British did first was to treat climbing as a sport. They didn't go as far as codifying rules as they had for sports like football, but they did create a whole culture around climbing, with its own literature, customs and clubs.

British interest in visiting the Alps grew in the 1840s and 1850s, thanks to men like the art critic John Ruskin, who encouraged the appreciation of mountain scenery, and impresario Albert Smith, who climbed Mont Blanc and produced a show about it, watched by hundreds of thousands in London. With greater leisure time enjoyed by the British upper middle class, and improved train links to the Alps, mountaineering quickly became very popular. An 1854 ascent of the Wetterhorn by Alfred Wills, grandfather of Edward Norton, is considered to have launched a 'golden age' of alpine mountaineering, with first ascents of many peaks in the 1850s and 1860s. By 1864, unclimbed summits were scarce enough for Adolphus Moore to write of the 'ardour shown in hunting for new peaks'.[19] The golden age culminated in the first ascent of the most sought-after alpine peak, the Matterhorn, by Edward Whymper's team, although four of them fell to their deaths on the descent, a tragedy which attracted great attention back in Britain. There was something of a public backlash against the mountaineers, but interest remained strong. There had always been risks and accidents, but that did not remove the appeal of climbing; some would even say it was part of it.

In 1857 the Alpine Club was formed in London to unite the increasing number of active British alpinists. It functioned as a typical Victorian gentlemen's club, with premises in Central London and a membership which was entirely male and from the higher social classes: among the first 281 members were 57 barristers, 23 solicitors and 34 clergymen, as well as 19 landed gentry. There was a requirement to have alpine climbing experience, although the criteria were not particularly well defined or onerous; moving in the right circles was critical, since election required a proposer and seconder before going to a vote, and candidates with too many anonymous 'black balls' were excluded. Although other clubs would be formed in Britain, the Alpine Club was for many years the elite British climbing club and the one which, together with the Royal Geographical Society, ran the Everest expeditions.

It did not take other countries long to follow the British lead: the Austrian Alpine Association was established only five years later, with advertisements for members explicitly challenging Austrians to compete with the 'daring activities ... [of the] ... English Rival'.[20] The Swiss and Italian Alpine clubs were founded a year later; the French in 1874. Seven years after the creation of the Austrian Alpine Club, a rival organization, the German Alpine Club, was created. It had similar aims of promoting knowledge and exploration of the Alps, but, whereas the original Austrian Club was centralized and based in Vienna, the German one was highly federal with local sections enjoying a good degree of autonomy. This was popular in Germany, where loyalties were sometimes more to the city or region than the overall country, which was not even unified until two years after the founding of the club. The new club grew quickly in Germany and Austria, and eventually absorbed the Austrian Alpine Club to create the Deutscher und Österreichischer Alpenverein (DÖAV), an important organization in our story.

The rapid industrialization and urbanization of Germany in the latter part of the nineteenth century created both a desire to get away from the cities into the natural beauty of the Alps and a burgeoning middle class with the income and leisure time to go. Soon the DÖAV was the largest alpine club in the world: by 1914 it had more than 100,000 members, organized into 400 sections. The (British) Alpine Club remained much more elitist and still had fewer than 1,000 members in 1890. The more egalitarian DÖAV's wider membership was still primarily middle class, but it also included mid-level civil servants, merchants and university students, and the broadening of the social classes involved increased over time: mountaineering historian W.A.B. Coolidge noted in 1908 'a distinct decline (far more marked on the Continent than in the case of English climbers) in the social status of those who tried high ascents'.[21]

The British continued to play a leading role in pushing alpine climbing standards in the last decades of the nineteenth century, but there were also plenty of significant ascents by continental European climbers. An important caveat is that many of the hardest climbs in this period, and particularly those of the British, were done using the services of professional mountain guides, who were generally from alpine villages. It was normally these guides who led in the difficult sections: when the huge East Face of Monte Rosa was first climbed in 1872, the party included three Alpine Club members, but their guides led all the way, and hence it was they, rather than their British clients, who were pushing the standards of climbing. When the Alpine Club was new, guideless climbing was not completely unheard of, nor especially criticized, but when in 1876 three British climbers made an independent ascent of the Matterhorn it was 'much discussed by the Alpine Club',[22] which had come to frown on guideless climbing as irresponsible, if not ungentlemanly. Although guideless climbing did become a trend even for Alpine Club members by the end of the nineteenth century, many were still using guides in the twentieth. The DÖAV members, who often lacked the financial resources of the Alpine Club elite, used guides much less.

The birth of Himalayan climbing

Albert Mummery, a British pioneer of increasingly difficult routes and guideless climbing in the Alps, was the first to attempt an 8,000-metre peak, Nanga Parbat. Mummery, who had already visited the Caucasus twice and was fascinated by high unexplored mountains, was a respected figure in the Alpine Club, even though his first application to join had been blackballed. It is disputed whether this was because of his connection to 'trade' – his father owned a successful tannery – or because of jealousy and disapproval of some of his pioneering Alpine climbs.

In 1895 Mummery and two teammates travelled through India to the foot of Nanga Parbat, where they were visited by Charles Bruce, who had brought two Gurkhas to climb with Mummery, together with many bottles of Bass beer, 'a priceless treasure in those parts'. Mummery identified a route on the Diamir Face, following a series of rock ribs leading to the summit snowfields. Whilst his teammates were suffering from the altitude, Mummery climbed to 6,100 metres with one of the Gurkhas, Ragobir, spending two nights on the mountain before turning back because Ragobir was unwell. Mummery considered the climbing to be 'excessively difficult but not impossible', and was 'fearfully disappointed'[23] to retreat, because he believed that with another night on the mountain he would have reached the summit. Future experience suggests this was vastly overoptimistic.

Mummery was keen to make another attempt, but heavy snowfall made the rocks difficult, and he decided to explore the Rakhiot Face of Nanga Parbat, which he expected to be easier angled than the Diamir. Whilst his teammates took a low route to the Rakhiot Valley with most of the equipment, Mummery and the two Gurkhas set off to cross a high pass. They were never seen again, probably killed by an avalanche. In these early years, climbers – even very talented ones like Albert Mummery – did not appreciate the scale of the challenge of high Himalayan peaks, the time required for acclimatization or the extent to which they would slow down as they got higher.

Oskar Eckenstein was more of a maverick than Mummery; he was never a member of, and indeed was frequently in conflict with, the Alpine Club, although he did climb and socialize with some of its members. A great innovator of mountaineering techniques and equipment, Eckenstein was reputed to be the first boulderer and the inventor of the short ice axe. In 1892 he was a member of an expedition to the Karakoram range in Northwest India, led by Martin Conway, later a baron and president of the Alpine Club. The two men were poles apart in character and outlook and had such bitter disagreements that Eckenstein left, frustrated at Conway's lack of ambition to make ascents. Ten years later, Eckenstein returned to the Karakoram with the goal of climbing the world's second highest mountain, K2, wanting to show Conway and the Alpine Club establishment that he could do better than them.

Eckenstein, whose father was German, regularly climbed with continental Europeans, and his team for K2 included a Swiss doctor, Jules Jacot-Guillarmod, and two Austrians, Heinrich Pfannl and Viktor Wessely. There was also Eckenstein's most notorious climbing partner, Aleister Crowley, the great eccentric, provocateur and occultist. Crowley shared Eckenstein's disdain for the Alpine Club, writing that the average member 'qualifies by paying guides to haul him up a few hackneyed peaks. He is not expected to do any new climbs whatever; and it is an outrage to the spirit of the club to do anything original.'[24] Despite strong climbing credentials from the Alps, they had a completely unrealistic view of the difficulty of K2, which Eckenstein expected to be an easy mountain. With volatile characters like Crowley and Eckenstein involved, it was a turbulent expedition: at one point a feverish Crowley threatened a teammate with a revolver. They made it up to the foot of K2, and Jacot-Guillarmod and Wessely climbed to 6,500 metres on the lower slopes, before bad weather, arguments and illness led to them abandon the expedition.

Crowley and Jacot-Guillarmod returned to the Himalayas three years later to try the world's third highest peak, Kangchenjunga. With two other Swiss climbers and an Italian hotelier they had recruited in Darjeeling, it was not a strong team, and the erratic and argumentative Crowley did not have the calming influence of Eckenstein, the only climber he respected. They established camps some way up the South-West Face but were out of their depth on the climb and in management of their porters, who complained of being beaten by Crowley. Some had run away, and one fell to his death whilst descending. A few days laters a group including Jacot-Guillarmod triggered an avalanche while descending in the late afternoon. Alex Pache, a Swiss Army officer, and two porters were swept to their deaths. From the camp above, Crowley heard the frantic cries, but refused to go and help because it was getting dark and there was 'no indication as to why they were yelling. They had been yelling all day.'[25] In the morning Crowley left for Darjeeling, where bitter arguments continued. Crowley's account of the accident in the *Daily Mail* was disputed by the others. The *Alpine Journal* concluded that, with 'a leader ... capable of writing the extraordinary letters printed ..., trouble in camp and disaster on the mountain were to be looked for.'[26] Beset by scandals, Crowley had a notorious reputation in the first half of the twentieth century; in recent decades, however, many have viewed his anti-establishment iconoclasm and rock-and-roll lifestyle in a more positive light. Be that as it may, his behaviour on Kangchenjunga does not seem defensible, and it proved to be practically the end of his climbing career.

Himalayan expeditions became quite frequent in the years before the First World War: for example, 7,700-metre Kamet was attempted six times between 1910 and 1914. Most involved fairly small teams, sometimes only a single climber, with an alpine guide or two and some native porters. Following this model, Tom Longstaff climbed the first 7,000-metre peak, Trisul, with two alpine guides and a Gurkha; and Alexander Kellas summited the 7,128-metre Pauhunri with two Sherpas. The war interrupted this activity: the *Alpine Journal* recorded little climbing and listed members serving in His Majesty's Forces, including many who would later go to Everest. As we saw in the previous chapter, when the war was over the climbers of a traumatized Britain focused their attention on the most prestigious prize, Everest.

The Munich School and the Great Piton Debate

The British saw themselves as the natural pretenders to Everest, but they weren't necessarily the best equipped to attempt it. The development of technical climbing standards accelerated in the early part of the twentieth century, with the Germans and Austrians clearly climbing harder routes than their British counterparts. A particularly inspirational figure was Austrian Paul Preuss, a cultivated and educated man who spoke four languages and studied biology and chemistry at the universities of Vienna and Munich, where he had to convert to Protestantism because Jews were not allowed to be awarded doctorates. Despite childhood health problems which confined him to a wheelchair for months, from the age of 11 Preuss spent all his free time in the mountains, where he felt in his element, climbing naturally and gracefully.

Preuss was a talented communicator with visionary ideas and a purist free-climbing philosophy. In 1911 he published an article on 'artificial aid on mountain routes',[27] questioning the use of pitons and abseiling: 'if you can't go down somewhere, you shouldn't go up'. Others disagreed, arguing that the ideals of Preuss risked killing inexperienced and overambitious climbers, and accusing him of being 'a cold-hearted monster' who was demanding that climbers 'die in beauty'. Preuss clarified free-climbing principles remarkably similar to those still espoused by many in the twenty-first century: for example, he thought that pitons should only be used for safety in the case of an emergency and not as an aid to climbing. There was a so-called 'Great Piton Debate' between the 'Vienna School' of Preuss, advocating free climbing, and the 'Munich School' led by Hans Dülfer and others, who advocated the use of technical aids to allow climbing standards to be increased in relative safety. Dülfer was also a brilliant climber, making over fifty first ascents in a short climbing career. He developed new climbing methods, including an innovative abseiling technique and the use of diagonal abseils

Siegfried Herford and George Mallory, Pen-y-Pass, Snowdonia, Wales, 1913.

to overcome sections that were too blank to climb freely. Together with Karl Planck, son of the famous physicist Max, Dülfer proposed a grading system for climbing, with five levels of difficulty. The debate was lively but based on mutual respect: when anti-Semites in the DÖAV tried to suppress the memory of Preuss's climbs, his opponents in the piton debate fought to keep his legacy alive. His finest climb was a free solo first ascent on the rock spire the Guglia di Brenta, which did not see a second ascent for seventeen years. Eventually Preuss's luck ran out: he fell to his death when climbing solo on the North Ridge of the Mandlkogel, aged only 27.

One of the most influential British climbers trying to push standards in the pre-war period was the aristocratic and bohemian

Geoffrey Winthrop Young, who recognized the brilliance of Preuss, writing of his regret for his loss and 'pride that there are still men of the highest intellect in our generation who, with full knowledge of all the easier and more profitable alternatives that life has to offer, continue to match their skill as it increases against increasing difficulty, and accept the issue with calm courage'.[28] In the years before the war, Young organized informal gatherings of leading British climbers in Snowdonia, inviting up-and-coming stars of British climbing such as Mallory. Another was Siegfried Herford, a Briton of German origin, who made some very difficult technical climbs. Young, a conscientious objector, served as a volunteer ambulance driver in combat zones. He eventually lost a leg in an explosion. Herford, who was unable to get a commission on account of his German ancestry, served as a private. He was killed in action in 1916, aged 24. The war destroyed many of those capable of raising climbing standards. Herford's 1914 route, Central Buttress on Scafell, remained probably Britain's hardest climb until the 1930s.

The VIth grade

The other main European climbing nations were also combatants in the war, including Germany, which suffered even higher casualties than Britain. Dülfer was killed in 1915 near Arras. Those climbers who survived continued to push standards after the end of hostilities. As the great Italian climber Riccardo Cassin wrote, 'immediately after the First World War it was the German climbers, driven by will-power and stubborn determination, who achieved greater feats than those previously accomplished.... The Munich school was born, and Bavarian technique spread.'[29]

Otto Herzog, a carpenter from Munich, who had already been one of the strongest pre-war climbers, returned from the trenches with a hand injury, but trained hard in the gym and by bouldering outside Munich. He was soon back at the cutting edge of climbing. The 'Munich School' had won the Great Piton Debate, and the use of climbing hardware allowed them to rapidly increase climbing standards in the 1920s. A leading figure was Willo Welzenbach.

Born in Munich in 1900 to a family of civil servants, he started climbing in the Berchtesgaden Alps when his father was transferred to Salzburg during the war. He was drafted into the infantry in 1918, but had not been sent to the front before the war ended. Welzenbach started climbing obsessively whilst studying engineering in Munich and was one of the first to apply rock-climbing techniques on ice routes. His skills as both a climber and a communicator meant he gained a reputation as the leading climber of the day. In 1923, ten years after Dülfer and Planck had defined five grades of difficulty, Welzenbach proposed adding a sixth to reflect the increasing severity of climbs being undertaken.

The following year Felix Simon and Roland Rossi climbed the first grade VI route: the 850-metre-high North Face of Monte Pelmo in the Dolomites. A year later Rossi and Fritz Wiessner climbed the even harder South-East Face of the Fleischbank. Short and unimpressive physically, Wiessner learnt to climb on the sandstone towers of Saxony, one of the first places where really hard technical climbing was done. Three days after the Fleischbank, Wiessner and Emil Solleder climbed the North Face of the Furchetta, a route which had defeated Dülfer. Solleder, born in Munich and a locksmith by trade until he became a mountain guide, found climbing a mystical world which provided an escape from the misery of post-war Germany, writing that 'the reckless mountaineer is often reproached for pushing his game too far. But can a man who is a stranger to such a game understand what it means to the mountaineer?'[30]

Whilst Solleder clearly had personal, if rather mystical, motivations to climb hard, there was also significant encouragement from institutions like the DÖAV, and this would ultimately take German climbing in undesirable directions. Several influential figures within the DÖAV saw mountaineering as having an important role in the rebirth of a German nation devastated by the defeat in the First World War. They wanted a spiritual renewal away from the pursuit of purely materialistic goals to 'strengthen a sick people' who had lost the war because they had given up the struggle. They also saw climbing as a way of restoring Germany's reputation internationally and, most disturbingly, as physical and mental training for a possible future armed conflict. Whilst not quite as explicit in their links to military factors, some of the motivations for the British to climb Everest were not that different. Francis Younghusband had played a key role in the militaristic imperialism of the Lhasa Mission, but his thinking had now evolved into a more spiritual vision of British imperial rule as a positive force for civilization. He argued that, whilst climbing Everest was 'no more use than kicking a football about, or dancing, or playing the piano ... if man stands on Earth's highest summit, he will have an increased pride and confidence in himself in his struggle for ascendancy over matter'. He believed the British were racially superior and would provide an example to strengthen the spirit of the local people of the Himalayas, who were 'tame and meagre', fearful and unenterprising'.[31]

By contrast with the leading lights of the Munich School, the British 1920s Everest teams were generally not cutting-edge technical climbers. Edward Norton climbed classic rock routes in the Alps, but he did so with guides. One of the others who went high on Everest, Geoffrey Bruce, had no previous climbing experience. Sandy Irvine didn't have much either, arguably being selected because he had the right social background and had manifested physical endurance in university rowing crews. Howard Somervell had spent a few seasons in the Alps, climbing fairly hard routes like the Dom–Täschhorn traverse, but was not forging new routes or repeating the hardest climbs of the day. Possibly the best technical climber of the 1920s Everest teams was George Finch, who studied in Switzerland, where he was exposed to developments in continental European alpinism. He had already ruffled feathers in an article written before the war, pointing out the technical limitations of those who relied on alpine guides and describing British mountaineering as being controlled by 'men who looked with suspicion on enterprise beyond traditional limits'.[32]

There is no single measure of climbing difficulty covering all the many types of mountaineering. At a purely technical level, considering how physically hard individual climbing moves are to make, scales of difficulty can be defined, but ability on short technical climbs in places like the English Peak District or the sandstone towers of Saxony does not necessarily translate into longer mountain routes requiring endurance, route finding and management of objective risks like avalanche and rockfall. Surprisingly often it does: Felix Simon and Fritz Wiessner both started climbing in Saxony and graduated to long, hard alpine routes, before eventually going to the Himalayas.

Mallory is sometimes described as a brilliant climber. However, whilst he was certainly a good one, it is not certain he was much more than that as a technical climber. Everest historian Walt Unsworth rated him as a 'competent rather than great climber'.[33] In the Alps he made few new routes, the most famous being that on the North Face of the Aiguille du Midi, which is today given a moderately hard grade; respectable for the day, but far below what people like Wiessner and Welzenbach were achieving.

The fact that they were not at the cutting edge in terms of technical difficulty should not detract from what the British climbers achieved on Everest. Some of the highest mountains do not have great technical difficulties, but require outstanding fitness, endurance and mental toughness, qualities the best of the Everest climbers had in abundance. With the equipment of the 1920s, the climbs to well over 8,000 metres in 1922 and 1924 were remarkable achievements. Experience of high-altitude Himalayan climbing was the one area where the Germans were at a disadvantage compared to the British, who were helped by their empire. The only Himalayan climb made by the Germans was that in the mid-nineteenth century by the Schlagintweits, three brothers from German nobility who, during their extensive explorations in Central Asia and India, reached an altitude of 6,785 metres during an attempt on Abi Gamen. By the 1920s this was no more than a historic memory and inspiration, but plenty of the leading German alpinists were keen to show they could apply the skills they had learnt in Europe to the world's highest mountains. The 1920s attempts on Everest were watched with great interest in Germany. Authoritative figures in the DÖAV were pushing for Germans to have the chance to compete with the British in the Himalayas, where it was felt success would bring benefits in terms of global prestige and influence for the whole German nation. There was frustration that, 'while English mountaineering youth ... will settle only for the highest goals, German youth is supposed to seek new routes in the Eastern Alps, to puzzle over where on a difficult face with ten routes an eleventh or twelfth one is still possible.'[34]

Germans and Austrians were the most active in pestering Mount Everest Committee secretary Arthur Hinks either to get involved in the British Everest expeditions or to launch one themselves. In February 1927 Hinks was contacted by the splendidly named Tyrolian Philipp Pulsator von Peisser, who wanted advice about funding for a German Everest expedition. Von Peisser had been trying to launch an expedition since 1924, getting some press coverage in Germany, but never seems to have got very far in his organization. The India Office was able to reassure Hinks that, although Everest remained blocked for the British, there was 'no reason to suppose ... the Tibetan Government ... would treat a foreign expedition more favourably',[35] but the requests from Germany continued to arrive. Ludwig Zoeller from Zweibrücken wrote with a detailed plan for a German–American–British team involving 'caves in the rock and ice ... fitted with oxygen apparatus for sleeping and recuperating'.[36] Herr Lichtenauer from Munich suggested landing the climbers by aeroplane at Camp III and starting the climb from there, and in 1928 Walter Stock from Salzburg offered to act in any capacity, including as a porter. They were all rejected by the indefatigable Hinks, who told Stock that 'the Committee has never engaged ... porters other than those of Himalayan races'.[37] But the desire of German climbers to visit the Himalayas could not be held back for ever, and the next year finally saw a very strong team heading for India. They were led by a man who was canny enough to leave Everest to the British and attempt one of the other great Himalayan giants instead.

THREE

The orphaned hand

On 3 October 1929 a team of German climbers reached a height of 7,400 metres on Kangchenjunga. Having overcome the difficult and intricate snow flutings and towers of the North-East Spur, they believed easier ground would lead to the summit, far higher than any climbed at the time. That day, several attempts to progress further had been repelled by difficult snow conditions, but with a well-stocked series of camps and ice caves they were confident of climbing higher. As they stood in front of the highest ice cave, watching the evening sky, the leader Paul Bauer and one of his companions Eugen Allwein noticed a huge bank of cloud to the south. The sky above the neighbouring peak of Simvu had a strange threatening green appearance. Later that evening bad weather arrived, dashing their hopes of pulling off a spectacular ascent and leaving them a desperate and dangerous struggle to get down. They spent the night in the cave with two of the Sherpas supporting the expedition. By morning the entrance was snowed up, and when they went out to clear it, a mass of snow blew in. They had to shovel almost continuously to keep the entrance clear; by the evening more than 2 metres of snow had fallen.

Further down the mountain the rest of the team were suffering similar conditions. Before the days of radio communications, climbers in different camps had to decide independently how to react to changing circumstances. Peter Aufschnaiter and Ernst Beigel had spent an uncomfortable night at the second highest cave, buffeted by wet and frozen snow. When they crawled out in the morning they could hardly see their hands in front of their faces, but it was clear they had to descend. As they edged their way almost blindly along the ridge, huge masses of snow broke away from the towers around them, noiselessly at first, before sliding into the depths with an ever-increasing roar. All day, they were up to their chests in snow. On a narrow ridge a snow cornice gave way, sending Beigel plunging down one side of the mountain. Aufschnaiter had no choice but to jump down the other side, hoping the rope would catch on the ridge between them: fortunately it did. He was only able to regain the ridge by discarding his rucksack, and when darkness overtook them they had to pass the night sat shivering under a cornice without jumpers or windproof jackets.

Up at the top snow cave, Bauer, Allwein and the two Sherpas got ready to descend. Bauer, like most of his team, was a veteran of the First World War, an experience which indelibly marked his character. He wrote afterwards that 'the German war generation is certainly not molly-coddled; it is used to bowing to hard necessity and seeing its cherished dreams fade away, and yet here it cut me to the very heart to think of turning back.'[1] His companions had already set off and Bauer knew there was no choice but to retreat, but he hesitated, his heart rebelling against what common sense was telling him. On the floor of the ice cave he spread out the flags they had brought to fly on the summit of Kangchenjunga: their own German one and the British one to honour the empire which had allowed them to approach the mountain.

Then he left, now fully focused on the task of getting the team safely down. Bauer and Allwein had begun the day 'burning with the lust of battle',[2] but outwardly calm and collected. The very experienced Eugen Allwein led the way, his huge strength allowing him to force a path through the snow, using his big overboots to kick loose any avalanches. He left a trench behind for the two Sherpas to follow, with Bauer at the back to safeguard in case those in front of him slipped. It was terribly slow work, requiring two hours to cover the first 50 metres. They were all burdened by heavy packs, particularly the Sherpas, whom Bauer frequently had to pull out of the snow when they collapsed into it. Allwein managed to dislodge the first avalanches without being carried away himself, and one big slope had already avalanched, allowing them to descend easily down the groove it had made, but on the next section their luck ran out. As Bauer watched the others descend into the mist he heard a shout and realized that a snow slab must have given way and precipitated a fall. Bauer jumped down onto the snow of the crest of the ridge. The rope grew taut, the tension increasing as he strained to hold on, before finally easing. Bauer recovered his composure and peered down: the Sherpas were lying motionless, whilst Allwein was sat up in the snow, but none of them uttered a sound. In their precarious position the Sherpas were unable or unwilling to move, and Bauer had to shout encouragement and tug at the rope to get them going. They slipped a couple more times. Initially Bauer was able to hold them; then he fell himself, his frozen hands unable to grip his ice axe properly, but he was skilfully held by the Sherpa Pasang and left dangling on the rope, gasping for breath in the thin air.

They reached the ice cave that had been left by Aufschnaiter and Beigel, but had to dig for half an hour to free the entrance before they could get inside. It provided a secure shelter for the night, whilst they steeled themselves to face the most difficult section of the route. The two Sherpas had been unnerved by the day's drama, and in the morning were reluctant to traverse a difficult section of towers. Bauer and Allwein escorted them back to the ice cave and then descended without rucksacks to make a track through the towers, before returning to the cave, where they all spent another night. They started to wonder about the fate of the rest of the team: on the lower part of their route on the North-East Spur there was no sign of movement, and they worried some accident must have befallen their teammates. Looking down, all they could see was a trail in the snow from the glacier to the start of the Spur, but it stopped there.

Descending the North-East Spur of Kangchenjunga in 1929.

After continuing their descent to the ice cave of Camp VIII, they found a message from Alexander Thoenes, saying that the heavy snowfall made transporting supplies on the Spur impossible and that he assumed Bauer and Allwein would be retreating. The message was dated 6 October, but it was now the 10th and Bauer and Allwein had seen no sign of anyone for days, leaving them worried. They met the others the next day when they reached Camp VII. Aufschnaiter and Beigel's desperate night in the open had left the former suffering from snow blindness and Beigel with bad frostbite, but at least everyone was alive. Thoenes and Karl von Kraus were also there and for the last three days had been rubbing Beigel's feet, trying in vain to restore some feeling. The next day Beigel refused to be carried, limping along with his swollen feet in his overshoes and slipping frequently. Two more of their teammates, Julius Brenner and Wilhelm Fendt, were waiting at the base of the route, unable to go higher because of the severe avalanche danger.

Once congregated at the foot of the mountain, they started the months-long journey back to Germany, first through the foothills of the Himalayas, the frostbitten and suffering Beigel carried by porters. As they crossed British India they were invited to receptions and meetings, including with the Governor of Bengal. A congratulatory telegram arrived from the British Commander-in-Chief in India. The German Consulate in Calcutta reported home that the expedition had succeeded in replacing an initial mistrust of Germans with a great respect for their mountaineering performance. Finally, they returned to Europe by boat. Despite their not reaching the summit, the Germans' attempt was one of the boldest yet made on a Himalayan peak. Most importantly for Bauer, it attracted admiration from around the world, helping to restore German pride, so damaged in his eyes by the First World War.

Bauer's team were from the Munich Academic Alpine Club, the Akademischer Alpenverein München (AAVM), a small but elite group of university students and graduates who played a huge role in the rapid development of climbing standards in the 1920s and 1930s. Bauer's team for Kangchenjunga were 'a close fellowship of men endowed with special spiritual gifts', which he found in the AAVM, where he could choose men 'unswayed by outside influences, men trained to a hair, in body, and in mind'. The influence of Bauer's war experience was clear in his desire for a team based on 'a kind of military discipline', with 'unquestioning obedience' of the leader's orders.[3] Some well-known mountaineers baulked at this type of organization, but Bauer's teammates accepted it and resolved to organize another expedition as soon as possible to complete what they had started in 1929. This approach to leadership was in contrast to the more consensus-based approach of British expedition leaders, even those like Bruce and Norton who were professional soldiers. This mirrored the countries' different traditions in military discipline and political climate, where Britain's well-established parliamentary democracy contrasted with the unstable governments of the Weimar Republic, which some saw as responsible for the country's economic crises and political violence.

Ten years earlier

Back in 1919, things had been very different for Paul Bauer. The year after the armistice had put an end to the fighting in the First World War he was released from allied captivity in a station building on the Rhine guarded by French soldiers, ordered to remove his uniform and given 'incredibly shabby' civilian clothes. With all his possessions on his back, he made his way back home, passing 'all that had meant his world – and that of hundreds of thousands'[4] of his comrades – lying in ruins. The bitterness of this experience took many years to pass.

Born in 1896, Bauer was the son of a printer and publisher of a local newspaper in Kusel in Rhineland-Palatinate. Life in the small town was stifling and Paul and his two sisters wanted to get out and discover the world: Maria, one of the first women to study philosophy at Munich University, wanted to go to the German colonies with Paul, but they were lost as a result of the First World War. From the ages of 10 to 17, Bauer attended boarding school in Neuburg, where he met Julius Brenner, his first climbing partner. In their last school year they went on a long bicycle and climbing tour through the Alps. They experienced a problem with their bikes in Switzerland, just outside the Grand Hotel Glacier du Rhône in Gletsch, and the two heavily laden young boys attracted the sympathy of the guests, who invited them in for food and drinks.

This pleasant childhood was rudely interrupted by the outbreak of war. Entire classes were mobilized, and Bauer was drafted and sent to the front before completing the final school exams of the *Abitur*. The effect of the war was devastating: in Bauer's extended family only two of fourteen young men survived. Bauer himself suffered a serious wound to his lung, which troubled him for the rest of his life and made swimming difficult and painful. In 1916 he fought in the Battle of the Somme, one of the deadliest in human history, with more than a million killed and injured. Many of the leading British climbers, including Mallory, Norton and Odell, had fought on the opposite side of the same battle. Historian Paul Fussell considers the Somme to be the battle in which the 'innocent [British] army fully attained the knowledge of good and evil',[5] changing forever the outlook of those involved.

In the war Bauer first faced the British, who would later be both rivals and friends in the field of mountaineering. In 1917 he was captured and sent to England, where life as a prisoner of war was very hard and food was scarce. He attempted to escape by digging tunnels. Even after the war had ended, the guards teased the prisoners about how long it would be before they were sent home, but with food shortages in England it made little sense to hold them, and Bauer eventually returned to Bavaria. Like many returning soldiers, he felt a sense of alienation – 'outcasts in our own country'.[6] In *All Quiet on the Western Front*, Erich Maria Remarque, eighteen months younger than Bauer, notes that things were harder for his generation than for 'older men who ... have wives, children, occupations and interests, ... a background which is so strong that the war cannot obliterate it. We young men of twenty ...have only our parents, perhaps a girl ... a few hobbies and our school. Beyond this our life did not extend. And of this nothing remains.'[7] Bauer and his friends found an escape from this desolation in the mountains, which 'had the power to restore that which the town environment threatened to steal'. Climbing provided a 'means of proving that he who was dauntless and undeterred, he who was prepared to make the greatest sacrifices, and he alone, could aspire to the highest attainments.'[8] But whilst they were to achieve great feats in the mountains, Bauer and his companions were forever marked by their traumatic wartime youth. Bauer talked explicitly about climbing being a substitute for war: 'when we had to hand in our rifles, the orphaned hand reached out for the ice axe.'[9]

The same alienation was felt on the British side – poet Siegfried Sassoon noted that a veteran was 'everlastingly differentiated from everyone except his fellow soldiers',[10] but at least the British could return to something like a normal homeland. The way in which the war ended shaped the attitude of many Germans and Austrians who had fought in or grown up during it. As in other belligerent countries, the outbreak of war in 1914 led to a surge of nationalistic fervour, with many young men volunteering to fight. In the first months, the German armies pushed into Belgium and northern France, but were unable to strike a decisive blow, and the war became the cruel stalemate of trench warfare. The Germans more than held their own on the battlefield, but a British naval blockade meant ever-worsening shortages in Germany, with many suffering malnutrition and starvation. Although Germany was nominally ruled by Kaiser Wilhelm II, it effectively became a military dictatorship under Field Marshal Paul von Hindenburg and General Erich Ludendorff. The Germans applied counter-pressure on the British by using their U-boats to sink transatlantic shipping, but this led to the USA joining the war. In early 1918 Ludendorff decided that the only remaining chance of victory was a swift and decisive attack before US forces fully entered the war. Stormtrooper units reached 120 km from Paris, but at the cost of heavy casualties. Morale in Germany was disintegrating, and anti-war marches were frequent. In August 1918 the allies launched a counteroffensive, and at the Battle of Amiens German resistance crumbled. By September Ludendorff and

Hindenburg knew the war was lost, telling the kaiser they could not hold the Western Front. He appointed a new chancellor, who told the kaiser that Ludendorff must be removed, but that Hindenburg should remain as a figurehead for the army. With defeat inevitable and Germany's allies abandoning the war, Ludendorff was keen to hand over to a civilian government who could take the blame for the defeat, saying 'they can eat the broth which they have prepared for us!'

In late October the Italians overran the troops of the Austro-Hungarian Empire, leading the Austrians to request an armistice. In Germany sailors mutinied at the port of Wilhelmshaven and the revolt soon spread over the whole country. By 9 November the kaiser felt obliged to abdicate and a republic was declared, with Social Democrat Friedrich Ebert as chancellor. Germany was in an impossible position, and two days later a delegation drove across devastated northern France to a railway carriage to accept the harsh terms dictated by the French Marshall Foch. As well as the immediate cessation of hostilities, release of allied prisoners and withdrawal from occupied territory, Germany also had to surrender a large quantity of military material, give up the disputed Alsace-Lorraine region and allow the occupation of the Rhineland. Technically the war was not over, but the fighting had stopped. No part of the German territory was occupied, and no foreign soldier had set foot on German soil. The Allies had ample supplies of men and materials to invade Germany, but no desire to fight on. The German armies had suffered heavy losses in the fighting of 1918, but were essentially intact and returned to their home bases.

It was a bitter disillusionment to many Germans, one AAVM member writing that 'the war ended differently than we hoped. Worn down from within, our fatherland collapsed, undefeated by the armies of its external enemies. We now stand powerless, abandoned defenceless to hateful enemies, brought to the brink of ruin by inner unrest. No glimmer of hope seems to illuminate the gloomy future.'[11] The situation led to the growth of a right-wing conspiracy theory, the *Dolchstoßlegende*, the stab-in-the-back legend, which claimed the war had not been lost on the battlefield, but defeat was due to the betrayal of citizens on the home front, particularly socialists, Marxists and Jews. The myth was encouraged by Chancellor Ebert, who told troops returning to Berlin that 'no enemy has overcome you'. It built on antisemitism and prejudices within parts of society and the German army. By the time the Nazis came to power, the *Dolchstoßlegende* was well established and those who had signed the armistice were referred to as the 'November Criminals'.

The return of the troops to Munich was a sombre affair: the journal of the Hochland section of the DÖAV reported the entry into the city 'of a field formation that was moving in a long column of cars ... The soldiers sat in silence on their vehicles ... seriously and silently the people stood on the streets and there were only a few who took off their hats to welcome the homecomers.'[12] The threat of a resumption of fighting was real; under the terms of the armistice the naval blockade continued and prisoners of war in allied countries, like Bauer, continued to be held, only being released gradually during 1919 and even into 1920. The Allies saw this as a way to put pressure on Germany to comply with the armistice terms, but it caused protests there.

Civil war and revolution in Berlin and Munich

Germany after the armistice was a violent and lawless country in a virtual state of civil war. The Social Democrat Chancellor Ebert sided with conservative and nationalist forces to prevent a revolution, like the one in Russia a year earlier, but the situation risked getting out of control. Ebert was challenged by the left-wing Spartacist League, led by Rosa Luxemburg and Karl Liebknecht, backed by mass demonstrations in Berlin. Only two hours after Ebert declared a parliamentary republic, Liebknecht declared a socialist one. The army promised Ebert support in return for his commitment to reinstate the military hierarchy, threatened by the establishment of soldiers' councils. The situation was explosive, with both the Social Democrats and the workers' and soldiers' councils claiming to be in control; but Ebert's government had the upper hand, and the

Spartacists felt they had to attempt a violent seizure of power. In the first days of 1919 they formed the German Communist Party, and with huge crowds of working-class supporters on the streets of Berlin called a general strike, driving Ebert to crush the rebellion.

A key role in suppressing the Communist uprisings was played by the *Freikorps*, paramilitary groups formed from soldiers returning from the war, often feeling ill at ease in civilian life. Many were angry at the sudden and unexplained defeat and were determined to put down Communist uprisings and exact revenge on those they held responsible for the mythical stab in the back. Several of the leading Bavarian climbers were members of *Freikorps*. In Berlin the *Freikorps* brutally cleared buildings, executing occupiers on the spot, whilst others were shot surrendering. Rosa Luxemburg and Karl Liebknecht hid, but were discovered by the *Freikorps*, beaten unconscious and shot.

The situation in Bavaria was equally chaotic. King Ludwig III fled and Kurt Eisner became president of a newly proclaimed People's State of Bavaria. However, after losing elections in January 1919 he was shot dead by a right-wing extremist, leading to a gun battle in the parliament. Although the Social Democrats managed to form a parliamentary coalition under Johannes Hoffmann, his government had to flee to northern Bavaria after the Revolutionary Workers' Council proclaimed a Soviet Republic. The Communists, knowing their hold on power was uncertain, arrested members of the upper classes as hostages. Hoffmann's government, supported by 8,000 German troops and 20,000 *Freikorps*, defeated a Soviet Republic force at Dachau, and surrounded Munich. Panicking, the Communists executed ten hostages. With 20,000 members of the 'Red Army' defending Munich, the *Freikorps* entered the suburbs and in bitter fighting worked their way towards the centre. There was a coordinated uprising in the city by a vigilante 'Republican Protection Force', which contained many conservative Munich mountaineers and young climbers of the AAVM, who in regular meetings had prepared for the overthrow of the Soviet Republic. The 'Reds' put up a stubborn defence, but eventually their resistance was broken. The *Freikorps* combed the working-class districts of Munich searching for revolutionaries, making indiscriminate use of the martial law which had been imposed: more than a thousand people are estimated to have been massacred. Otto Herzog, one of the leading Munich climbers, could easily have been a victim. He had fought and been injured in the war but, as a dedicated Communist, had been at the forefront in the Soviet Republic. When the 'Whites' arrived, Herzog was hidden by right-wing mountaineering friends, saving him from the fate of many fellow Communists.

The Soviet Republic set the Bavarians against left-wing rule and created an environment in Munich in which the Nazi Party could incubate and grow. The views of the Bavarian public were mirrored in the AAVM, which before the war had been apolitical but afterwards was strongly nationalist. Twenty-seven of its members died in the war, more than 10 per cent of the total membership. The club's annual report concluded: 'let us go about raising men who uphold the traditions of our fathers, men who still enjoy fighting and victory.'[13] One member suffered a serious gunshot wound during the storming of Munich's main station, which was occupied by the 'Reds'; but by the summer he was out climbing hard new routes in the Alps.

Eugen Allwein, such a tower of strength on Kangchenjunga, had in 1917, aged only 17, volunteered with his whole high-school class to fight in the war; only four survived. After the armistice, Allwein did not return to school, but immediately joined the *Oberland Freikorps* and was involved in the battle against the Red Army at Dachau and the 'liberation' of Munich. He was in action again for the *Freikorps* in Upper Silesia, where there was fighting between ethnic Poles and Germans in the disputed territory, and missed his last chance to graduate from high school. In view of his 'services to the Reich and the Fatherland',[14] Allwein was allowed to continue his medical studies. Bauer, like many Munich students, joined the *Freikorps*, where he soon commanded a company. Officially the *Freikorps* were disbanded, since the Treaty of Versailles limited the size of the German army and they were considered to be within the numbers; however, many reformed as unofficial associations, some of which were later merged into the *Sturmabteilung* (SA), literally the storm division, a paramilitary organization which supported Hitler's rise to power.

The 1923 Munich Beer Hall Putsch was Hitler's first unsuccessful attempt to seize power. Inspired by Mussolini's March on Rome and with the support of the wartime leader Erich Ludendorff, the Nazis wanted to seize power in Munich and then march to overthrow the government in Berlin. Wilhelm Fendt, a member of Bauer's Kangchenjunga team, was present and would have been with Hitler and Ludendorff when they were fired on by government troops, but he had been sent with a pistol to defend Oberföhringer Bridge. On his application to join the AAVM, Fendt did not mention mountaineering achievements, but simply wrote 'I was in the *Freikorps*'.[15] Paul Bauer was there too, but didn't join the Putsch after being alarmed by Hitler's speech, and instead stayed in a *Biergarten* with friends; when they heard shooting and chaos, they were glad they had not participated.

Campfire by the River Isar

After his return from the war, Paul Bauer had been at a loss as to what to do with his life. He considered taking over a farm, but his sister convinced him he should continue to study. He first tried philosophy, but didn't like Schopenhauer and Kant; so he changed to law, which he enjoyed and was good at. He soon joined the AAVM, remaining active in the club even after graduating.

Although the new Weimar Republic brought some political stability in the early 1920s, the economic situation was highly volatile, with continuing food shortages. Germany had borrowed heavily to finance its war effort, hoping to pay off its debts by annexing resource-rich territories in the east, and its financial situation was severely exacerbated by the reparations imposed by the Treaty of Versailles, which had to be paid in gold or hard currency. The Weimar Republic, with massive debts and few economic resources, began printing money to purchase the required foreign currency and pay government expenses. This led to an inevitable collapse in the value of the mark, which dropped from 4 to the dollar at the start of the war to 320 to the dollar by early 1922. By late 1923 a loaf of bread in Berlin cost 200 billion marks, compared to 160 a year earlier. Hyperinflation brought misery and wiped out the savings of the middle class.

In this period, Bauer and his old school friend Julius Brenner started to make plans for climbing abroad, which eventually took them to Kangchenjunga. The inflation of 1922 had left the two students penniless and unable to travel far, so they visited the Isar Valley, which goes up from Munich towards the Alps. Their total wealth consisted of a cooking pot, some 'sausages' made from dried peas, and some cheese, but they had a campfire to keep them warm; the city seemed distant and nature close. Even in such a place, Bauer's thoughts turned back nostalgically to the war and 'how often had a golden evening sky helped us to forget the hardest day's fighting [or] the severest losses'.[16] Munich and the whole of Germany, 'which for five long years' they had defended, had now grown 'so terribly strange to us'.

As their campfire lit up the rolling waters of the Isar, their thoughts turned to distant mountains that were inaccessible to them, reminding Bauer of his childhood frustration that his home region of Palatinate didn't contain the mountains and glaciers he read about. Now the frustration was because they were encircled 'by a wall of falsehood, enmity and poverty'. Bauer and Brenner talked all night and hatched a plan for a six-week trip that summer to visit the highest peaks of Switzerland and Italy, travelling long distances by bicycle and living in tents to save money. For Bauer, the trip was necessary to 'escape at last from the crushing narrowness into which Germany had been forced by the war'.[17] It was a success, with twelve 4,000-metre peaks climbed. This was the time of the first British Everest expeditions. For German climbers, though, the Himalayas were still an unrealistic dream, making Bauer feel disadvantaged by historical circumstances.

Bauer moved to Königsberg (later the Russian city of Kaliningrad) to finish his legal studies, taking him away from the Alps, but he climbed with locals on the sandstone cliffs close to Dresden. After his studies, Bauer returned to Munich and took a job in a prestigious notarial firm, whose offices opposite the *Rathaus* had a stone facade. When he worked late in the evening, his AAVM friends would climb the facade and knock on his window, to the consternation of Bauer's fellow notaries. The AAVM were a tight-knit group, partying and climbing hard. They called him Bäuerle (little Bauer) on account of his modest stature. One weekend he was buried by an avalanche, but was able to make himself a breathing hole until his friends dug him out. The next day he was back at work, still feeling chilled and spending much time by the heater. When his boss asked him why, Bauer explained and was duly sent home to rest.

The AAVM leads a jump in climbing standards

In the 1920s the AAVM yearbook reported its members' incessant activity throughout the Alps. In April 1927, for example, Joachim Leupold and Karl Wien made the first winter traverse of Mont Blanc; in May, Willy Fendt the first ascent of the North Ridge of the Außeren Höllentalspitze; in June, Eugen Allwein a hard new rock route in the Karwendel; in August, Peter Aufschnaiter the first ascent of the West Face of Monte La Bianca in the Dolomites; in September, Bauer and Karl von Kraus the Peuterey Ridge on Mont Blanc; in October, Bauer and Ernst Beigel the first ascent of the North Side of Grundschartner in the Zillertal Alps, and so on. The most active climber of all was Willo Welzenbach, who was chairman of the AAVM in 1925 and 1926. He climbed with various partners, including Bauer: Welzenbach considered the new route they made together in 1925 on the North Face of Schönangerspitze close to the limit of what could safely be achieved, with vertical rock, brittle cracks and overhangs. The following Easter, Welzenbach and Bauer climbed a new route on Piz Scerscen in Switzerland, with the superb ice climber Welzenbach leading a 60 to 70 degree 'ice nose', and Bauer following with a mixture of admiration and envy. Welzenbach also undertook very hard climbs with Eugen Allwein, including their 1925 first ascent of the very steep North Face of the Dent d'Herens.

As Germany's economy improved in the 1920s, the distant peaks of Asia started to be a realistic goal for its climbers, and in 1928 two expeditions gave valuable high-altitude experience to several of them. During a joint German–Soviet expedition to the Pamirs, Eugen Allwein, another AAVM member, Karl Wien and Austrian Erwin Schneider made a lightning dash to the summit of the 7,134-metre Peak Lenin, the highest mountain yet climbed. At the same time, Bauer led an expedition to the Caucasus, which climbed a total of forty-six summits, including a series of first ascents. For some in the DÖAV, however, these expeditions were not ambitious enough: the influential Walter Schmidkunz criticized them for not attempting an 8,000-metre peak, which, with Everest out of reach, was the ultimate goal for German mountaineers.

By 1929 Bauer was ready to take up this challenge and started negotiations with the British Consulate to get permission to go to India. He sent a circular letter to twelve AAVM members whom he saw as candidates for the expedition, beginning 'it has become clear to me that in 1929 we must go to the Himalayas'.[18] He wanted a tight-knit team, united by shared experiences and with impressive climbing records, but above all who had learnt mountaineering in a way that stressed security, self-denial and unshakeable good humour. Eugen Allwein, who had completed his medical studies, was an obvious choice. Peter Aufschnaiter lacked the mountaineering credentials of some of the others, but had a strong interest in Asian languages and spoke some Nepalese, which was a big asset. Julius Brenner and Ernst Beigel had been in the Caucasus with Bauer and were again in the team. The others recruited had the same mixture of academic and mountaineering achievements: political economists Wilhelm Fendt and Joachim Leupold, medical student Karl von Kraus and engineer Alexander Thoenes.

Bauer's first letter laid down various rules and regulations, and stated the three most important principles for the expedition. The first was unconditional obedience to the expedition leader. This

The 1929 Kangchenjunga team at Camp III. Standing from left to right: Peter Aufschnaiter, Wilhelm Fendt, Paul Bauer, Joachim Leupold, Alexander Thoenes; sitting from left to right: Eugen Allwein, Harry Tobin, Karl von Kraus.

caused Heinz Tillmann, the strongest climber in the 1928 Caucasus team, to decide against joining, after Bauer told him that 'a captain on the high seas has the right to shoot a sailor who refuses to follow an order. An expedition leader should have the same right.'[19] Bauer was undoubtedly a forceful character: a cartoon in the AAVM newsletter shows him arriving late for a meeting, with a speech bubble reading 'No matter what the previous speaker said, I am against it!'[20] He was also a loyal friend and campaigned for the release of Otto Herzog, the Communist mountaineer arrested after the fall of the Bavarian Soviet Republic. The second principle was the willingness to carry loads on the mountain and non-reliance on indigenous porters, to save costs and improve climbers' fitness.

The third required a spirit of camaraderie, with members happily providing support to those who made the final summit push and voluntarily standing aside for others better placed than them.

Bauer's desire for individual ambition to be subordinated to the common goal saw the individual mountaineer as a 'soldier' and Himalayan climbing a continuation of the struggle of war, which could only succeed with team effort. He believed personal ambition was not enough for a months-long fight in the ice and snow of the Himalayas. Instead, 'deeper sources of power',[21] such as patriotism and selfless teamwork, were needed. The Bavarians, lacking the resources of the British Everest expeditions, could not afford artificial oxygen and huge teams of porters, but Bauer felt they could compensate by having a military-style organization and great team spirit. His personal experience fighting against the British at the Somme made Bauer doubt whether they were capable of extreme performance. For him, the struggle in the war for honour and victory for the fatherland was replaced by sporting competition in the mountains.

Bauer was by then working as a notary in the town of Nabburg. Night after night he sat at his typewriter, producing endless communications to the team, requests for money, enquiries about supplies and equipment, letters to England, to India, to Nepal. The whole team was involved in preparation: mothers, sisters and aunts were sewing equipment; Beigel and Fendt went from house to house among climbing friends in Munich, collecting spare boots and clothing for the porters. Decades later Fendt explained that 'we had no money but we had another asset, which was our team spirit';[22] this encouraged them to make financial and personal sacrifices. Finally they were ready to board the train from Munich to Genoa, and the boat to India, and the start of their great adventure.

FOUR

Hours to illuminate a lifetime

When Peter Aufschnaiter looked out of the overnight train to Siliguri at the foot of the Himalayas, the sight almost took his breath away: in the early morning light the arsenic-green paddy fields were intersected by irrigation ditches and separated by banana and palm trees. Ahead were dark wooded hills and, when the heavy clouds lifted, towering high above, the mighty snows of Kangchenjunga. Aufschnaiter came from the Alpine resort of Kitzbühel and was very used to mountains, but seeing the Himalayas was a lifelong dream. In high school he was fascinated by Swedish explorer Sven Hedin's *Transhimalaya*, a graphic account of his four expeditions to Central Asia in the late nineteenth and early twentieth centuries. At school Aufschnaiter learnt English and Italian, but also began to study Hindi, Nepali, Tibetan and Farsi. In 1917 Aufschnaiter received an early leaving certificate from high school so that he could enter the Tyrolian Imperial Rifles in the Austro-Hungarian army, fighting the Italians in the Alps. Like Bauer, he became a prisoner of war, captured at the armistice, his nineteenth birthday his last day of freedom; he was not released until August 1919. After graduating in agricultural studies at Munich, and unsure what to do, Aufschnaiter applied for an American immigration visa. But it was Bauer's invitation to Kangchenjunga that changed the direction of his life.

It had taken the nine climbers just over a month to reach this point from Munich. Bauer's account of the voyage is often through the lens of the war: when passing through the Suez Canal he noticed the 'isolated trenches and the remains of barbed wire', and seeing memorials to the allied war dead caused him to remember when Germany 'possessed the strength and courage to stretch out a hand towards this technically important centre of communication'.[1] On leaving Europe they still did not know whether they would be given permission for their favoured objective, Kangchenjunga, or for one of the two alternatives, Nanga Parbat or Kamet. The highest mountains in the world could only realistically be approached through British India, meaning that Bauer was dependent on the goodwill of his historic foe.

British power in India still seemed secure following the First World War, but with nearly 1.5 million soldiers of the British Indian Army fighting, the war inevitably impacted on how Indians viewed being part of the British Empire. Many had gone to war with little understanding of the geopolitical issues involved: General Bruce, who had led Gurkha regiments at Gallipoli, observed that many Indian soldiers had 'no real conception either of what they were fighting about and being called to lay down their lives for, or of who the people were whom they were going to fight against'.[2] Indian nationalists had originally supported the war effort, seeing it as a path towards greater freedom from Britain, even if not full independence. The war raised Indian soldiers' awareness of the inequalities inherent in the imperial system, and demobilized soldiers were prominent in political protests against injustices.[3] In 1919 British Indian troops opened fire on unarmed protestors in Amritsar, killing several hundred, and changing the attitude of Indians to British rule. From this point, Mahatma Gandhi started his campaign of non-cooperation. Bauer's expedition arrived in India with tensions there high: a year earlier the visit of a British parliamentary commission studying possible constitutional change had led to widespread protests.

While they were at sea, a telegram arrived granting them permission to climb Kangchenjunga, which lay in the independent state of Sikkim. The arrival in Madras (Chennai) felt like a scene from the *Arabian Nights*, with the silhouettes of palm trees blowing in the wind and antique boats tossed on the wild sea, but the

Bavarians found the reality of India less attractive: the heat was exhausting, they got lost in the maze of narrow streets and were assailed by persistent beggars. Bauer felt more positively towards the Indians as he came to know them, although he was prone to racial stereotyping, like referring to 'their unpretentious simplicity, mystic fanaticism and good nature, in spite of dirt, neglect and beggary which seem omnipresent'. Bauer felt affinity with the English, whom he considered 'our closest blood-relations in the world. With a glance, a handshake, we can understand one another', but found it hard to read what the Indians were thinking. He believed Germans sympathized with the Indian demands for independence because they too were victims of political oppression, with 'righteous indignation' at the Treaty of Versailles, and because Germans 'regard ourselves as a nation of poets and thinkers, and so consider the reflective Oriental with his inscrutable look nearer akin to us than the practical, materialistic Englishman'.[4] As they approached Calcutta (Kolkata), some newspaper reporters came on board, but Bauer asked them to say as little as possible about the expedition as he wanted it to remain low key until he had seen what they could achieve.

The Himalayan Club

In Calcutta they visited the German Consulate-General, and the Himalayan Club, which had been founded a year earlier 'to encourage and assist Himalayan travel and exploration, and to extend knowledge of the Himalaya'.[5] One of the co-founders was Major Kenneth Mason, who, despite never being a dedicated climber, was a significant figure in Himalayan mountaineering and exploration. Born in 1887, Mason, inspired by books like Younghusband's *Heart of a Continent* and fired by patriotic enthusiasm for the Boer War, decided aged 11 that he wanted to be a soldier. He wanted to serve in India following in the footsteps of relatives, including his Uncle Alec, reputedly the inspiration for the character of Colonel Creighton in Rudyard Kipling's novel *Kim*. After studying at the Royal Military Academy in Woolwich, Mason joined the Royal Engineers; he was posted to the Survey of India, a colonial body responsible for much of the early exploration of the Himalayas. In one of the last acts of the 'Great Game', Mason surveyed the Indo-Russian border, connecting the British triangulations with those of the Russians: in 1907 the two empires had ended their rivalry in Central Asia in a new alliance focused on opposing Germany.

Mason's boyhood dream of exploring the Himalayas was interrupted by the outbreak of the First World War. The surveyors were transferred back to the Engineers and sent to the Western Front. Mason fought in the Second Battle of Ypres in 1915 when the Germans used poison gas for the first time, surprising the allied troops, who did not have gas masks and were told to urinate on their handkerchiefs and hold them to their noses to combat the gas. With the allied line broken, the Mason's Lahore Division counter-attacked, but came under heavy fire. Mason was in a party of twelve soldiers hit by an enemy shell: he was the only survivor. His injuries were fairly minor, and he returned to action on the Western Front and then in the Middle East. After the armistice he returned to the Survey of India and was bitterly disappointed to miss out on the 1921 Everest Reconnaissance, denied leave by his superior, who objected to the Mount Everest Committee suggesting which surveyor to send together with Henry Morshead. He did go on a major survey and exploration of the Karakoram in 1926, following in the footsteps of his boyhood hero Younghusband.

Mason had extensive knowledge of the Himalayas and was the first editor of the *Himalayan Journal.* His contacts around the world included the German climber Rickmer Rickmers, who wrote to Mason on behalf of Bauer and his friends, who 'wanted to test themselves against something difficult in the Himalaya'.[6] They were recommended to try Kangchenjunga. Mason met the German team when they arrived in Calcutta, and at a dinner he and Bauer discovered they had been opposite each other in the trenches in France in 1915. Mason asked Bauer

> whether he had been with the Bavarians on the La Bassée front. He replied by asking whether I remembered them hanging a pair of pants on their wire with a notice attached: 'Try these'. The incident

> at once came back to me, and I replied that our men raided their wire, collected the pants and hung them on our wire, with a notice: 'We do'. Bauer then remarked that they had had information that a highland battalion had taken over the line and that our notice had puzzled them greatly. I enlightened him by telling him that the Highland Light Infantry did not wear the kilt![7]

This light-hearted banter between opposing sides in an otherwise bloody war is indicative of an attitude where soldiers are fully dedicated to their opposing national causes without feeling any lasting personal enmity. The pair became friends, and Mason and the Himalayan Club provided valuable support to the Bavarians. Bauer knew that cultivating good relations with the British was important for his Himalayan climbing ambitions, but he also genuinely valued these friendships. Mason later wrote that Bauer was 'desperately envious of everything in the British way of life'.[8]

After taking the train to Siliguri, Bauer was approached by a man with a piece of paper explaining that he was the sirdar, or head porter, and had been sent by Lieutenant-Colonel Harry Tobin of the Himalayan Club. Tobin, another man who remained a lifelong friend of Bauer, had arranged for motor cars to take the Germans through the malarial Terai jungle to the hill station of Darjeeling. At a dinner with top officials at the Darjeeling Club, Peter Aufschnaiter was pleased to find himself sitting next to the police chief Laden-La, a Tibetan-looking gentleman with a spectacular moustache. Anglophile to the core, Laden-La entered the Indian Imperial Police service, and later became the right-hand man of Charles Bell, the British Political Officer in Sikkim, who did much to foster closer relations between Tibet and British India. Aufschnaiter found Laden-La fascinating company, 'educated, intelligent, funny and – naïve'.[9] His role in securing permission for the first British reconnaissance of Everest had earned him a fellowship in the Royal Geographical Society.

Also at the dinner was Edward Shebbeare, another founder member of the Himalayan Club and transport officer of the 1924 Everest expedition. The Germans' equipment was ready, but Bauer realized it would be hard to convince Shebbeare it was adequate.

German financial resources were much more limited than those of the large British Everest expeditions, and Bauer wanted to dispel any doubts about their preparedness. So, when the team returned to their bungalow long after midnight, he ordered them to take off their smart dinner clothes and spend several hours unpacking and repacking their equipment. Working off the excess alcohol, by 7.30 a.m. the Bavarians were ready to display the equipment to the satisfaction of Shebbeare.

They also had to select the Sherpas who were going to accompany them on the mountain, and the large team of porters. At this time, many of the Sherpas who supported the Everest expeditions were based in Darjeeling. The Himalayan Club helped to organize those working as mountain porters, defining pay scales and issuing personal record books with mountaineering CVs. Today, climbing Sherpas are well capable of managing their own activities, but in the 1920s such paternalism was accepted without question. The Himalayan Club assumed recruitment would be done by one of the experienced sirdars, but the Germans were not keen on delegating this responsibility. Bauer believed that 'methods of handling subordinates are fundamentally the same all the world over ... [having] ... studied them as a private in the war, and later practised them ... as platoon and company commander.'[10] He believed it was possible to get cooperation from anyone provided the superior takes an interest in the subordinate's welfare, remains at his post in times of danger, gives few orders but insists on these being obeyed, and punishes lapses of duty. The selection started with a medical examination by the two doctors, Eugen Allwein and Karl von Kraus. Keen to be chosen, the candidates pressed up against the window of the room where the inspections were taking place. When selection was complete, the porters were given an advance payment, which they immediately handed over to their waiting wives, who gave them a drink of rice wine and a white silk scarf to bring luck for the hazardous journey.

The Germans were able to do a short stretch by car, accompanied by Laden-La, who warned them to respect the sacred mountain of

Kangchenjunga and allow the porters time to pray to it during the full moon. They descended from Darjeeling into the steaming hot and luxuriantly vegetated Teesta Valley, a wild labyrinth of ravines. The Germans were approaching Kangchenjunga, which lies on the border between Nepal and Sikkim, from its north-east side. They did not follow the Teesta Valley due to the unbearable heat and risk of malaria, but crossed several side valleys and ridges, meaning more ascent and descent. Only once they had entered the Zemu Valley, descending from the North-East Face of Kangchenjunga, did they start to continuously ascend.

Into Sikkim

They crossed into Sikkim, an important travel crossroads between India, Tibet and China, where Tibetan pilgrims in rough woollen clothes mixed with Hindu holy men in loin cloths, and merchants and artisans from the Indian plains. Alexander Kellas had made various trips up the thickly forested Zemu Valley between 1907 and 1911, but since then others had given up without reaching the Zemu Glacier, after days of hopeless struggle in the jungle. The Bavarians were happy to discover that among their porters was a man named Nursang, who had been with Kellas as a young man and dimly recalled the route. Nursang's involvement in Himalayan expeditions would have made a European a major figure in climbing history; being an Asian, his name appears only fleetingly, albeit recurrently. After portering for Kellas, he joined a Gurkha regiment of the Indian Army, becoming a sergeant and fighting in the First World War on the same part of the front in Belgium as Bauer himself, although of course on different sides. Nursang had worked on Everest in the 1920s and would continue to be involved in most expeditions to the great peaks during the 1930s, working as a reliable sirdar for the British and Germans alike.

Nursang was able to find vague traces of a track through the rhododendron jungle, which was so dense that they only caught glimpses of the sky above. Having hacked through this impenetrable labyrinth, they were astonished to find a well-maintained path and a group of Tibetans, who crossed to the upper Zemu Valley from further north to graze their cattle. Despite some difficulty in communication, they managed to get directions and camped below the snout of the Zemu Glacier, a mist-shrouded mix of ice and moraines with a huge torrent gushing out of its base.

Above the snout the valley was wide and level, its bottom filled by the glacier. They placed Base Camp by a mountain lake and started building a wall to protect the camp from the cold winds. Bauer describes with a typically paternalistic attitude how at first the porters 'would not lift a finger to try and improve their condition', and that he had 'often noticed that simple folk ... show very little understanding of how to cope intelligently with Nature's treacherous onslaughts'.[11] In Bauer's account, once the porters had seen the example set by the Germans in moving rocks and cutting turf to build a wall, they 'took fire', vying with each other to see who could move the largest rock. Base Camp was gradually transformed into a small village with high walls, a dining room and a kitchen.

When they started to look for a viable route up Kangchenjunga, Bauer found six men crossing the Green Lake Plain who seemed 'very much like an advance, as if the infantry were moving up to attack', and commented that, 'however much war may be solemnly denounced',[12] his old fighting spirit rejoiced. Bauer's expedition book is full of military analogies; the war clearly dominated his psyche. But we should remember that the 1920s British Everest climbers were also war veterans and used similar analogies: Norton's book about the 1924 expedition was titled *The Fight for Everest*; he likens the approach to the Rongbuk Glacier as being like the Great War, with 'the fertile fields of France behind and the stricken battlefield ahead'.[13] Bauer, Brenner, Tobin and the Sherpa Pasang set out to explore Kangchenjunga, spending three days stumbling along the moraines. Every night it snowed, and the mornings were bitterly cold, but by midday the tropical sun reflected off the snow made it oppressively hot, sapping their energy and slowing progress.

On the fourth morning they woke to the sight of the vast North-East Face of Kangchenjunga towering above, glittering in the morning sun, their proposed route on the North-East Spur sweeping up to its junction with the main North Ridge. With the practised eyes of mountaineers, the old school friends Bauer and Brenner spent ages looking for a possible route, without exchanging a word. Heading back across the glacier, they were thinking the same thing: the North-East Spur, at least on this side, looked desperately difficult. Even if the crest could be reached, there was then a series of vertical ice bulges, each like the one on Piz Scerscen in Switzerland, which Bauer had climbed with Welzenbach, but repeated over and over. But the bold increases in standards achieved by the Munich climbers in the 1920s had taught them to be cautious in declaring anything to be impossible. They explored the other side of the North-East Spur, but the approach to it was manifestly threatened by ice avalanches. Bauer's thoughts turned back to the 'terrifying' North-East Spur. He studied it again and came away convinced they could find a route and determined to make a serious attempt. They had been happy with the performance of the porters and selected twelve Sherpas and five Bhotias for work on the mountain, sending the rest home.

Finding a route

At the foot of the North-East Spur, they set up Camp VI as a base for their attempts, and for 'wearied fighters' returning from the mountain to rest. Above the camp was a 200-metre-high icefall, which led to a glacier basin at the foot of the precipice below the lower section of the Spur. They trained the porters how to use crampons, ice axes and ropes and set up Camp VII protected by overhanging rocks above. They zigzagged up steep snow above, keeping an eye out for rockfall and avalanches, before being turned back by bad weather. When good weather arrived, they could see multiple ice gullies divided by jagged snow crests running up to the lowest part of the Spur. In the misty conditions, traversing across this slope seemed possible, but a clear view changed their minds. They tried going straight up, but gave up after finding themselves insecurely spread out on steep slabs, one above the other. If anyone fell, they risked sweeping all of the other climbers away. Allwein and

Thoenes climbed a steep ice gully to the crest, but this was far too difficult for the porters. They reported that the Spur was festooned with huge snow towers, ranging from 10 to 20 metres in height, and with a sheer drop on the other side.

The climbers were depressed, feeling that their attempt would fail so soon after starting. Bauer wondered whether the East Ridge on the other side of the valley could be an alternative route, but decided not to abandon the Spur before one final try. That night, as the Bavarians gazed from their camp across the glacier to Kangchenjunga, a distant flash of lightning lit up the summit. The conversation turned to the fairy-tale beauty of the marble chateau of Hollebeke in Belgium, the centre of some of the fiercest fighting in the First World War battle of Ypres. The chateau was first held by the British and then the Germans before being completely destroyed. On 31 October 1914 British dispatches talked of a critical moment, as they struggled to hold out against massive waves of German attacks, but by the afternoon the chateau was full of Germans. A week later, at Hollebeke, Bauer was hit by fragments from an artillery shell and suffered his serious lung injury. He spent the next few months in hospital before returning to combat at the Battle of Arras in June 1915. The events at Hollebeke must have been hugely marking for Bauer, coming when he was still 17 and less than a month after he had first seen action.[14] Bauer recalls how

> young volunteers and bearded veterans had lain on costly carpets and marble flooring, waiting, rifle in hand, for another day of fighting, while the enemy's shells played havoc.... In the glowing light of a lofty fire-place and to the last sob of a damaged piano, there sprang up there, born of the experiences of the last days, of the visions of home, of presentiments of a hidden destiny, a hallowed emotion such as falls upon a circle of men who have become one to the death, – Hours such as these, I think, can illuminate a whole lifetime.[15]

This passage is typical of Bauer, reflecting the writing of Ernst Jünger, who portrayed war as a mystical experience which tested the capacity of the human senses and revealed the nature of existence. Jünger, a year older than Bauer, had rebelled against a

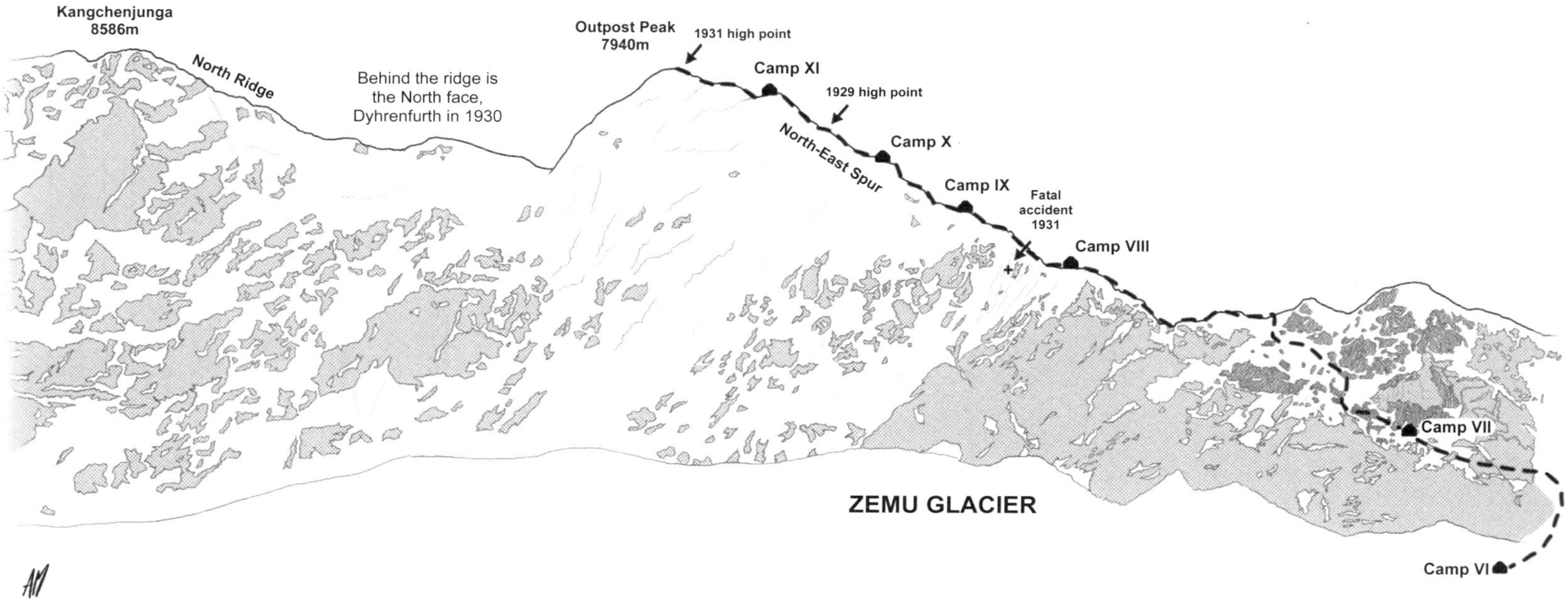
Kangchenjunga
8586m
North Ridge
Behind the ridge is
the North face,
Dyhrenfurth in 1930
Outpost Peak
7940m
1931 high point
Camp XI
1929 high point
North-East Spur
Camp X
Camp IX
Fatal
accident
1931
Camp VIII
Camp VII
ZEMU GLACIER
Camp VI

Kangchenjunga North-East Spur route.

Kangchenjunga map.

privileged upbringing by joining the *Wandervogel*, youth groups who protested against industrialization by hiking in the countryside and communing with nature. Like Bauer, Jünger fought in the Battle of the Somme; his book *Storm of Steel* is one of the most vivid accounts of the First World War. Later works called for the creation of a society run by warrior–worker–scholars and rejected liberal values, advocating that men should be judged by their capacity to withstand pain and sacrifice.

The following day the weather was terrible, but the Bavarians resolved to make a final effort to reach the crest of the Spur by a rising traverse across its flank, forcing their way through numerous corniced snow ridges. As the snow swirled around, it seemed very daring for even a well-belayed climber to trust their weight on these snow structures, precariously attached high above steep slabs, but they proved more stable than they looked, with thick icicles embedded in the snow attaching them to the mountain. The lead climber used his ice axe to hack out a path that could be followed by heavily laden porters. After an hour and a quarter of hard work they had cut a path through the first ridge and into the gully on the far side. They had to change the lead frequently as it was hard work at high altitude. By the time driving snow forced them to retreat back to Camp VI they had not reached the Spur, but had learnt how to deal with the strange ice structures and were convinced a way could be forged.

Bad weather forced them to halt operations on the mountain, and the whole team reunited in Camp VI for the first time since leaving Darjeeling, the crowded tents animated by conversation and Bavarian songs. Camp VI was comfortable: it had running water, and their cook, Tenchedar, always had something ready to eat and drink. Early in the morning they usually found him gazing out at the holy mountain of Kangchenjunga and praying. Tenchedar was an extraordinary man, with great Buddhist religious knowledge, and able to speak and write English. During the bad weather they made plans to attempt Kangchenjunga, extending their stay in India by a month and sending Leupold down to Camp III to maintain communications with the outside world.

The team moved Camp VII to a new position on the face leading to the North-East Spur, which they called the 'Eagles' Eyrie' because it was on a narrow ledge with steep walls below and a huge rock tower above. After two days' hard work, they reached the crest of the Spur, which towered 2,000 metres above with a series of ice pinnacles, up to the junction with the main North Ridge of Kangchenjunga. Two more days of hacking and digging allowed them to pass three towers on the first horizontal part of the Spur, which then started to rise steeply. The magnitude of the task began to dawn on them: whilst each of the towers would have been climbable by the Germans, this would have served no purpose, because to stock the camps and make further progress they needed a trail that the porters could follow safely. They tackled the steep slope leading up to a first snow terrace, identified as a possible site for Camp VIII. Night overtook them before they reached the terrace, so Beigel and Bauer dug a place for their small tent on a snow arête so dizzyingly narrow that at one point they could see through the cornice to the glacier far below. Despite this they managed to sleep. As soon as the sun reached them, they set to work on the tower ahead, hacking away ice so they could pass its left-hand side and then cutting a deep zigzag path up a steep slope towards the terrace.

The ice towers

The ice structures on the Spur were quite different from those in the Alps, and the Germans had to develop new techniques to climb them. The next section looked so difficult that they seriously doubted further progress was possible. At Camp VI both Germans and the porters spent a lot of time outside the tents watching the tiny black dots climbing on the improbable ice structures high above. The Germans were pleased to see the porters' support, but, like the British on occasion, probably had an idealized view of their attitudes. Bauer believed that, because the Germans shared the food equally when it was in short supply, and 'when our route lay over difficult ground, we Europeans were far more concerned for the lives of the porters than ... our own'; the porters were willing to follow, 'to the last man in desperate places, with a trust and enthusiasm beyond rewarding, which had no thought of payment but sprang purely from ethical motives, from noble natural instincts'.[16] Bauer implies here that his team had a more egalitarian attitude towards the porters than the 'imperialist' British, and this resulted in them being more motivated. Few contemporary accounts from porters exist, so we cannot be sure of their motives; even if on occasion they showed genuine enthusiasm for the climbing, they were ultimately in paid employment. Ang Tharkay, who participated in many expeditions from the 1930s onwards, wrote in the first autobiography of a climbing Sherpa that he was not sure what drew him to the dangerous world of high-altitude portering. Although his imagination was fired by the poetic descriptions of adventures given by a porter who returned to his village from one of the early Everest expeditions, the prospect of gaining a better living was also clearly a driver for Ang Tharkay, who had grown up in crushing poverty in a small village and discovered a new cosmopolitan world when he visited Darjeeling for the first time.

Above Camp VIII was a series of spectacular towers, each a climbing challenge in its own right, which the Germans gave names like *die Wendeltreppe* (Spiral Staircase) and *der Twins Turm* (Twins Tower), which hung like a gigantic mushroom 25 metres above the Spur, and was passed on unstable powder snow with a huge drop to the glacier below. The next towers proved to be the most troublesome. Allwein and Kraus could see no way around the fourth tower, which had a vertical crest and overhanging flanks, but on the left a narrow ledge led into a deep recess in the ice, topped by huge cornices. The only possibility was to drive a vertical shaft upwards from the recess. Kraus tried first, squeezing his way in and burrowing up with his ice axe. It was very tiring, and the dislodged snow soaked them with icy water, but they eventually dug a path big enough for someone with a bulky rucksack to pass. They made further progress along a very narrow crest, before bad weather drove them back to the camp.

The following day a large party led by Bauer arrived at Camp VIII too late to go down. There was no space in the tents, so he suggested digging a snow cave. This took three or four hours but provided better shelter than the tents during bad weather. After two weeks of hard work on the Spur, they had still not broken through to easier ground. They had agreed signals to indicate to the lower camps when everyone should move up for the summit push, but time passed and the signal never came. They pitched Camp IX and enlarged the ice caves so they could hold six to eight men, making the entrance as small as possible to keep in the warmth: the temperature rarely went below −2 or −3 degrees Celsius, even though outside it could be −30 at night. They used their imaginations to imitate architectural styles when sculpting the ice caves, with one even having Gothic arches.

On the North-East Spur with the summit of Kangchenjunga behind, 1929.

Above Camp IX the route got a little easier. On a few occasions slab avalanches swept the lead climber off his feet, but they were well belayed and did not fall far. One slope required great caution when first crossing it, but was less dangerous once they had made a trail. Camp X, again an ice cave, was placed at 7,000 metres, and they started making preparations for the final summit push. They expected that, with the monsoon over, the weather in October would be settled, but for eight days there was almost continuous light snow. On 3 October Beigel and Bauer, with two porters, moved up to Camp X, where they found Thoenes finishing the ice cave. Allwein and Kraus went up to survey the route ahead, sinking up to their knees in snow. At 7,400 metres they turned back, optimistic that the way ahead looked feasible, with two more camps needed before attempting the summit. However, this proved to be the highest point reached in 1929.

In Camp X they had supplies that would provide for ten men for five or six days, as well as tents and sleeping bags for the planned Camps XI and XII. With everyone physically fit, success seemed within their grasp. There was a festive atmosphere in the ice cave, with Beigel pulling out a little surprise for every man from the depths of his rucksack: one got a packet of cigarettes, another some tobacco, and there were even three fresh apples from Darjeeling. But this was the moment their luck turned: 4 October saw ominous black clouds and by the evening it was snowing hard. They had to alter their plans and prepare for a siege. As the heavy snow continued through the next day, they realized that success on Kangchenjunga that year could only be achieved by taking unacceptable risks.

On 6 October the weather improved, and for the first time in forty-eight hours it wasn't snowing. Allwein and Bauer, with two porters, tried to climb the peak at the summit of the North-East Spur, but the snow had a hard but breakable surface covering slush underneath, and they only gained 75 metres in two hours. Abandoning their packs, they managed to carry on for another hour and a half. The view was stunning, with the 7,000-metre peaks around the Zemu Glacier below them and the red hills of Tibet stretching into the distance, but the improvement in the weather was over and they were faced with a battle to get back down alive, as we saw in the previous chapter.

Even without making it to the summit, the Bavarians were enormously proud of what they had achieved and determined to return. At the dinner held for them at the Himalayan Club in Calcutta, Kenneth Mason gave a speech praising their achievements. He referred to 'the Spirit of Locarno', citing the treaty that had improved Germany's relations with its First World War enemies. With all the major peaks still unclimbed, Mason observed that 'one great attribute possessed by the Himalaya ... is room for all the climbers of all the nations of all the world'. Bauer replied, praising the British Himalayan pioneers, including Mallory and Irvine, who 'will always live in the memory of those who try to follow in their footprints'.[17]

FIVE

Champagne on high

Before Bauer and his team got another shot at Kangchenjunga, an attempt would be made by Günter Oskar Dyhrenfurth. Like Bauer, Dyhrenfurth was a German First World War veteran, but the similarities end there. Visiting the Himalayas was a long-standing dream for Dyhrenfurth, who was born in 1886 in Breslau (Wrocław), then the sixth largest city in Germany, before becoming part of Poland after the Second World War. His father ran a successful medical practice and was himself a mountaineering enthusiast. His mother was the daughter of a painter and took the young Günter Oskar around Europe to see museums, palaces and churches, but his real passion was climbing. From the age of 10 he kept a record of all his ascents, with 917 entries by the end of his life. Aged 17, he climbed his first 4,000-metre peak, and soon he started to climb without guides.

In 1906, when Dyhrenfurth was 19 and a geology student, he became engaged to the 14-year-old Hettie Heymann, the only child of a wealthy Jewish industrial family. Their engagement was secret at first, but they already had plans: a first child in 1913, a first Himalayan expedition in 1914; a second child in 1915, a second Himalaya expedition in 1916; a third child in 1917, and finally a third Himalayan expedition in 1918. They actually had three children – in 1913, 1915 and 1918 – but the war delayed plans to go to the Himalayas for many years.

In 1914 Dyhrenfurth assembled a team for an expedition to Kangchenjunga, but the outbreak of war meant the plan was abandoned. He volunteered for service and got transferred to the Austro-Hungarian army so that he could serve on the Ortler front in the Eastern Alps, a region he knew and loved. Hid duties, including the training of soldiers in mountaineering, gave him the opportunity to make an astonishing number of climbs – 195 during the war years, including seventeen ascents of the 3,778-metre Monte Cevedale. The war ended chaotically for him, with the Austro-Hungarian army decisively beaten by the Italians. Wanting to get back to his family as quickly as possible, he decided to desert and return home via Switzerland, but first informed his commanding officer, who thanked him for his service. Instead of crossing the mountains to Switzerland during the night, as he had planned, he managed to get a lift from the Swiss border police after explaining that he had worked there surveying for a geological map before the war. The contrast between the panic and confusion in Austria, where the war was lost and the empire dissolving, and the calmness of Switzerland was huge. Technically Dyhrenfurth was interned, but conditions were very relaxed: he was allowed to stay in a hotel and go for mountain walks.

Prior to the war, Dyhrenfurth was managing the significant wealth of his family, and that of his wife and mother-in-law, but the inflationary period of 1919–23 shrunk this, forcing him to sell assets, including the beloved family home, Carlowitz Castle (the five domestic staff had to be released). Their last family Christmas at the Castle was that of 1922. Dyhrenfurth received Howard-Bury's book about the first British Everest expedition from his mother, who dedicated it thus: 'Many dreams have been shattered ... With the heartfelt desire that one day some of these dreams will still come true.'[1] Dyhrenfurth had not given up hope of going to the Himalayas, and when he heard that Charles Bruce was training for the second Everest expedition in Switzerland he arranged to bump into him. Günter Oskar sent Hettie, whose English was better, to engage Bruce in conversation with the hope of getting an invitation, but in the nationalistic spirit of the post-war period the British would not consider a German for their team.

As well as being Professor of Geology and Palaeontology at Breslau, Dyhrenfurth gave mountaineering lectures to DÖAV sections, but the mood among elements of the club was becoming ugly in the 1920s. Antisemitism already existed before the war, with some sections inserting Aryan paragraphs limiting membership to 'Christian baptized German citizens'. The AAVM, of which Bauer and his team were members, was founded in 1910 for 'academically educated gentlemen of Germanic descent',[2] although this was not strictly applied before the war – the Jewish Paul Preuss became a member, for instance. After the disastrous end of the First World War, many Germans were susceptible to antisemitic conspiracy theories blaming Jews for Germany's problems. Talented climber and rabid anti-Semite Eduard Pichl introduced an Aryan clause in the important 'Austria Section' of the DÖAV. When the excluded Jewish and other liberal Austrian mountaineers formed their own 'Donauland' Section in 1921, anti-Semites in the DÖAV managed to expel it. Some liberal mountaineers resigned and formed a new club, and many who stayed in the DÖAV were unhappy, but the anti-Semites got their way. With some mountain huts displaying posters declaring 'Jews and members of the Donauland section are not welcome',[3] Jewish mountaineers would clearly have felt uneasy within the DÖAV.

In 1926 the Dyhrenfurth family moved to Switzerland, putting them closer to the high Alps and further from the hostile atmosphere of Germany. Dyhrenfurth once again started planning a Himalayan expedition, even though his financial situation was much less comfortable than in 1914, when he had expected to meet all the costs himself. By late 1928 Dyhrenfurth's plans for an expedition to Kangchenjunga had matured enough for him to submit an official application to the DÖAV Expedition Committee, but he was pre-empted by Bauer and had to delay to 1930. After his bold attempt in 1929, Bauer wanted to try again as soon as possible, but the British authorities considered it impossible to have more than one expedition per year and had already given Dyhrenfurth permission for 1930. There was an unseemly battle between the two, with Bauer calling Dyhrenfurth's expedition a disloyal attempt to steal the victory from the unfinished work of his team, and asking for it to be stopped or denied support.

Bauer was struggling to finance a second expedition after the Wall Street Crash and needed sponsorship from the DÖAV. They promised to support Bauer in 1931, as long as Dyhrenfurth had not reached the summit. Dyhrenfurth still thought that both his and Bauer's expeditions would leave in 1930 and wrote that it would be a 'deeply sad spectacle ... [to have] ... two German Himalayan expeditions in fierce competition'. Bauer commented that the 'spectacle is undoubtedly sad ... but to call ... [Dyhrenfurth's expedition] genuinely German is a naughtiness that must be properly rejected, above all, if it comes from a man who is not a German by race',[4] referring to Dyhrenfurth's Jewish ancestry. The argument worsened and risked getting coverage in the press, leading Philipp Borchers, the main Committee member responsible for foreign expeditions, to tell Bauer to back down.

The International Himalayan Expedition

Dyhrenfurth wanted to climb in the pre-monsoon season to avoid the autumn weather, which had hampered Bauer, and worked round the clock to prepare, so they could leave on a ship from Venice in February. Short of money, he changed his original plan for a German expedition to an international team, allowing him to pick strong climbers from other countries and access additional sources of financing. This caused a stir in Germany, by rejecting the norm for purely national expeditions and having both British and German climbers in the same team, only a decade after the end of the First World War. For those who saw Himalayan climbing as a way to restore German national prestige and Britain as the key competitor, a joint team was problematic. The attitude in Britain wasn't very different: when Germans asked the Mount Everest Committee about a joint expedition, they were told the Committee did not 'favour the idea of making high climbing parties international'.[5]

The highest profile foreign recruit was Englishman Frank Smythe. Born in 1900, Smythe narrowly escaped the call-up for the First World War. Like Sandy Irvine, he received news of former school-mates killed in action, black-edged cards with their names being placed on the wall of the school chapel. Whereas the life-shaping experience of the British and German generations who went to the trenches was fundamentally similar, for those young enough to miss going to war it was very different. While this 'war youth generation' in Germany passed into adulthood in the post-war chaos, violence and economic collapse, people like Smythe had ostensibly a calm and normal early adulthood. Indeed, when Smythe went to Austria for engineering training in late 1921, he was shocked to see the devastating impact of the economic collapse, with 'a defenceless people fast sinking into ruin'.[6] Some of the German 'war youth' contemporaries of Smythe, who lived through the war but did not fight in it, felt that 'a traitorous armistice had cheated them of their right to fight for the Fatherland'.[7] Many became supporters of the Nazis. In Britain 'the generation that had been just too young to serve in the war ... felt itself misunderstood. It had come to manhood in a time of insecurity, after an education that presupposed security, and was made to feel inferior simply because it had not fought for King and Country.'[8]

A complex and sometimes difficult and temperamental character, Smythe was not a 'good mixer': Hugh Ruttledge, who twice led Smythe on expeditions, wrote that when discussions degenerated into arguments he 'would retire into his own tent for peace and meditation'.[9] Smythe had made his name with two significant new routes on the Italian side of Mont Blanc in 1927 and 1928, both with Thomas Graham Brown. The second climb led to a bitter and lifelong feud between the two men, who disputed what happened at a key moment. Smythe had been considered for the 1924 Everest expedition, but Howard Somervell, who assessed him in the Alps, concluded that he was 'a bad mountaineer always slipping and knocking stones down and an intolerable companion. Nobody in our party could stand him for more than a few days'[10] – an interesting assessment given that Smythe became one of the most successful Himalayan climbers. Smythe was bored at school and dreamt of the mountains he read about in the school library. He left without qualifications. Following unsuccessful attempts to make a career in engineering and the Royal Air Force, he decided to try to become a professional climber, something very unusual at the time. With a rare talent for communicating to a wider public, Smythe had written a successful book about climbing and skiing in the Alps. He was excited by Dyhrenfurth's invitation, although it came with a catch: Dyhrenfurth asked him to contribute £500 towards the expedition's cost, a very material sum in those days. It was more than Smythe could afford, but he managed to convince *The Times* to sign him up as a special correspondent, pay his costs and provide additional sponsorship. He also got a contract for a book about the expedition, a significant step in establishing himself as a professional climber financed by writing.

Hermann Hoerlin was one of the younger members of Dyhrenfurth's team. Born in 1903 in Baden-Württemberg, he started climbing whilst studying in Stuttgart, soon amassing an impressive set of ascents. On a trip to the Alps he met a short Austrian engineering student with thick black hair called Erwin Schneider. Schneider and Hoerlin were very different characters, but made a formidable partnership in the Alps. Schneider had also climbed the 7,000-metre Peak Lenin in 1928. As well as the Dyhrenfurths, Smythe, Hoerlin and Schneider, there were another six members of the team, including German Uli Wieland and Briton George Wood Johnson, who had learnt to climb in the English Lake District, before becoming a tea planter in Darjeeling. Marcel Kurz, a pioneer of winter Alpinism, had climbed as a student with George Finch and was proposed for the 1920s Everest expeditions, before these were limited to British climbers. Now he had his chance.

Hettie Dyhrenfurth was more noted as an international tennis player than a climber, but she had been on many climbs with Günter Oskar. The involvement of women in Himalayan climbing expeditions at the time was unusual – the Mount Everest Committee was firmly opposed – but there was an important precedent in the American Fanny Bullock Workman, who had overcome what she felt was 'sex-antagonism'[11] to make multiple expeditions and reach nearly 7,000 metres with her husband in 1902. Hettie threw herself enthusiastically into preparing the equipment, clothing and rations, whilst her husband managed political and financial matters.

On the boat to India, Günter Oskar insisted that everyone got up at 6.30 a.m. to do exercises on the deck. Hettie took lessons in Hindustani from a young Indian and one evening danced with him, whereupon Smythe explained to her that 'it simply wasn't done for a white lady to dance with coloured people'.[12] On arrival in Bombay (Mumbai), Dyhrenfurth received a telegram saying that the DÖAV was supporting the expedition financially, but the positive view from Germany was certainly not unanimous. As well as the official reports in *The Times* and *Scherl Verlag* in Berlin, articles also appeared in other newspapers, such as the *Münchner Nachrichten*, which described the luxury provisions in detail: 'more than a ton of chocolate ... as well as caviar and goose liver paté and 500 bottles of Munich beer, boxes of whisky, rum, champagne, schnapps and various types of liqueurs, apparently intended for gastric disposition and victory celebrations'. As well as having enough drinks for a team of alcoholics, reports also claimed that they had dynamite to 'explode suitable platforms for bivouacking and setting up tents'.[13] Press reports in nationalist newspapers talked about serious conflicts within the team and ill-treatment of local porters: Dyhrenfurth published a detailed contestation after returning to Europe.

Both Smythe and Dyhrenfurth had taken advice from General Bruce, who with his knowledge of local languages and care for the porters was much loved by the indigenous people he took on expeditions, but who comes across as a typical colonial figure. At Victoria Station in London his last advice to the departing Smythe had been a whispered 'Don't forget to worm your porters.'[14] The doctor checked the health of porters before selection, but did not find many cases of worms; however, scurvy was a problem and they decided to vaccinate them against smallpox, due to a recent outbreak. In Darjeeling they were joined by Lt-Col. Tobin, who was accompanying them as he had the Bavarians the year before. Dyhrenfurth had not warned him of their need to hire 400 porters, and Tobin had his work cut out trying to find enough candidates, despite men arriving from hill villages looking for work. They ended up with a nucleus of what Smythe called 'keen, reliable men', but also others whom he derogatively referred to as 'Bazar wallahs', who were just trying to make money and had 'no intention of working or serving the expedition faithfully'.[15] Each of the European members had a personal servant. Bruce had given Smythe a letter to his personal servant on Everest, Lhakpa Chedi, describing Smythe as his grandson. Bruce's reputation meant that this (incorrect) description gave Smythe high standing among many of the porters. Lhakpa Chedi, who was one of the first Sherpas to carry to over 8,000 metres back in 1924, was working as a waiter and unable to come, but Smythe also got a recommendation for Nemu, Irvine's servant on Everest in 1924, who was keen to join. Other veterans of the Everest and Kangchenjunga expeditions carried tatty and dirty letters of recommendation. Chettan, who served as Erwin Schneider's personal servant, was one of the most experienced Sherpas, having been on all three Everest expeditions, and with Bauer in 1929. The fact that men like Chettan worked for rival expeditions is consistent with the (at least superficially) chivalrous and gentlemanly nature of the rivalry.

Dyhrenfurth wanted to attempt Kangchenjunga through Nepal, in part to avoid accusations of taking advantage of Bauer's explorations, but initially did not receive permission to enter the country. They were about to set out along Bauer's Sikkim route when permission arrived from the Maharajah of Nepal. Dyhrenfurth didn't hesitate in moving to the Nepalese route, but failed to appreciate that it meant a much more difficult approach to Base Camp, with two high passes to cross. This proved a serious problem, especially since they only had boots for the porters who were going to work above Base Camp. Some of the porters refused to cross the snow-covered Kang La and many loads had to be relayed across later.

The ice wall

On 26 April, Base Camp was established on the Kangchenjunga Glacier, 5 miles from the 3,000-metre-high North Face of Kangchenjunga. They started to look for a feasible and reasonably safe way to the summit. Douglas Freshfield, who had visited in 1899, felt that 'the whole face of the mountain might be imagined to have been constructed by the Demon of Kangchenjunga for the express purpose of defence against human assault.'[16] The North Face is made up of a series of ice terraces, one above the other, with the lower edges of the terraces being steep ice walls. The mornings were typically fine, but clouds always arrived around midday and a cold wind swept across the glacier. The upper ridges were 'smoking' with snow blown from a westerly wind, so fierce that there was no chance of climbing Kangchenjunga unless it dropped. After heading up a narrow trough in the glacier, they looked for a site for Camp I safely out of range of any ice avalanches from Kangchenjunga. This forced them into the centre of the glacier, which contained many hidden crevasses. Dyhrenfurth fell into one unroped but was fortunately blocked by a snow bridge: a plunge into the depths could well have been fatal.

Dyhrenfurth gave three blasts on a small horn each morning to signal that the climbers should get up and start working, something Smythe and Wood-Johnson found grating. Wood-Johnson even stole the horn, only for Dyhrenfurth to produce a spare. The only feasible route seemed to be up the face below the summit of Kangchenjunga. If the first terrace could be reached they could traverse left and climb a slope to reach the crest of the North Ridge, approaching it from the opposite side to the Bavarian route. Reaching this first terrace meant overcoming a 300-metre-high ice wall which stretched for miles across the face. Towards the left it was broken up into a series of subsidiary walls, and at one place a steep shelf seemed to offer a possible way through, although it was very exposed to ice falling from unstable pinnacles above.

On a terrace below the ice wall they placed Camp II. They were again concerned about concealed crevasses and told the porters not

North Face of
Kangchenjunga from
Base Camp in 1930.

to stray far from the tents. As they rested in the afternoon, they heard shouting from across the glacier. At first they thought it came from porters coming up the trail from below, but then they realized that Wangdi Nurbu was missing. Wieland and Smythe rushed in the direction of the cries and found a single set of footprints with no returning steps leading to a 60 cm hole in the ice, revealing the depths of a crevasse from where despairing cries could be heard. They managed to haul Wangdi Nurbu out; fortunately he had no broken bones, but was badly bruised and very cold after spending two hours wedged in the crevasse walls. Smythe described Wangdi Nurbu, who supported all six of his Himalayan expeditions, as 'a little fellow, all bone and wiriness, and ... one of the hardest men I know'.[17]

The ice wall was frighteningly impressive as they neared it, with tier upon tier of hard green ice, laced with snow. They managed to pass a first ice block but then arrived at a 25-metre overhang. A shelf sloping upwards seemed to offer a way past, but was overlaid with 30 cm of powdery snow, which they had to shovel away before cutting steps in the tough ice below. Wieland and Smythe fixed ropes to help the laden porters, anchoring them with ice pitons. The leader drove a piton as high into the ice as he could reach, clipped the rope into it, and then hung on to it whilst cutting steps with the other hand until high enough to place another piton. Smythe doubted whether ice this hard had ever been climbed; the porters said this ice wall was even harder than the 1929 Bavarian route. At one point Smythe had to stand on Wieland's shoulders in his nailed boots to place a piton past a steep place. Progress was desperately slow, and they were acutely aware of a 100-ton ice flake hanging menacingly above; they hoped two more days would see them at the top of the ice wall. Schneider, a splendid ice climber, managed to overcome another overhanging section; work was then interrupted by heavy snowfall and they had to descend. Soon the steps were filled and the ropes buried; several people slipped and fell, mercifully being held by the rope.

The next day, Schneider and Hoerlin reached the foot of the final wall and made plans to go up with a team of porters to complete the route and establish Camp III on the terrace above. Using the siege approach developed on Everest, porters would need to keep going up and down the route to create a supply chain to feed the climbers and stock the camps; but, whereas on Everest the terrain was simple enough for porters to move on their own, here each convoy would need to be led by a European climber. They worried that it would not be possible to keep the supply chain going after heavy snowfall, and worst of all feared that if part of the ice wall collapsed the climbers above would be stranded and unable to descend. In the Alps they were used to passing sections threatened by falling ice, but generally this was only done once and done quickly, keeping the probability of an accident very low. On Kangchenjunga, establishing higher camps and reaching the summit would require porters to be carrying loads for many days, making the chance of an accident much greater.

After sleeping badly, Smythe stayed back at Camp II with the cook, watching the others leave, with Erwin Schneider off first as usual, accompanied by his personal servant, Chettan; the others followed with a large team of porters. Smythe returned to his tent to write some letters, but half an hour later he heard a horrible roar, and rushed out to see that an enormous portion of the ice wall had collapsed. Huge masses of ice were still falling as his companions, a line of black dots on the slope, rushed to the left to get out of the line of fire, before being engulfed by the cloud of snow and ice. The avalanche was now approaching the tents. Realizing they were in danger, Smythe shouted at the cook to run. They had only made it 20 metres when the avalanche stopped, 200 metres above the camp. Seeing no sign of the others and fearing they had all been killed, they grabbed their ice axes and set off to help, but as the snow dust settled a hugely relieved Smythe started to make out figures on the slope away to the left.

Reaching the edge of the avalanche debris, Smythe saw a track disappear under the piles of ice blocks. The porters were paralysed by fear, with Nemu prodding the debris. Smythe asked whether a man was buried there, but Nemu was worried more about the load he had cast aside when running for safety. Smythe counted the people: two were missing – Schneider and Chettan, who had been in the lead. Wieland saw Chettan's hand sticking out of the snow; he was already dead when they dug him out. He had been carried 100 metres down the slope and crushed by the ice blocks. Schneider arrived, having had a miraculous escape, running to the left and avoiding being hit by 5 metres. Chettan, further back, was unable to get out of the way. The rest of the party had been on a part of the track where it swung further to the left and were able to run clear, although some of the porters were bruised by pieces of ice. They carried Chettan's body down to Camp II and buried him in the snow, the porters saying prayers and throwing rice over the

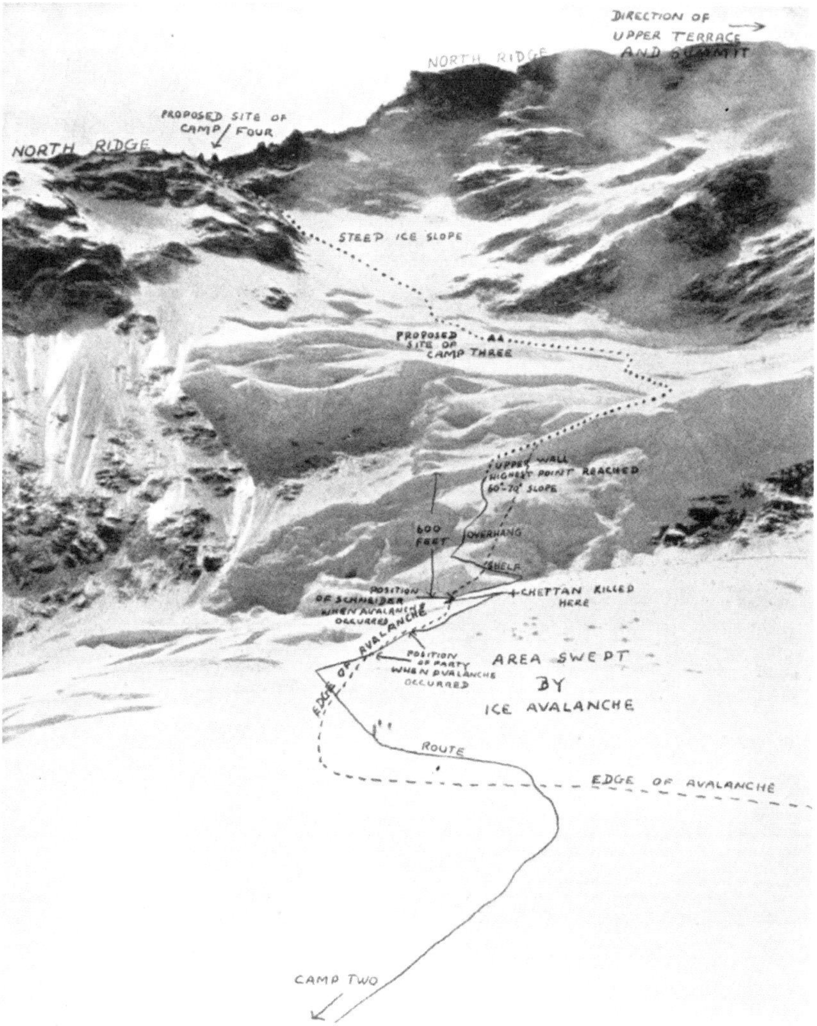

The route up the Great Ice Wall on the North Face of Kangchenjunga, 1930.

body, whilst the Europeans stood around solemnly. Chettan was one of the most experienced climbing Sherpas, and was respected and well liked by the European climbers he worked for. Tom Longstaff's obituary lamented the loss of a 'companion and a friend', one who had the skills to develop into a 'real [alpine] guide'.[18]

Other targets

Another crack had opened up in the ice wall. Fearing a further collapse, the team descended to the safety of Camp I. The next day Dyhrenfurth arrived from Base Camp to discuss the next move. He wanted to continue the attempt on the ice wall, but this was rejected by all those who had tried to climb it. Apart from the danger, the avalanche had completely obliterated the lower part of the route, which would need to be remade. A suggested alternative was the North-West Ridge, which led towards a terrace under the western summit of Kangchenjunga. Smythe was not keen on this idea and instead proposed attempting the 7,462-metre high Jongsong Peak, but no one supported this plan. Smythe overheard conversations in other tents where he was referred to as 'the English coward'.[19] Instead, they moved camp to the base of the North-West Ridge, which rose up 1,300 metres, in a serrated edge of rock towers separated by snow arêtes. Smythe judged it to be even harder than the North-East Spur and felt very pessimistic about their chances of success.

Hoerlin, Wieland and Smythe climbed a long steep snow couloir dropping from one of the gaps on the ridge. It was topped by a cornice, which Hoerlin hacked through to reach the crest. The ridge was incredibly loose with rocks ready to crash down at the slightest touch, leaving the Germans cursing the rock quality. At one point, Hoerlin turned to Smythe and said in perfect English, 'These rocks are shit!' The next section looked possible, but then there was a 100-metre-high pinnacle connected to another pinnacle by an ice ridge. Even if they had been able to fix ropes along all of this section, they doubted it would be feasible for loaded porters. They had lost a lot of ropes in the avalanche, making rope fixing all the way impossible. Despite the pessimistic verdict of the three climbers on their day's explorations, Dyhrenfurth wanted to continue trying, but another attempt only confirmed the difficulty. Given the risk that the monsoon would break whilst they were on the mountain, they decided to abandon the attempt on Kangchenjunga and focus on more achievable smaller mountains.

Dyhrenfurth wanted to use the time available to explore as much new ground as possible and decided to split the team up. Their main target was Jongsong Peak, which would require crossing the Jongsong La pass and setting up a new base camp beyond. Whilst most of the team went in this direction, Wieland and Schneider explored the area of Nepal Gap, the pass between the Kangchenjunga and Zemu glaciers. After Wieland had to stop, Schneider summited the 7,177-metre Nepal Peak, beating his own record from Peak Lenin for the highest peak ever climbed. On the crossing of the Jongsong La the porters were restive, feeling they had worked hard and not been treated well. Their complaints do not seem unjustified given the difficult approach to Base Camp, and Dyhrenfurth's insistence on forced double marches because they were behind schedule. It is worth noting that Wood-Johnson, who was one of the transport officers, was later felt by his Everest teammates to have a bullying attitude towards the porters. Many of the clothes they were promised had been lost or stolen, and Wood-Johnson had to provide the cash equivalent to persuade them to carry on. Schneider and Wieland arrived fresh from their successful trip to the Nepal Gap, and Hettie Dyhrenfurth somehow produced a small crate of champagne to celebrate.

After three days on the Jongsong Glacier, they crested the pass and looked down on the yellow, brown and gold of the hills of Tibet. Jongsong Peak seemed within reach, but the clouds flooding up from the Teesta Valley made them fear the monsoon would break before they climbed it. This led to a first attempt being made by Schneider, Hoerlin, Wood-Johnson and Smythe from a camp that was further from the mountain than they had planned. They descended a heavily corniced ridge before crossing a glacier basin to the summit block of Jongsong Peak, climbing as two pairs, Schneider and Hoerlin on one rope and Wood-Johnson and Smythe on another. Wood-Johnson was unwell, and was slowed by his inexperience of technical snow and ice climbing. Eventually he had to stop, and Smythe tried to catch up with Hoerlin and Schneider, but they were going too fast and Smythe turned back. Hoerlin and

Schneider made it to the summit, once again breaking Schneider's record for the highest summit ever climbed. On their way down to Base Camp, they met Dyhrenfurth, Kurz and Wieland coming up to make their own attempt, and Smythe joined them to repeat the ascent of Jongsong Peak.

They now split into three groups: a main party descended the valley towards Darjeeling; a group led by Dyhrenfurth explored the upper Lhonak Valley; and Hoerlin and Schneider, who climbed another difficult peak just under 7,000 metres before crossing into the Zemu Valley, where they encountered a dangerously crevassed glacier and deep snow. Fortunately, some of the porters had been on the 1929 Bavarian expedition, and were able to find one of the camps, with well-preserved earth huts. They spent three days there waiting for the weather to improve, before being rewarded with a spectacular view of the North-East Face of Kangchenjunga and descending into Sikkim.

The main group, including Hettie Dyhrenfurth and Smythe, made a less adventurous descent back to civilization. In Gangtok, the capital of Sikkim, the first thing Smythe noticed when entering the bungalow was 'a bottle of whiskey standing like a Serjeant-Major before a row of tins containing various delicacies, a gift of the Maharajah's'.[20] At a dinner at the palace Smythe was in his element recounting stories to the Maharanee, the wife of the Maharajah, and drinking one glass of champagne after another. As they returned to the drawing room, Smythe turned to Hettie and groaned 'I'm sick'. Seeing his pale green face, she escorted him as inconspicuously as possible into the garden, 'from where he came back visibly refreshed after a quarter of an hour',[21] later saying he would be grateful for her presence of mind until his dying day. Smythe's account of the evening is more circumspect than Hettie's, merely saying it was convivial, but mentioning that at the 'annual dinner given by the Maharajah to the Lamas of the Sikkim Monasteries ... it is considered an insult to the hospitality ... if the Lamas are able to leave the Palace on their own legs. I can well believe that they never do.'

The International Himalayan Expedition failed in its primary objective, Kangchenjunga: the routes attempted proved too dangerous and too difficult for the capabilities of the time. On lower neighbouring peaks they did much better, breaking the record for the highest mountain climbed twice, but not reaching anything like the altitudes achieved on the British Everest expeditions. The consensus was that Kangchenjunga was a much harder mountain than Everest, and they suspected it might take generations until it was climbed. Dyhrenfurth's experiment of an international team had not solved the problem of climbing one of the world's great peaks.

SIX

A new guard cuts its teeth

Seven years after the last expedition, the Mount Everest Committee in London had not given up hope of organizing another attempt, and started putting out feelers about getting permission from the Tibetans. Frederik Bailey was no longer Political Officer in Sikkim, but his successor reported that the Tibetans were still upset about the affair of the Lamas, who had still not returned to Tibet, where they faced punishment, but preferred to eke out an existence in exile in Darjeeling. The India Office was sensitive to the issues of British national pride, given the recent expeditions of Bauer and Dyhrenfurth and the reported interest from the Americans. Francis Younghusband encouraged these sensitivities by pointing out that Britain should have priority to make another attempt given that the bodies of Mallory and Irvine lay near the top of Everest.

Frank Smythe was a Briton with ambition to match that of Paul Bauer. Building on his experience on Kangchenjunga, he organized his own Himalayan expedition in 1931. Smythe's end goal was Everest, which he dreamed of climbing as much as did Mallory. After returning from Kangchenjunga, Smythe had written to the Alpine Club hierarchy saying that it might be possible to get permission from the Maharaja of Nepal to approach the North Col of Everest through Nepal via the Arun Valley, and that he believed plans were afoot for an international attempt this way by Dyhrenfurth. He urged speedy action because of the 'very strong sentimental reasons why Everest should be climbed by a purely

British party'.[1] With Tibet seemingly blocked, the India Office also asked the Committee if an approach through Nepal was practicable, but the British Envoy in Nepal advised that permission was unlikely to be given there either. With Everest blocked, Smythe targeted the 7,756-metre Kamet in India, 300 metres higher than any mountain climbed at that time. Even though not as important as the 8,000-metre barrier for continental climbers, measured in feet Kamet would represent the first 25,000er ever climbed, as well as being an 'ideal training ground for ... Everest candidates'.[2]

Smythe's book about Dyhrenfurth's expedition, *The Kangchenjunga Adventure*, had been highly successful. Some leading mountaineers were privately snooty about Smythe's writing – Edward Strutt described one of his books as 'psychological bilge'[3] – but his exciting and sometimes spiritual descriptions of mountains appealed to the wider public, and Smythe's plans to make a career in mountaineering seemed feasible. Kamet had already repulsed nine attempts, all by British climbers, so a lot was known about the approaches to the mountain and possible routes, making it a good target to further Smythe's Himalayan climbing career. His six-man team included Raymond Greene, a doctor and brother of the novelist Graham. Greene had been at school with Smythe and remembered him as 'a rather frail fair-haired boy who was said to have a weak heart'.[4] In fact, Smythe's supposed childhood ill health may have been largely a figment of his overprotective mother's imagination, but it had the effect of implanting 'a determination to prove his physical strength'. The rest of the team fitted the typical profile of British Everest expeditions, including Romilly Holdsworth, a Classics master at Harrow School and first-class cricketer, and Eugene Birnie, a serving British officer in India.

The youngest member would go on to be the most famous: Eric Shipton, born in Ceylon, where his father was a tea planter. There are important parallels in the background of Shipton and Smythe: both had lost their fathers at too young an age to remember, and both had close but complex relationships with their mothers. They had both had difficult times at school, becoming interested in climbing after reading the books of Edward Whymper. Although neither had excelled at their studies, Shipton did win a place at Cambridge, but decided against taking it up and instead emigrated to Kenya to grow coffee, the start of a lifelong wanderlust.

Shipton had already shown good potential in a couple of alpine seasons, and in Africa he made some impressive new routes on Mount Kenya. Although Shipton and Smythe made some of their key climbs together, they were very different in temperament – Shipton easygoing and sociable, Smythe highly strung and temperamental – and they were never close friends. Shipton described Smythe as 'an agreeable companion ... but not a stimulating one', and technically he viewed Smythe as a 'sound rather than brilliant' climber. Indeed, when Smythe was out of practice he had some embarrassing failures on British rock routes, but he did have a remarkable endurance. Shipton described how in adverse conditions Smythe had 'a fakir-like ability to shut himself in a mental cocoon, where he was impervious to fatigue or boredom, discomfort or psychological distress, and thus emerged with his resources quite unstrained'.[5]

Smythe's 'extraordinary gift' was later hugely valuable on Everest, but Kamet did not present enough of a challenge to require it. He was able to stick closely to a well-designed plan. Within a fortnight of starting above Base Camp, the team were camped on Meade's Col, at 7,000 metres and within striking distance of the summit. Progress was almost too fast from the perspective of acclimatization, but with the weather holding good Smythe decided to attempt the summit. Shipton, Smythe, Holdsworth and the Sherpa Lewa were the first to make it, although Lewa suffered bad frostbite during the descent. They were followed two days later by another group, which included Birnie and Greene. After this success and his experience on Kangchenjunga, Smythe was Britain's leading Himalayan climber and had his eyes firmly set on Everest.

Bauer versus Welzenbach

Dyhrenfurth was not Paul Bauer's only rival wanting to launch a German Himalayan expedition. Fellow AAVM club member Willo

Welzenbach had drawn up a plan to try Nanga Parbat in 1930, the same year as Dyhrenfurth's expedition. German authorities were worried that two German expeditions in the same year would create resentment, given that 1.5 million Indian soldiers had taken part in the war, and that too many expensive German expeditions would create the impression of a financially strong country, something they were keen to avoid during the reparation negotiations. So, a disappointed Welzenbach had to postpone his plans for Nanga Parbat to 1931. Arguing that success on an 8,000er would allow German mountaineers to maintain the advantage in reputation that they had gained over the British in recent years, Welzenbach got the backing of the AAVM, and the Munich and Bayerland sections, but he needed support from the main DÖAV and faced competition from Bauer, who wanted funds for a second Kangchenjunga expedition in 1931.

Welzenbach and Bauer were former climbing partners and the two leading figures in the AAVM, but neither could accept being in an expedition led by the other. Unsuccessful attempts were made to mediate between them, suggesting they could divide the available financing and travel to Asia together to reduce costs, before heading towards their individual objectives. With many Germans suffering financially, some AAVM members asked why now, of all times, were they being asked to contribute to expensive Himalayan expeditions. The Committee replied that the time for the conquest of 8,000ers was ripe, and since AAVM had the top climbers in the world they should not miss out due to a lack of funds.

The dispute between the two was heated, with Bauer threatening to use his good relations with the British authorities against Welzenbach and telling AAVM member Heinz Tillmann that he would 'squeeze Welzenbach against the wall'[6] if he did not stand aside and give him priority. In December 1930 the AAVM approved support for only the Kangchenjunga expedition, which they felt had a better chance of succeeding, given Bauer's experience from 1929. They compared the British attempts on Everest, which were a 'matter of the entire English nation',[7] with the attempt on Kangchenjunga, which was similarly important for the 'reputation of the German name abroad'. The British now viewed Kangchenjunga as 'a German mountain', and if Welzenbach was successful on Nanga Parbat it would look like the Germans wanted to climb every mountain in British India. Ironically Nanga Parbat would later be presented by Nazi propaganda as Germany's 'Mountain of Destiny'.

Bauer set out this concept of particular mountains being targets for certain nations, writing that Everest was a national goal for the British Empire and that 'Pioneers ... like Sir Francis Younghusband, marched like heralds and standard-bearers before the serried ranks of English Everest fighters.' Bauer was 'not concerned in getting there before the English. In the Great War, Germans and English fought often enough for possession of a trench, a farm, or a few trees.' He pointed out that by the late 1920s both nations compete in sport, but 'in the struggle to conquer the world's highest peaks, man is face to face with such overwhelming natural forces, that all nations should be allies. In those altitudes, it would be presumptuous to attempt rivalry or a race for priority. Whatever our pride ... [in] ... our own national efficiency may be, respect is due to other nations who are striving towards the same goal.'[8] Bauer was fiercely competitive and ambitious, but he was also keen to look dignified and chivalrous. This respect for the 'enemy' recalls Ernst Jünger, who in *Storm of Steel* wrote that 'it was always my endeavour to view my opponent without animus and to form an opinion of him based on the courage he showed. I would always try and seek him out in combat and kill him, and I expected nothing else from him. But never did I entertain mean thoughts of him.'[9] Bauer wanted to emulate the attitude of the British, for whom 'all that the country can offer is devoted to this one goal'[10] of climbing Everest. 'Having forced a breach, German climbers should concentrate all their efforts upon Kangchenjunga', which the 1929 team felt to be 'our higher duty' and a 'personal obligation',[11] sentiments which recall Sandy Irvine's attitude on setting out to Everest. Once again, Welzenbach had to delay his plans for Nanga Parbat.

A strengthened team

Five of the 1929 Kangchenjunga team were returning, including Eugen Allwein and Peter Aufschnaiter. Bauer also added four younger climbers: Hermann Schaller, Hans Hartmann, Hans Pircher and Karl Wien. Wien was the most notable addition, the son of the Nobel Prize-winning physicist Wilhelm Wien, who made discoveries instrumental for the formulation of quantum mechanics. Wilhelm was a committed nationalist. In the First World War he had been the lead signatory in a proclamation by eminent German physicists declaring that they should no longer publish in English journals, and that German publishers should only accept articles written in German. This proclamation was part of the *Krieg der Geister* (war of ghosts), the cultural war which went on during the First World War, when academics and intellectuals supported their home countries' war aims and conduct. Given Wilhem's background, it is not surprising that his son, Karl, born in 1906, would share the nationalist political views of Paul Bauer. Karl was also a talented climber. He joined the AAVM whilst studying in Munich, becoming chairman in 1926. His mentor was Willo Welzenbach, whose friendship Wien valued: 'countless times we climbed as a rope on difficult routes, we savoured all the joys that the mountains can give two mountaineering friends and we wrestled with the difficulties and dangers in ice and snow and storm.'[12] Wien had made a number of first winter ascents and traverses in the Western Alps and had high-altitude experience from the Soviet–German Pamirs expedition in 1928, where he summited Peak Lenin.

Hans Hartmann was born in 1908 in Berlin. He went to Munich to study medicine in 1927, soon joined the AAVM and spent all his free time climbing. In the spring of 1929 Hartmann and Wien climbed the Biancograt on the Piz Bernina in wintry conditions and were overtaken by a storm. Despite Wien rubbing his feet all night to try to revive them, Hartmann suffered severe frostbite and amputations were required, but this did not keep him away from the mountains for long; within a year he was climbing hard routes in the Dolomites.

When Bauer's team reached Darjeeling, they found that many of the porters who had supported them in 1929 had for weeks been awaiting their arrival. Two of the 1929 Sherpas, Lewa and Nima, were away with Frank Smythe on Kamet, but the others had brought younger men from their villages in Nepal, who were keen to work. Over 400 men were camped around the bungalow where the Germans were staying, eager to be signed up. After the warm greetings, the Germans discovered there were tensions among the porters, with the Sherpas complaining they had been paid less than the Bhotias by Dyhrenfurth's expedition. This is the only time Bauer mentions Dyhrenfurth in his book about the expedition, despite them having attempted the same mountain in successive years. Bauer clearly felt he did a better job of managing the porters than Dyhrenfurth, but maybe he had fewer problems because of heavier-handed methods. In 1931 he refers to 'controlling our unwieldy band of porters with strict supervision'.[13] The Sherpas demanded that Bauer should employ only them, and refused to come if Bhotias were also employed. Using his historical relations with the porters and the influence of Laden-La, Bauer convinced both Sherpas and Bhotias to participate.

Summer rains

Bauer's expedition had left Europe a month earlier than in 1929, meaning they started operations on the mountain during the monsoon period rather than the typically more settled post-monsoon weather of October–November. The monsoon has never become a popular period for Himalayan climbing, but it was proposed for Everest in the 1930s by Eric Shipton, who thought winds would be lower, temperatures higher and conditions easier, apart from the heavy snowfall. Low on Kangchenjunga, this translated into rainfall; on some days the Bavarians had six to eight hours of it. They were grateful to have the shelter of the walls and turf huts from the 1929 Camp III, which they found intact on the Green Lake plain. When the clouds cleared enough to let them see the North-East Spur, they recognized the platforms on which they had placed camps, but between them there were many changes to the old route: between camps IX and X there seemed to be two new towers and a sharp cleft in the ice ridge, and the 'Great Tower' seemed to have grown some 80 metres in height. Two years earlier it had taken them twenty-five days to reach Camp X. They wondered how long it would take this time.

Seven weeks after leaving Munich, they set up Camp VI at the foot of the North-East Spur. The mountains were active, with avalanche after avalanche pouring off Simvu and Kangchenjunga, which 'aroused ... a lust of battle' in the Germans. The porters watched the avalanches nervously, but Bauer believed the Germans 'could depend upon the loyalty of the best of them, if needs be, to the death',[14] an attitude which was to have fatal consequences for some of the porters. Based on their experience in 1929, the Germans expected avalanches and rockfall in July, but they were surprised by the force of them, meaning they had to work cautiously on the route. The 200-metre icefall above Camp VI proved testing for the porters, many of whom grew nervous and hung on to the ropes, whilst others were overconfident and had to be warned to be more careful.

Above the icefall, the glacier flattened off before the steep rocky slopes up to the crest of the North-East Spur. In September and October 1929 these slopes had been quiet, and only during August did they have problems with rockfall, but in July 1931 the warm winds loosened frozen debris, making it so dangerous that they paused operations. Allwein, Aufschnaiter and Pircher spent two days taking it in turns to note down the avalanche activity and the time and direction of rock and ice falls, to determine when it was safe to climb this slope. This allowed them to plan a cunning route across the areas dangerously exposed to rock falls, and rush from one safe place to another, keeping an eye out for danger, ready to shout a warning to others when rocks fell. They made an absolute rule that this lower section could only be climbed between 5 a.m. and 8 a.m., before it got too warm. If anyone arrived too late, they had to wait until the next morning. Above the Eagles' Eyrie camp they could be a little later, but still only up to 10 a.m. Bauer likened the few occasions when a descending party was late on this section to a wartime enemy barrage, with masses of rock crashing down and smashing into thousands of hissing stone bullets. They needed nerves of steel and learnt to tell by the sound it made what falling debris was particularly dangerous. The porters watched from the safety of the Eagles' Eyrie chanting the Tibetan prayer *Om mani padme hum*, as those caught on the face above disappeared behind a cloud of dust and debris. Even with their risk-reduction tactics, it was only by chance that Bauer's team operated there for two months without a serious accident.

Above this precipice the rockfall danger disappeared because the mountain was plastered in snow and ice. A series of ice ridges festooned with bizarre ice formations were divided by avalanche-swept gullies. On 22 July they reached the crest of the Spur, but the exceptional hot weather, with temperatures rarely below zero, caused the paths they had stamped out to collapse and cornices to break away from under them. They experimented with waiting until the temperature dropped and the mountain was quieter in the evening, but it started to rain and the snow bosses, already softened by the hot sun, melted and became very slippery. At the Eagles' Eyrie, Allwein was suffering from sciatica due to the damp; most of the others had colds and terrible coughs; and some of the porters even had mumps and had to be isolated. It snowed every day; with the temperature above zero, this turned to slushy water, not weather conditions conducive to curing their illnesses.

When the weather improved, avalanches thundered down from the neighbouring peaks, their tracks covered by a metre of fresh wet snow. Whilst Hartmann and Bauer looked nervously at a very difficult-looking tower they planned to climb the next day, it obliged them by leaning forward, toppling into space, and crashing onto the glacier far below. In 1929 the strange ice formations on the ridge were frozen, providing difficult but quite secure climbing; in 1931 they froze only on the surface, remaining watery inside, even at night. The techniques they had used in 1929 were useless; they had to make a firmer path, either by stamping down the snow until it was hard or by clearing it away completely. This was slow work, but day after day they gradually advanced along the ridge. Bauer had to deal with the tragic death of one of the porters, Babu Lall, a veteran from 1929, who had probably died from malaria or blackwater fever. In 1931 there were various epidemics and the Europeans were not immune: Fendt got a paratyphoid fever; Leupold, Hartmann and Pircher all caught malaria, despite regularly taking quinine.

A fatal accident

Route-making towards Camp VIII proceeded slowly, with the last part of the crest so soft that Schaller and Pircher had to traverse the face under it until they reached the foot of a gully leading back to the ridge. Pircher tried to climb the right side of the gully, but the snow was too soft and he slipped back down. There was no other choice but to go up the gully, which was swept by avalanches. Pircher had only advanced a few metres when a mass of snow fell on him. Then Schaller tried and climbed a rope's length up the gully, before moving out onto the left-hand rib and finding a way to the terrace above.

They had been working for two and a half weeks on this section and were behind schedule, so this breakthrough was a major relief. A team of heavily burdened men went up to establish Camp VIII on the first terrace, with Hartmann and Wien going ahead to improve the route for the porters, whilst the others followed. When Bauer arrived below the difficult section, he and Schaller sat together for a short rest in the warm sun. Schaller then roped up with two porters, Tsin Norbu and Pasang, and set off, with Pircher, Bauer and another porter, Bagde, following. When Bauer saw the route, he felt an intuitive dread that it was too hard for the porters, who might panic faced with the exposure or an avalanche. He wanted to call down to the others to find a safer way, but Schaller and the two porters were already at the gully. Bauer watched anxiously from the start of the traverse as Schaller climbed carefully, before disappearing from view. Pasang followed, while Tsin Norbu stood at the foot of the gully belaying.

To his horror, Bauer saw Pasang suddenly shoot out of the gully, followed by Schaller, who bounced over Pasang, before they both crashed at the foot of the gully and were flung out down the face below. One of them had been knocked off balance by a snow slide and pulled the other off. Bauer held his breath, praying that the rope would hold, but it was severed by sharp rocks where Tsin Norbu was belaying, sending Schaller and Pasang further down, together with dirty snow and debris. Bauer saw a dark object roll, then come to a stop on an avalanche cone 550 metres below. He realized there was no hope for them. Bauer made sure the hysterical Bagde, who he feared would throw himself down too, was securely tied on. He and Pircher tried to make sense of what they had just seen, doubtless thinking of Schaller's parents back in Germany. Bauer must have felt he had done all he could to make things as safe as possible, but now wondered whether they should carry on with the expedition. According to Bauer, his doubts were checked by Pircher, who hit a defiant note: 'But our great goal, Captain, surely we won't give that up?'[15] Himalayan climbing is a very risky activity and it is not unusual for an expedition to continue following a death. For example, Alexander Kellas had died early in the first British reconnaissance of Everest; after burying him, the team continued across Tibet, almost as if nothing had happened. Wade Davis suggests the team may have 'lost the very capacity to be touched by something as commonplace as death'.[16] However, the 1930s also saw the growing prevalence of another current in the German climbing community: the narrative of a higher objective which merited sacrifices. As Isserman and Weaver pointed out, one of the origins of such ideas was 'the enormous [British] publicity surrounding another famous expedition: "the race to the pole" together with the extravagant national commemoration of Scott's martyrdom ... [which] suggested an entire rhetoric in which to couch Himalayan aspiration, a high rhetoric of struggle and honour and fellowship and sacrifice'.[17]

Before continuing the attempt, they wanted to bury the fallen climbers with a proper ceremony, but the immediate problem was

Tsin Norbu, who was petrified at the foot of the gully. The Germans brought the porter across the traverse and left him with Bagde. They then had to go back up the gully to tell Hartmann and Wien what had happened. They, in the meantime, had improved the track to the terrace, coming out onto a broad horizontal section of the ridge, before going further to find a site for the camp. Schaller and the porters had been carrying the tents, and Hartmann and Wien were worrying why they had not arrived yet. They heard a call and saw Bauer was quite close, saying they should come back because the route was too hard for the porters. Hartmann begged him to let them stay there, saying they had a tent sack and could dig an ice hole that night and improve the track for the porters in the morning. Bauer calmly insisted they should come down. This puzzled Hartmann and Wien, since it was obvious they could not reach camp below before nightfall. They descended carefully, Pircher cutting huge steps in the gully, and reached the place where Tsin Norbu and Bagde were crouching against the rocks. Only then did Bauer tell Hartmann and Wien about the accident. They all had to bivouac between some rocks. In the morning they saw Allwein and Aufschnaiter below on the avalanche cone, dragging a black form from the rocks and laying it down on the snow, before placing a second body beside it. Bagde collapsed at the sight of the two bodies, making it a struggle to get him down to Camp VI. The victims were duly buried with Buddhist and Christian prayers, on a rock island in the Zemu Glacier marked with a large stone cairn.

The renewed assault

Bauer wanted to continue. The team knew the risks, and he believed each member would want the others to carry on, even if he himself was killed; but it would not be easy. Schaller had been one of the strongest climbers; the others had not been in such a good state. Leupold and Fendt, who had been managing the supplies, were both unwell, as were Brenner and Allwein. This left only five of the team able to work on the route. Of these only Wien was fit; the others suffering from colds.

Hans Hartmann, Hans Pircher and three porters moving up the North-East Spur of Kangchenjunga near Camp VIII in 1931. The scene of the fatal accident is the gully on the left.

The attitudes of the porters changed after the accident. There were some thefts, to which the Germans responded with 'a sharp control', and many now seemed to want to do as little work as possible. This was not unreasonable given the great risks they were facing, but Bauer viewed it as offensively disloyal, and felt that malcontents were trying to influence the 'honest and enthusiastic' porters. Whilst Bauer recognized the reasons for discontentment ('the bad condition of the ridge, the poor state of general health and the grim disaster'), he still expected more from the porters. The exceptions were 'the men of 1929, and especially Tenchedar ... [who] ... remained true to us'.[18] Matters came to a head when the Germans tried to move camp from a spot at risk of rockfall. The porters, led by Tsin Norbu, the man who was with Schaller when the accident occurred, and whom Bauer calls 'the arch conspirator', were comfortable and did not want to move. Bauer thought Tsin Norbu wanted to use the accident to 'enlarge his sphere of influence at our expense', but none of the other porters disobeyed orders. Eventually even Tsin Norbu picked up his pack to move, under the stern glare of Bauer, who seemed to be unaware of the trauma caused by the fatal accident. Perhaps the experience of death in the trenches desensitized veterans like Bauer, and his British equivalents, so much that they did not understand the impact on others. The writer Robert Graves, who in 1916 fought on the opposite side of the same trenches at the Somme as Bauer, wrote of the latter period of his time in the trenches that 'there was no excitement left in patrolling, no horror in the continual experience of death'.[19]

They also heard the worrying news that Danatbank, one of Germany's four big banks, had collapsed, leading to a run on the banks and a suspension of bank deposits. The Bavarians wondered whether it was right to continue the expedition, spending money on climbing instead of being back at home with their families. They knew, though, that nothing they could do then would make any difference.

When they returned to the North-East Spur the porters were initially unwilling to follow. Bauer realized they had to come of their own free will, and a few days later first Tenchedar, then three others, came to him saying they would return to work. Bauer appeared to believe they were inspired by the example of courage shown by the Germans, but we have no direct testimony of their motivations. The porters were not willing to climb the gully where the accident had occurred, so they followed the crest of the ridge, which had been rejected before as too difficult. It was dizzyingly narrow and covered in ice mushrooms, which had to be tunnelled through or hacked away, often whilst standing on unstable snow, trying not to bring the whole structure down. Hartmann climbed the hardest part, squeezing past the highest tower, before getting onto it and collapsing it. It was slow and difficult work involving many days of tunnelling and digging, alternating the pair in the lead to keep the team fresh.

Hans Hartmann cooking in a snowhole during the 1931 Kangchenjunga expedition.

Although progress continued on the route, they were worried about the supply chain below. They had a system to communicate with Aufschnaiter in Camp VII, but he had no porters willing to bring supplies up, so Bauer went down to organize reinforcements. At Camp VI only Allwein was in good enough shape to work on the North-East Spur; the others were still too weak. Aufschnaiter had been in Camp VII for weeks, maintaining the supply chain, but once they had enough supplies for the summit climb he handed over management of the camp to Tenchedar and went higher up himself.

They managed to persuade another two porters, Pasang and Dordshi, to return to work, but they were very nervous at the site of the accident and threw themselves in the snow, begging not to have to continue. Dordshi put down his load, untied himself from the rope, and tried to run back down the mountain, forcing the Germans to grab him and push him up the short remaining section

Karl Wien at 7,275 metres on the North-East Spur of Kangchenjunga in 1931, looking towards Siniolchu.

to the terrace. Pasang, who had been one of the strongest Sherpas during the retreat in 1929, had in Bauer's view 'been corrupted by various influences and circumstances'.[20] Since he was a relative of the other Pasang, who had died in the accident, his fear does not seem surprising. Dordshi seemed so demoralized that the Bavarians realized he couldn't carry on, and Pasang was suffering from snow-blindness, so they left them in the ice cave at Camp VIII with blankets, food and fuel for several days.

When the three porters who had been working on load-carrying heard that the others weren't coming up in support, they were disconsolate. Bauer decided to give them a few days' rest, with the Germans taking on most of the load-carrying themselves. When the three porters saw that their employers were determined to go on, they declared themselves willing to help create two or even three more camps. This, and the settled weather, gave the Bavarians a chance: they were at 7,000 metres, with six climbers and three porters, and supplies for a fortnight, but with no possibility of being resupplied from below they had to push on as fast as possible. A party led by Allwein, who carried a large shovel, went up to Camp XI in beautiful weather. With no level place for a tent, Allwein started digging an ice cave. Then he, Aufschnaiter and the porters went back down, leaving Hartmann and Wien to expand and sleep in this cave. Only one of them could work at a time, and Hartmann's damaged feet were very cold by the time they got inside. He had a difficult night, exhausted and coughing badly.

Bauer was not able to participate in this final assault. He had been so slow on the way up that Aufschnaiter told him to turn back. Bauer was surprised, as he had had no thought of giving up, but realized he would endanger his comrades if he chose to continue. Once he turned round he realized how weak he was and thought of Alexander Kellas, who had died of heart failure on the 1921 Everest reconnaissance. At Camp X there was no sleeping bag or blanket, and to make matters worse a crack in the ice cave let in a bitter wind. Bauer had one of the worst nights of his life but managed to drag himself down to Camp IX in the morning. Finding a sleeping bag there, he decided to wait for the main party above, hoping they would reach the summit.

Outpost Peak

Camp XI was on the last level section before Outpost Peak, the highest point of the North-East Spur, before it descended slightly and merged with the main North Ridge of Kangchenjunga. After the cold night in the ice cave, Wien and Hartmann woke to a beautiful day. They went up the snow arête towards Outpost Peak, expecting that a similar arête on the other side would lead them to the main North Ridge. The position was spectacular, with huge drops on either side. Kangchenjunga, going in and out of the mist, looked quite close. They couldn't reach the top of Outpost Peak that day because of deep unconsolidated snow. They did not have a complete view, but it was clear that instead of the arête continuing to the North Ridge, as they had assumed, the Spur actually ended in a broad snow saddle. This was a good site for Camp XII, but a steep snow slope above would have to be overcome to reach the North

The main summit of Kangchenjunga seen from Outpost Peak (7,940 metres) in 1931.

Ridge. They could only see the upper third, but there were suspicious traces of slab avalanches.

When Wien and Hartmann returned to Camp XI, Allwein, Pircher and Aufschnaiter were already there with a tent. That night in the snow cave Hartmann's feet hurt terribly, and in the morning a small part of his right foot was black, raising the fear that it would eventually have to be amputated. Allwein's medical advice was that Hartmann should descend as soon as possible. It was also very cold in the tent. Aufschnaiter, who had a bad cough, stayed behind, but Allwein and Pircher set off, with Wien following twenty minutes later. They hoped to reach the planned site of Camp XII, dig an ice cave there and explore the route to the North Ridge. Pircher was tired and Wien easily caught him up. Allwein was going really well and pulled further ahead. Wien only caught him up at the top of Outpost Peak. Allwein expressed a worry regarding the risk of a windslab avalanche on the snow slope to the North Ridge, although he had not seen the whole of it on account of the mist. Looking again, Allwein told Wien they had to turn back. The slope appeared harmless at first sight, even to the experienced climbers, but they took note of two jagged edges where snow slabs had detached, as well as various suspicious cracks. The lower part was highly convex, a dangerous shape for avalanches. On the left was a fluted snow wall; on the right steep rock faces above overhanging masses of snow. There was no way to bypass the slope. Wien and Allwein sat for a long time discussing whether there was a way to overcome this section. They knew, though, that the attempt on Kangchenjunga was over. Allwein had a reputation in the AAVM as a risk-taker who had known narrow scrapes with avalanches, but this time his experience told him they must turn back. As they headed down, the clouds closed in and then opened up again, showing Kangchenjunga close but inaccessible. Wien hung back from the others, reluctant to forsake such a place.

When Allwein reached Camp IX the next morning, Bauer was sat outside looking at the view. He took the news of failure hard. They descended the North-East Spur with their minds full of memories of the weeks of struggle. They had always known that an obstacle might stand in their way but had not expected it after overcoming the whole North-East Spur. They were too tired and supplies too short to wait for conditions to improve. They returned to the rock island on the Zemu Glacier to erect a bronze gravestone that had been sent by the Himalayan Club. Bauer lacked the strength to get to the island. He lay on the glacier, where he experienced a wartime vision:

> I saw ... my battalion commander standing before me, just as I had seen him for the last time. His eyes filled with tears as I was laid down in front of him, badly wounded. We could not speak, for I had a bullet through my chest and he could not trust his voice. He fell soon after. This picture accompanied my fevered dreams. I could

> not quite understand it. For a nineteen-year-old lieutenant, fighting was a natural profession, and even when mortally wounded, he felt a joy and a satisfaction in it. Now I realized that these joyous fighters have a lonely destiny. They must fight and fall in the forefront of the battle, alone, miles away from the dull aspirations of the masses, as outposts of humanity. We who are older and wiser do well to veil our heads in sorrow when one of the younger recruits is reft from the ranks.[21]

This 'vision' surely relates Bauer's second First World War injury, suffered at La Bassée during the Battle of the Somme in August 1916. When he was first injured in 1914 the war was still mobile, but by 1916 it had been reduced to the murderous grind of trench warfare. At La Bassée the Germans repelled repeated Allied attempts to advance; their dispatches in 1916 making reference to

> A whole system of shafts and mine tunnels in which work is carried out ceaselessly day after day, night after night. The outsider has no idea of the dedication and perseverance that is being shown. Sack after sack of excavated soil has to be brought to the surface through the long shafts, and often enough the arduous work of weeks and months is ruined by enemy or water. But the digging is tireless, always listening out for the enemy. Are they to our right, our left, above or even below us? Are they going to blast us?[22]

It was here in August 1916 that Bauer suffered the chest injury that would cause him discomfort for the rest of his life. Less than three weeks earlier, Mallory's friend and fellow climber Robert Graves suffered a similar chest and lung injury, so severe that he was reported dead. The parallels between trench warfare and the struggle to climb the North-East Spur are obvious, as is that between the loss of Hermann Schaller and Bauer's fellow soldiers. The tragedy is that not only did Bauer and millions like him have to endure the horror of war, but it also marked them so indelibly. In Bauer's case he seemed unable to experience mountain adventure other than through the prism of his experience in the trenches.

SEVEN

Not a reasonable and amusing sport

Three attempts on Kangchenjunga had failed in three years, but Bauer's 1931 attempt had got the highest and was widely considered one of the hardest climbs yet made in the Himalayas. Success on the great Himalayan peaks seemed imminent: Francis Younghusband wrote that 'Every year now, mountaineers from Europe – from Italy, Germany, and England – go forth to the attack of the Himalayan peaks. And we may be certain that giant after giant will be vanquished till the mightiest of them all has lain under the foot of man.'[1] The British had been frustrated that permission for another attempt on Everest was elusive, but that was about to change.

Bauer's team returned to a Germany in economic turmoil, starting to undergo changes which would impact climbing and ultimately have terrible consequences for the country and the world. The first years of the presidency of Hindenburg, the First World War leader elected in 1925, were relatively calm, helped by the Dawes Plan, which set a more achievable schedule for war reparations and provided loans from US banks to rebuild Germany's industry. The Reichstag, the German parliament, was very fragmented, but the Nazis remained a fringe party. This calm was ended by the Wall Street Crash of 1929, which had domestic US causes but affected Germany's already faltering economy more than any other country. The loans made under the Dawes Plan started to be withdrawn, causing a slowdown in economic activity and mass lay-offs of workers.

Heinrich Brüning was appointed chancellor by Hindenburg in March 1930. He tried to steer Germany through the crisis by freeing it from the burden of reparations and foreign debt, using what was at the time a conventional austerity approach. It was Mallory's university friend, economist John Maynard Keynes, who first proposed that governments should instead actively intervene to correct economic downturns. The Reichstag rejected Brüning's austerity proposals and Hindenberg called fresh elections in September 1930. They took place against a background of political violence between the Nazis and the Communists and brought significant gains for extremist parties and a further splintering of German politics. The Nazis, who had won just 2.6 per cent of votes in 1928, now got 18 per cent, becoming increasingly difficult to ignore as a political force. Previous governments had been 'grand coalitions' involving all the centre-right and centre-left parties, but this no longer produced a majority and Brüning had to rule through presidential emergency decree, which undermined the democratic mechanisms of the Weimar Republic.

The banking crisis, which blew up during the period of the 1931 Kangchenjunga expedition, only made Brüning tighten the screws further, increasing taxes and cutting public spending. This avoided a complete economic collapse, but at a severe cost, with unemployment peaking at over 30 per cent. Brüning, believing the overriding goal was to convince other countries that Germany could not continue to pay reparations, did not deviate from his strategy, earning the name 'the Hunger Chancellor'. The still-fresh memory of early 1920s hyperinflation discouraged politicians from considering any more inflationary economic policy. Mass unemployment brought crime, psychiatric problems and alcohol abuse; suicides increased; many children and young people formed gangs. Despite the presence of emergency kitchens, malnutrition was common, and by late 1931 there were 400,000 migrant workers looking for work. Unemployment boosted support for the extreme parties on both the right and the left. The traditional view was that the Nazis' core support was among the 'working poor', like shopkeepers, small farmers and artisans. In fact, many in the professional classes were supporters, including eventually 50 per cent of the medical profession. Such professionals were typical members of the AAVM; several of Bauer's team were doctors.

For Germany's climbers the economic crisis curtailed activity, although the 1931/32 AAVM yearbook saw a silver lining in the greater collaboration between older graduate members, who had cars and motorbikes, and undergraduates, who were looking for free pillion seats and car space to go to the mountains. Many young climbers dreamt of the Himalayas, but organizing expeditions was problematic, and money was tight.

After losing out to Bauer in the race to launch an expedition in 1931, Willo Welzenbach planned to lead a team to Nanga Parbat in 1932, but was forced to withdraw again because the austerity policies meant that his employer, the city of Munich, could not give him paid leave. It was increasingly difficult for Welzenbach to balance his professional career with trying to organize an expedition, and he was bitterly disappointed having to give up again. A possible way round the funding problem was to collaborate with climbers in other countries. Welzenbach agreed to hand over to his climbing partner Willy Merkl, who managed to organize a joint expedition with the Americans Rand Herron and Elizabeth Knowlton.

Whilst most Himalayan climbers in this period came from the business or professional classes, Merkl was born in 1900 to a single mother and had attended the technical high school rather than the more selective gymnasium. During childhood, Merkl went to live with his grandmother in Traunstein at the foot of the Bavarian Alps and was soon spending all his free time in the mountains, recording his ascents from the age of 12 in a notebook. He started proper climbing three years later with a school friend, Fritz Bechtold. At the age of 17 Merkl was called up. He was a private, not an officer, given his social class, and after a short training saw active service in Flanders before the war ended.

After studying at Nuremberg, Merkl became an engineer for the state railway. He continued to make many new routes in the Eastern

Alps. In 1929 he went on an expedition to the Caucasus with his childhood climbing partner Bechtold, who was also in the team for Nanga Parbat. Merkl moved close to Munich and met Welzenbach, who interested him in the hardest problems of the Western Alps, and later in the idea of going to the Himalayas. The pair spent sixty hours on the summit wall of the North Face of the Grands Charmoz, ravaged by thunderstorms but completing the first ascent.

Merkl had a strong team for Nanga Parbat, but they lacked high-altitude experience, something few yet had in the early 1930s. It did not help that the rivalry with the group around Bauer meant that there was no one in Merkl's team who had been on Kangchenjunga. The team included Felix Simon, one of the first to climb Grade VI routes in the Eastern Alps, and Austrian mountain guide Peter Aschenbrenner. The link between the Germans and Americans was Fritz Wiessner, who reacted to the grim German economic outlook by emigrating to America, where he built a successful chemical company making ski waxes. He was climbing four grades harder than any American and got in contact with the American Alpine Club, where he met Herron, a US citizen born in Italy, who had spent most of his life in Europe, dividing his childhood between a beautiful villa outside Florence and Geneva. In Europe, Herron pursued his passion for climbing in the Alps. The funds he raised in the USA were crucial, as the DÖAV had not been able to provide much support, given the ever-worsening economic crisis in Germany.

In March 1932 Hitler challenged Hindenberg in a presidential election for the first time, receiving around one-third of the vote, but was defeated in the second round. By then Brüning was in trouble. The paramilitary wing of the Nazis, the SA, was causing chaos, with street battles between opposing paramilitary groups common. Around 400,000 men belonged to paramilitary groups associated with the Nazis. When the Prussian government searched the Nazi Party offices, they found references to plans for a putsch. The federal government hesitated to take action and Hindenberg only banned paramilitary association after pressure from regional state governments. In May, Hindenburg replaced Brüning with Franz von Papen, but his government had almost no support in the Reichstag, and so Hindenburg dissolved it and called new elections. The country desperately needed strong leadership, but Hindenburg was becoming increasingly physically and mentally decrepit, his decisions ever more influenced by the scheming of the right-wing parties.

Merkl's first Nanga Parbat attempt

When the German–American expedition left Munich Station in April 1932 Paul Bauer and several other members of the Kangchenjunga team were there to see them off. Despite this public show of solidarity, there was clearly tension between the two groups. On the boat to India they met a 'quiet, thin, middle-aged Englishman',[2] Hugh Ruttledge, who was travelling with an alpine guide to attempt a first circumvention of Nanda Devi. Ruttledge had spent more than twenty years in India, doing much Himalayan exploration, and had a wealth of knowledge for Merkl's team to tap. Ruttledge turned out to be a significant figure in 1930s Himalayan mountaineering.

Lying more than 1,000 miles from Kangchenjunga in the North-West of British India, Nanga Parbat was the first 8,000-metre peak to be attempted, when Albert Mummery disappeared in 1895. Walter Schmidkunz, the German author, publisher and climbing partner of Paul Preuss, acquired the German rights to Mummery's autobiography in 1910. He planned to attempt Nanga Parbat but was thwarted by the First World War and the inflationary period. By the late 1920s Schmidkunz felt too old to try and instead suggested his idea to Welzenbach. Welzenbach's original plan was to try from the Diamir Valley, but Merkl thought it was dangerous and technically too difficult for the porters. Instead, he wanted to reach the East Ridge from the Rakhiot Valley, a route with less technical difficulty, but still with avalanche danger and very long, increasing the risk of being caught high up by storms. Both these risks would exact a terrible price in the coming years.

Merkl's team made Base Camp in a delightful spot they called 'Fairy Meadow' and started up the crevassed and dangerous Rakhiot

Glacier. After the windblast of a huge ice avalanche close to Camp I destroyed tents, cracking the bamboo poles like matchsticks, the porters were frightened and only willing to continue for very high wages. This negative experience with porters from North-West India led the Germans to believe they compared unfavourably with the Sherpas, but Merkl had to use local men because he was short of funds. The Germans ended up doing a lot of load-carrying themselves to supply the camps.

The glacier, with concave slopes which concentrated the sun's heat, was so hot that they had to stop working after 11 a.m. Camp IV was placed on the second terrace of the Rakhiot Glacier. The most obvious route ahead traversed around a very broken glacier below Rakhiot Peak to enter what they called the *Mulde* (hollow), below the main East Ridge of Nanga Parbat. They were concerned about avalanche risk, so Aschenbrenner and Herbert Kunigk explored an alternative route over the shoulder of 7,070-metre Rakhiot Peak. They climbed the peak but concluded it did not provide a viable route to the East Ridge of Nanga Parbat. Instead, the Germans crossed into the *Mulde*, where they had not seen avalanches falling despite the threatening-looking seracs. Just as Bechtold and Merkl were about to start, an ice tower crashed down in the area they planned to cross. They had been climbing together since childhood; rather than being put off they were determined to find a way through. Crossing the most dangerous section quickly, they established Camp VI at the top of the *Mulde*.

Finding a route up to the East Ridge proved more difficult than expected, but finally Bechtold, Wiessner and Merkl struggled through waist-deep snow to reach the ridge. The main technical difficulties seemed to be behind them, and they had a breathtaking view of Nanga Parbat before descending to fetch supplies to make a camp on the ridge the next day. Wiessner had to stay with a sick porter, whilst Bechtold and Merkl only reached the ridge at 7 p.m. It was bitterly cold, so they immediately put up their small tent and fell into a deep sleep. They believed they could reach the summit in five to six days, but the next morning it started to snow, forcing them back to Camp VI, and then further back down to avoid using up the supplies they had expended so much energy bringing up.

They waited in Camp IV hoping for the weather to improve, but when it did three weeks later it only lasted one day. Wiessner, Herron and Merkl had a final try, but the snow continued to fall and reluctantly they gave up the expedition. The descent was very dangerous, as they fought their way down in waist- or chest-deep snow, triggering huge avalanches, which fortunately didn't bury anyone. Below Camp III, a serac collapsed, flinging Wiessner 20 metres into a crevasse in a whirl of ice blocks. Herron and Merkl were sure that either the fall or the ice blocks must have killed him, but could not get near enough to the highly unstable crevasse edge to see him. After an agonizing wait, they heard a faint cry from Wiessner, who was bruised but did not have any broken bones and was even able to climb back out of the crevasse unaided. They continued to Base Camp, frustrated that they had not achieved more.

On the boat journey back to Europe they stopped in Cairo, where it was still possible to climb the pyramids at Giza. After Rand Herron and Elizabeth Knowlton climbed the first pyramid before breakfast, Herron announced he wanted to climb the more difficult second one, saying 'I've heard that that smooth coping at the top is really difficult, interesting climbing. Very few people ever do it.'[3] Herron climbed the hard part without difficulty. However, after descending to the easier part he started running, lost his footing on a loose pebble and fell to his death. Herron had packed so much into his thirty years: he was fluent in four languages, wrote poetry in Italian and left a half-completed novel. After having survived the dangers of Nanga Parbat, he was undone by hubris.

Germany sleepwalks towards the disaster of a Nazi regime

The Germans returned to an ever more chaotic country. Elections at the end of July took place in very tense conditions: a reduction in the duration of unemployment benefits took many below subsistence level, and whole families were living on the streets, moving around and desperately looking for work. Political arguments were increasingly fought out in the streets by paramilitary groups. Von Papen lifted the ban on the SA in June 1932, and within a month nearly 100 people were killed in political violence. Hitler campaigned under the slogan *Arbeit und Brot* (work and bread) and promised to create jobs, realizing that credible policies to bring down unemployment, like investment in public works, could provide power via the ballot box.

Despite the climate of violence, with another twelve people killed on polling day, the turnout was a record 84 per cent. The Nazis made huge gains, more than doubling their share of the votes to 37 per cent, but not gaining a majority. The Social Democrats and Communists, unable to work together despite the appeals of Albert Einstein among others, shared 36 per cent. Hitler assumed he would be offered the role of chancellor, but Hindenburg reappointed Von Papen, who toyed with the idea of turning Germany into a dictatorship. In September he again dissolved parliament, hoping to suspend elections beyond the constitutional limit of sixty days, but found himself outmanoeuvred by Hermann Göring, who had become president of the Reichstag following the July elections. New elections in November saw the Nazis remaining the largest party, but with a slight drop in support. Fearing their chance to get power democratically might be passing, the Nazis decided to do all they could to seize it. Von Papen's position was weak because the Nazis and Communists could always vote no confidence in his government and his attempts to negotiate with Hitler failed. He also faced a threat from his defence minister, Kurt von Schleicher, who viewed the Nazis as the only party that could attract voters from the radical left. Von Papen told his cabinet that he planned to have martial law declared and rule as a dictator, but Schleicher revealed the results of a war game showing that if martial law was declared the army would not be able to defeat the paramilitary groups and there would be a civil war. Von Papen had to resign when Hindenburg refused to back his plan for martial law. Hindenberg then appointed Schleicher as chancellor.

Schleicher planned to achieve a majority in the Reichstag by winning the support of the Nazis, who he believed were running short of money and distracted by infighting. Schleicher thought he could outmanoeuvre the Nazis and persuaded Hindenburg that by appointing Hitler chancellor he could be controlled by a cabinet with a majority of conservatives, a catastrophic misjudgement, both for Germany and for Schleicher personally – he would be murdered by the Nazis a year and a half later. Hitler immediately called new elections for March 1933 and launched a campaign of violence and terror against his opponents. SA militias attacked the offices and homes of Communists and trade unionists and broke up meetings of the Social Democrats, beating up speakers and the audience indiscriminately. Many newspapers were banned.

The cause of the Reichstag fire on 27 February 1933 is still disputed. It was blamed on a Dutch Communist, Marinus van der Lubbe, who was executed, but rumours persist that the Nazis started the fire themselves and framed Van der Lubbe. Whatever the cause, Hitler ruthlessly exploited the event to suppress his political opponents, persuading Hindenburg to issue a decree suspending most civil liberties. Despite the arrest of Communists, violence and voter intimidation, the Nazis failed to win a majority, taking just under 44 per cent of the votes. They had to rule in coalition with the right-wing National People's Party, but Hitler was determined to consolidate his hold on power. The Enabling Act gave the cabinet the right to enact laws without the consent of parliament. Hitler achieved the required two-thirds majority by arresting all the Communist deputies and preventing a number of Social Democrats from attending the vote. The only obstacle to complete power was Hindenburg, but Hitler had to move cautiously with regard to the president, who still had the power to sack him and was a popular war hero with support from the army. Hitler avoided offending the president, who was 86 and in declining health, meaning Hitler could wait until Hindenburg died the following year. Hitler then abolished the role of president and became undisputed head of state. After the election, hundreds of thousands joined the Nazis, many opportunistically as it was clear the party would have considerable control over Germany society. The new members were nicknamed the *Märzveilchen* (March violets) and were distrusted by the long-standing members, the *alte Kämpfer* or old fighters. Paul Bauer joined the party in May 1933, although he wrote afterwards that he had sympathized much earlier, but had seen party membership as an obstacle to his journeys to the Himalayas.

Bauer still wanted to organize another Kangchenjunga expedition and waited sceptically to see the outcome of the attempt on Nanga Parbat, with little confidence in Merkl's ability. Bauer had to abandon the idea of an expedition in 1933 because the British authorities said that no Sherpas would be available, since the British were returning to Everest after a gap of nine years. The India Office had written to the Mount Everest Committee with the unexpected good news that the Political Officer in Sikkim had obtained the consent of the Dalai Lama to a British expedition in 1933.

The British react to the German activity

The British mountaineering establishment had watched the German attempts on Kangchenjunga and Nanga Parbat with a strange mixture of admiration, envy and disapproval. When they failed only 200 metres below the top of Everest in 1924, the British were far ahead of other nations in high-altitude mountaineering and seemed to be in a position to maintain this lead, even if Germans and Italians were climbing harder routes than them in the Alps. The Germans knew the British would probably reserve Everest for themselves, but were keen to make the first ascent of one of the world's fourteen 8,000-metre peaks, something Edward Strutt, the editor of the *Alpine Journal* dismissed as 'an unworthy obsession without value of any kind'.[4] The logic that Everest is a worthy and noble objective, but other '8,000ers' are arbitrary goals is hard to follow, but Strutt clearly feared the Germans would claim to have achieved more than the British if they climbed Nanga Parbat or Kangchenjunga.

One reason for the different attitude to the 8,000ers was the metric system. Arbitrary height cut-offs, like 4,000 metres in the Alps or 8,000 metres in the Himalayas, have long had a bizarrely important influence on mountaineering ambitions. An alpine mountain just over 4,000 metres will see long lines of climbers heading to its summit on a sunny summer day, whilst its slightly lower neighbour below the crucial 4,000 metre cut-off will rarely see ascents. In the Himalayas in the twenty-first century, 8,000-metre peaks can see hundreds of ascents per year, but Gyachung Kang, the world's fifteenth highest mountain, less than 50 metres below 8,000, has not even been attempted for close on twenty years. Used to viewing the '4,000ers' as the great mountains of the Alps, continental climbers naturally viewed the 8,000ers as the greatest mountains of the world, and the first ascent of an 8,000er became a sort of holy grail. For Britons using the imperial system, the divide didn't work so neatly: Everest was over 29,000 feet, but there are three mountains over 28,000 feet, five over 27,000 and seventeen over 26,000: none of these works as a natural absolute category. If a 26,000er was climbed, it would still leave the problem of climbing a 27,000er.

Whilst dismissing the value of climbing an 8,000er, Strutt was confident that 'German mountaineers will, without bitterness, and with ... pleasure ... learn of the 1933 expedition's possible victory, not over an "eight-thousander"... but over the "world's greatest mountain", be the height what it may.'[5] Strutt was reacting to what he considered a 'patronizing and highly inaccurate' article in *Der Bergsteiger* magazine on the announcement of the 1933 Everest Expedition, which provocatively said it would be 'a difficult test of the comradeship of German mountaineers to be obliged to see without bitterness how British mountaineers, relying to a great extent on the last German Himalayan expeditions',[6] might achieve both the first ascent of an 8,000er and the world's highest peak. Strutt was positive about the expeditions of Bauer, Dyhrenfurth and Merkl, saying that Bauer had 'gracefully and thoroughly acknowledged this indebtedness [to British climbers].... British mountaineers have "followed" Herr Bauer's heroic Kangchenjunga struggles with the keenest sympathy, that when he found himself compelled to retreat for the second time, we felt for his gallant party as we should have felt had it been a British expedition.'[7] Ever politically astute, Bauer had written to his friend Strutt about the 'silly remarks' in *Der Bergsteiger.*

After participating in the 1922 Everest Expedition, Strutt was editor of the *Alpine Journal* from 1927 to 1937 and president of the Alpine Club from 1935 to 1938, a period in which it had 'declined into a stuffy, snobbish, backward-looking institution'.[8] Strutt 'had little sympathy for the revolution in Continental mountaineering which was taking place before his angry eyes, ... and the *Journal* too often appeared ... a shocked and censorious maiden aunt, appalled by the immoral goings-on of the younger generation.'[9] He believed that crampons were 'an invention of the devil', and saw the Munich School's heavy use of pitons as unsporting as shooting a fox or netting a salmon. Strutt's ire was raised again in 1934 by an article in the DÖAV newsletter by Bauer's rival Hermann Hoerlin. Strutt wrote a nitpicking critique, titled 'A Superiority Complex?', of the view that the Germans were better prepared for top-level Himalayan climbing than the British. He oscillates between admiration and disapproval when referring to the 'unjustifiable but wonderful conquest of the Matterhorn's North Face and foolish variations on the Dent d'Herens ... by guideless if misguided amateurs'. The 'foolish variation' was one of Welzenbach and Allwein's finest routes. A key point of contention was the use of guides. Hoerlin had written of the 'ancient English custom to climb in the Alps with professional guides', whereas Germans usually climbed guideless, meaning they were 'more prepared than the English for the struggle with the 8,000ers'. Strutt protests that during the Himalayan expeditions German mountaineers had 'not hesitated – in some cases ruthlessly – to avail themselves of the devoted services of British Empire porters to 'trudge through deep snow' carrying superhuman loads, for the glory of another country than their own'.[10] This is disingenuous: the work of an alpine guide could not be compared to what Himalayan porters did in the 1930s. When British climbers were making hard new routes in the Alps, the local guides led the key sections. The porters on Kangchenjunga played a crucial and dangerous role, but the Germans did all the route-making, and Hoerlin was right that climbing guideless in the Alps gave them better preparation to do so.

Strutt's implication that the porters would risk their lives for the glory of the British Empire gratingly assumes that porters, many of whom were Nepali or Tibetan anyway, saw the British Empire as 'their country' and were motivated to further its glory, even though white European climbers would go to the summit. There is little evidence that the porters felt any more loyalty to a British expedition than to a German one. Strutt concludes indignant that the British, who in his view had pioneered guideless climbing but 'despised gladiatorial displays',[11] had to endure such statements from the Germans.

However, despite being adversaries in the war, the feeling between the British and Germans was not necessarily always negative. Robert Graves found at Oxford University after the war that 'pro-German feeling had been increasing. With the war over and the German armies beaten, we could give the German soldier credit for being the most efficient fighting man in Europe ... Some undergraduates even insisted that we had been fighting on the wrong side: our natural enemies were the French.'[12] Bauer's expeditions were viewed positively by Strutt, who called the 1929 attempt 'a feat without parallel, perhaps, in all the annals of mountaineering',[13] and Edward Norton, who was 'full of admiration for [the Bavarians'] ... fine performance: the hardships the party endured, the grit and determination they showed in sticking to the route selected'. Comparing their route with the North side of Everest, Norton concluded, 'Kangchenjunga appears to me a more formidable and more dangerous proposition.'[14]

By 1933 Bauer had been elected to the British Alpine Club. Strutt's review of Bauer's book in the *Alpine Journal* remarked on 'the splendid and unselfish camaraderie of the Bavarians'. In the same piece he couldn't resist reviving the oxygen controversy, noting that the Bavarians had not 'handicapped themselves with the clumsy Everest oxygen apparatus'. Whilst this negative view of oxygen largely held sway in the 1930s, Strutt's prediction that 'despite Captain Finch ... the last of oxygen, carried on the back, has been seen in the Himalaya'[15] would turn out to be very wrong.

The team for Everest

In 1933, after four German-led expeditions to 8,000-metre peaks in the previous four years, the British finally got a chance to show what they could do. When the Mount Everest Committee put together a team for Everest, an obvious choice for leader was Frank Smythe, despite his reputation for 'irritability, tactlessness and being easily offended'.[16] Raymond Greene reckoned Smythe was the only man he knew whose temper improved with altitude. But, still yearning for the Victorian era of gentlemen climbers, the Committee did not approve of a professional mountaineer living off his writing and were unhappy to learn that Smythe had independently contacted the government of India about a possible expedition. The Committee's first choice for leader was the greatly respected Edward Norton, but when he declared himself unavailable they turned to 48-year-old Hugh Ruttledge, the man who met the 1932 Nanga Parbat team on the boat to India. Having taken early retirement from the Indian Civil Service, Ruttledge continued to be active in Himalayan exploration, but hadn't done any top-level climbing and was not expected to go high on Everest.

The core of Ruttledge's team came from Smythe's Kamet expedition. Eugene Birnie was a soldier, as were four of the sixteen-man Everest team, along with two university lecturers, four colonial civil servants and plantation managers: far from a representative cross-section of British society. This was still the era in which the Alpine Club was described as a club 'for gentleman who climb',[17] and when Ruttledge mentions receiving applications from 'pugilists, a barber [and] a steeplejack',[18] it is clear they are not the class of people he would consider for his team.

It was far from ideal that Ruttledge knew none of the likely climbers, and he soon realized that the team was 'not very well assorted'.[19] The process by which it was chosen was obscure and

Porters climbing on the slope leading to the North Col of Everest in 1933.

no note was made of how climbing records were checked: the result was that five of the team turned out to be 'dead failures'.[20] An important core of the team had studied and climbed at Cambridge University, where they had played a part in finally pushing standards higher than those before the war, even if not quite to the level being achieved in the Alps by Germans and Italians. Jack Longland's 'Javelin Blade' route in Snowdonia was one of the first to reach the extreme level in British climbing grades. Longland, Lawrence Wager and Percy Wyn-Harris were part of a new generation from Cambridge, who had learnt their alpine climbing without guides. Wager believed this 'tends to produce a safer and better attitude towards mountaineering than difficult expeditions led by a good guide, whose rapid and accurate judgement of conditions prevents the beginner from realizing the many dangers of climbing, and whose skills mask the difficulties of the technique.'[21] Edward Strutt would not have approved of such sentiments, but their philosophy was very much in line with that put forward by Hoerlin.

There were some important changes from 1924, when almost all the team, aside from the young Irvine, had seen action in the First World War. Even then there was a difference between the career soldiers, like Edward Norton or Geoffrey Bruce, and people with civilian careers who had served in the war, like Mallory, who was impressed by the military discipline of Norton and Bruce when organizing the logistics of moving equipment up the mountain. Now there was an even clearer divide between the military and civilian climbers, which led to conflict. This scope for tensions was understood even before departure, with Longland writing to Wager encouraging him to accept an invitation to participate because you 'can't leave Wyn [Harris] and Shipton and me to the tender mercies of Smythe and the Army'.[22] Although there were First World War veterans in German teams, active military men were much less of a feature because, until Hitler broke the terms of the Treaty of Versailles by reintroducing conscription in 1935, the German army was limited to a much smaller size than the British one.

There were some good climbers in the team, but the Committee did not select any of the strong up-and-coming climbers from the North of England, who did not quite fit the typical social profile of the team. Ruttledge was aware of the value of the northern climbers, but was worried they were 'a close corporation with, it seems to me, a contempt for everyone outside their own clan'.[23] The strongest candidate rejected was Liverpudlian Colin Kirkus, arguably Britain's best rock climber at the time. The British climbing establishment was narrowly closed within a certain social class, but Bauer's teams were drawn from an arguably even shallower pool of candidates from the Munich academic world. The difference was that the Munich academics were at the cutting edge of rising standards in

Alpine climbing; of the British, that could only truly be said of Smythe with his routes on the Brenva Face.

The Committee suggested Ruttledge should travel to talk to Bauer about his experience on Kangchenjunga, but he decided he could learn all he needed from Smythe. The journey by boat and train to Darjeeling and across Tibet to Everest passed without significant incident apart from some illnesses due to the altitude, cold dry air and unfamiliar microbes, but most people recovered quickly. They arrived at Base Camp twelve days earlier than in 1924, putting them in a strong position. The steep glaciated slope of the North Col presented the first serious mountaineering problem; given the fatal accident in 1922, Ruttledge took it very seriously. After inspecting it, Smythe sent a letter down to Ruttledge explaining that they could not follow the 1924 line because avalanche debris indicated severe danger. Terrifying ice cliffs ruled out a route further south, which left only the 1922 line, also with avalanche danger, although mitigated by a large crevasse across the slope midway up, which would catch smaller avalanches. Despite rotating teams, making the route took them a week, with Smythe's experience on Kangchenjunga invaluable on an overhanging section of ice. They reached an ice shelf below the North Col, where they placed Camp IV. Getting this far had taken a lot out of Shipton and Smythe, with many of the others not skilled or acclimatized enough to play a role in the route-making.

The summit attempts

As one of the first Himalayan expeditions to bring wireless equipment to monitor weather forecasts, they learnt on 12 May that the monsoon was on the east coast of Ceylon. This made them keen to establish two or three further camps and attempt the summit as soon as practical. During a first try at establishing Camp V by Eugene Birnie, fellow soldier Hugh Boustead and Percy Wyn Harris, there was a disagreement about the siting of the camp. Birnie insisted on turning around at 7,500 metres, 300 metres below the planned height, because he considered it too cold for the porters, and the camp was not made. There was no clear chain of command beyond Ruttledge and his deputy Shebbeare, neither of whom were expected to go high on the mountain. Wyn Harris, the more experienced climber, disagreed and came back down to Camp IV in an absolute rage about 'the fucking soldiery'.

For many of the climbers this incident showed the limitations of Ruttledge's leadership style. He was charming and well liked, but his goal of not losing his temper under any circumstance left him too weak to manage fifteen strong-willed men in harsh and stressful conditions. Greene felt that Ruttledge was too kind with Birnie, who had already given 'vent to his extremely bad temper',[24] and that he should never have allowed Birnie to go high on the mountain. Smythe thought afterwards that a more effective expedition would have been 'run on the same lines as Bauer's'.[25] Greene agreed that this might have radically changed the course of the expedition, although he was against a 'Hitlerite leadership'. The British never really reached a conclusion about the best way for expeditions to be led until after the Second World War.

Ruttledge was not assertive but he did have diplomatic skills, and went up to the North Col himself to resolve matters. Contemporary accounts tended to gloss over any disagreements, but Ruttledge still describes a 'long discussion' leading to a plan for a group led by Wyn Harris to place Camp V at not less than 7,800 metres. They managed to get 60 metres higher than envisaged, on the way passing a 1922 oxygen cylinder and an old roll of film, which they hoped could give a clue to what happened to Mallory and Irvine – when processed it was found to be unused.

They planned to establish Camp VI the next day, but the weather turned bad, blocking them in Camp V for three days, unable to communicate to those below. Smythe and Shipton came up, and the camp was overcrowded, so Wager and Wyn Harris were 'sent down by the senior party'.[26] This could have caused tensions, but the bad weather persisted and everyone descended to the North Col. On 28 May they returned to Camp V, and the following day Wyn Harris, Wager and Longland with eight porters managed to establish Camp VI at 8,350

The porters, referred to by the climbers as 'Tigers', who carried loads to establish Camp VI at 8,350 metres on Everest in 1933: Ang Tharkay, Da Tsering, Nima Dorje, Ang Tsering, Pasang, Tsering Tarke, Rinzing. Kipa Lama is missing from the picture; the exact positions of the others are unknown.

metres, significantly higher than the highest camp in 1924. The eight porters who carried to Camp VI had done a fantastic job, carrying heavy loads to a record height for local porters. Ruttledge called them 'as gallant a company as ever served an expedition',[27] and lists their names in his book – it says something about the times that even this slight level of recognition is unusual.

When they decided to place Camp VI higher than before, they established a rule that the porters who carried to it should always be led by an experienced climber, and this was Longland's crucial role. A storm had brewed up and Longland decided that it was too difficult to descend the way they had come up across open slabs, where a slip could easily occur. Instead, he traversed directly across, towards the North Ridge, where the risk of getting lost was much less. Soon visibility was down to 'a snow-swept circle of some twenty metres';[28] with their goggles freezing up, navigation was difficult. Every couple of hundred metres, Longland counted the men, fearful that a straggler might sit down in exhaustion and freeze to death. He was also worried that if they went too far across the face, they might miss the North Ridge and arrive at the precipice which fell to the East Rongbuk Glacier far below. Finally, they saw Camp V and met Birnie, Smythe and Shipton. Smythe noted that Longland's 'eyes were bloodshot and strained from the effort of peering into the blizzard. He spoke shortly, tersely, breathing hard the while; he was very tired but the fire of mental energy burnt as brightly as ever.'[29] He told them the 'splendid' news about the placement of Camp VI and how the porters 'had climbed magnificently'. Longland left the two most exhausted porters in the care of Birnie, before continuing with the rest down to the North Col. His contribution wasn't as spectacular as a summit attempt but was every bit as important.

Wyn Harris and Wager slept higher than any humans ever before. A significant dilemma was whether the best route to the summit was to make Norton's rising traverse across the North Face or follow Mallory's preferred route on the crest of the North-East Ridge, with its two famous rock steps. Wyn Harris and Wager had the task of exploring the Second Step to see if they could find a way over it onto the easier final part of the North-East Ridge. If they failed, they were to try Norton's route. An hour after leaving camp they made a dramatic discovery: an ice axe lying on a slab about 20 metres below the crest of the ridge. Only Mallory and Irvine had gone that high in that direction, so it must have belonged to one of them. They could see the mark of Willisch of Täsch in Switzerland, suppliers of several axes to the 1924 expedition, but they did not know which of them had dropped it or whether this had occurred on the ascent or when descending, perhaps after reaching the summit. Most of the 1933 team took the unromantic position that a fall on the way up was more likely.

Wyn Harris and Wager reached a point with a good view of the Second Step, which rose some 30 metres from the narrow crest like 'the bows of a battlecruiser', and decided it was 'impregnable to direct assault'.[30] They attempted to circumvent it via a gully on its right-hand side, but this proved to be a 'snare and a delusion', only a shallow scoop in the smooth dark rocks of the step. They switched their attention to Norton's traversing route; with Wager belaying from a bad stance, Wyn Harris was able to enter the Norton Couloir with a tricky section of climbing. Wyn Harris was fairly fresh and Wager wrote that he 'still hoped for the top and I was proposing to accompany him for 300–400 ft till he got through the grey band, then I thought I might go back over and rappel the First Step'. Afterwards Wager recognized that 'both our ideas were megalomaniacal and this little couloir of powder snow stopped us and ... [at 12.30 p.m.] decided us that we should turn back'.[31] They wanted to explore the area between the First and Second Steps again, but by the time they were back near Camp VI they realized how tired they were from the extreme altitude. Wager got onto the crest of the ridge just below the First Step and looked down the huge Kangshung Face on the other side. The ridge was narrow and did not seem a viable route up Everest. Wyn Harris picked up the ice axe they had found earlier and replaced it with his own. After nine years lying at well over 8,000 metres, it seemed undamaged.

The Yellow Band

At Camp VI, Wyn Harris and Wager met and debriefed Eric Shipton and Frank Smythe, who had come up to make their own attempt. Smythe and Shipton thawed four tins of Brand's meat essence and some canned fish, followed by coffee with condensed milk. Although it was bitterly cold, they poked their heads out of the tent before nightfall to get a fantastic view of the highest peaks appearing above a sea of clouds. They had an uncomfortable night on the sloping tent floor, during which Smythe frequently rolled onto Shipton, who kicked with his elbow or jabbed with his knee, 'hoping vaguely that the action would not reveal the temper that was undoubtedly behind the blows'.[32] They woke to snowfall and decided to wait, hoping for better weather. They lay in their sleeping bags all day, wondering

Frank Smythe (left) and Eric Shipton on Everest in 1933.

how long they could stay at such a high altitude and still have the strength to descend.

The second night was no more comfortable than the first, with blasts of wind driving snow against the side of the tent, but it dawned clear. If they were to attempt the summit, it would have to be that day. They delayed their start due to the cold and put on all their available clothes before venturing out. They took a thin rope but agreed not to use it on the slabs near Camp VI, which were not technically difficult, although slippery when covered in fresh snow, which is how Smythe suspected Mallory and Irvine came to grief. Shipton, who had already been going less well than Smythe up to Camp VI, had stomach trouble, but they moved steadily under the First Step on a series of narrowing ledges. Then Shipton's stomach worsened and he told Smythe to continue alone, just as Norton had when Somervell couldn't go on nine years earlier.

Smythe wanted to cross the Norton Couloir as high as possible and so kept traversing at the very top of the Yellow Band, finding a lot of snow, mostly soft and powdery, but occasionally hard, including 30 metres requiring steps to be cut. The angle steepened, and a couple of times he had to retrace his steps to find a viable way. Despite the fresh snow, Smythe was optimistic that he could traverse the couloir and find his way through the band of black rocks (Wager called them grey) on the far side to the easier-looking final pyramid. He was less sure once he looked into the couloir, which was steep and ended in some fearsome overhangs. A slip would mean falling to the Rongbuk Glacier, 3 kilometres vertically below. Even entering the couloir was tricky, with Smythe forced to turn inwards to the steep rock, his fingers clinging to indentations. He eventually managed to lower himself to a snow-covered ledge which led to the couloir.

To his surprise, it was full of hard snow, and he had to cut steps – very hard work in the thin air, leaving him panting. A subsidiary couloir forking off the main one seemed the only chance to break through the band of black rocks. Up to that point the climbing had been dangerous but not difficult; now it was both. Smythe's chances of reaching the summit were disappearing, but he was determined to carry on as long as possible, whilst keeping an eye on the weather. To reach the subsidiary couloir, he had to climb 15 metres up steep rocks covered in fresh powder snow. Smythe had to sweep this clear with his hands before levering himself up onto the sloping rock shelf he had uncovered, first kneeling and recovering his breath, before managing to stand. The process was repeated on the next step, but his hands became numb, and he was worried about dropping his ice axe. He started to rely on feeling the footholds through the deep snow rather than exposing them, but he nearly fell when a hold broke away, before managing to hang onto his axe, which he had jammed into a crack. His senses were so dulled by the lack of oxygen that he was barely scared, despite the prospect of a fatal fall. He had been in the couloir for an hour and barely gained 15 metres in height. Another 100 metres of difficult snow-covered rocks remained before easier ground. He could have carried on for another hour or two, but that wasn't enough time to make it to the summit, and going on just increased the risk of not making it back. Smythe stopped at more or less the same height as Norton, Wyn Harris and Wager.

Smythe shovelled away snow, so that he could stand securely and look at the summit 200 metres above. A continuous plume of snow blew from it, even though he was completely sheltered. After photographing the incredible view, he turned his mind to the descent. With oxygen deprivation impacting much less when going down, he was soon back in the couloir. The altitude played tricks with his mind: he saw UFOs and felt that he had an imaginary companion, offering him half of the mint cake he forced himself to eat. There was no sign of Shipton at the place Smythe had left him. Smythe was tempted to descend directly to Camp V, but he knew Shipton would assume an accident had taken place and come looking for him, so Smythe traversed across to the tent of Camp VI and found Shipton inside. They were so hoarse from the cold dry air that they needed a hot drink before discussing plans. Shipton wanted to descend to the more comfortable Camp V, whereas Smythe was very tired and stayed another night at Camp VI.

From the door of the tent, Smythe watched Shipton leave in worsening weather and then dozed for a while. After being woken by a violent storm, he cooked dinner and fell into a sound and unbroken night's sleep in the comfort of two sleeping bags, one inside the other. He woke feeling so refreshed that he contemplated going up again to look at the Second Step to 'settle the vexed question' of whether a viable route existed over it, but only an immediate descent was sensible. High grey clouds dulled the light; there was fresh snow on the rocks and signs that another blizzard was on the way. After a last glance at the tent where he had spent three nights, Smythe set off down. As he made a slow descent towards Camp V, he was hit by a hurricane so fierce that sometimes he could only make progress on his hands and knees. Some 100 metres above the camp, Smythe saw the figures of Birnie and Shipton emerge from the tents and, without seeing him, set off down towards the North Col. His hoarse shouts to catch their attention were lost in the wind and Smythe was so frustrated that he continued past Camp V without looking inside: if he had, he would have found a thermos of tea left for him. Smythe staggered down like a drunk, but as he neared the North Col he saw people helping Birnie and Shipton, whilst Longland came up to him with a flask of tea laced with brandy.

Ruttledge wanted to make another attempt, but his lead climbers needed rest in Base Camp. Snowfall continued; what had been a rocky black Everest when they first arrived became a snow-covered mountain. This would make conditions high up difficult, and increase avalanche danger on the North Col. Despite this, the team hoped a break in the monsoon would allow another attempt. On 11 June climbers who had passed an ad-hoc medical headed back up the glacier, but the earlier attempts had taken a lot out of them, with only Shipton and Smythe in half decent shape. The fixed ropes on the North Col were buried in 60 cm of fresh snow and an avalanche had half-buried the ladder on the ice wall. Each evening storms added to the load of snow on the mountain.

Some of the team hoped for a real break in the monsoon in July or August, although meteorological experts told them this was unlikely before the end of the monsoon in September. Ruttledge even proposed descending to a lower altitude to wait out the monsoon before launching another attempt, but the Mount Everest Committee replied saying funds were too low. At the start of July the expedition was abandoned. Given its size and cost, there was a lot of analysis on why they had not got higher than in 1924. Although Ruttledge was well liked by the team, some felt that he was not the right leader. They were unlucky with the weather, and would have attempted the summit earlier if not for the disagreement over the siting of Camp V. Eric Shipton felt strongly that the team was bigger than necessary and there would be as much chance with a smaller team, but most still believed that having plenty of reserve climbers maximized the chances of success.

Jack Longland felt that hard alpine experience was very useful for Everest and that 'the Bavarians who made those two great attacks on Kanchenjunga showed how far confidence and superb technique, learnt from the most difficult alpine climbing, can carry a party in the teeth of every natural and climatic obstacle.' He also felt that by

> belonging to a single great Munich climbing club [the AAVM], they were, almost before they left Germany, what any successful party on Everest has to be, a climbing team. ... They set new standards of climbing; they taught us that it was possible for Europeans to carry loads and pitch high camps themselves when porters failed, ... they were prepared to learn to get over the discomforts of double sleeping sacks to save weight high up on the mountain, and their team spirit was sufficient to send them back to the attack after their companion Schaller and the porter roped to him had been killed.[33]

Longland concluded that 'climbing Everest is not a reasonable and amusing sport; it's a kind of war'.[34] The British were determined to return to complete the job on Everest, and there was no shortage of opinions on what they needed to do to succeed.

EIGHT

The mountain of destiny

While Paul Bauer joined the party after the Nazi seizure of power, Günter Oskar Dyhrenfurth resigned his post at the University of Breslau following the book burnings carried out by the German Student Association. More than 25,000 'un-German' books, including those by Jews and left-wing writers, were burnt in Berlin, with a similar display in Breslau. Dyhrenfurth had read *Mein Kampf* and understood the ugly way things would go once Hitler seized power. Hettie's Jewish roots were well known; Günter Oskar's Jewish ancestors would also have shown up in the check of Aryan lineage required for university professors. After Kangchenjunga, Hettie had vowed never to go on another expedition, but was 'married to a man whose dream has been the Himalayas since childhood'.[1] Dyhrenfurth planned a new expedition in 1934 to the Karakoram mountains in the far North-West of British India, where four of the 8,000ers are situated. The family's financial circumstances had been devastated by the stock-market crashes and property left inside Nazi Germany, meaning they had to rely on scarce external sources of finance.

The Nazis were trying to control mountaineering, like all aspects of German society. Hans von Tschammer und Osten, an upper-class war veteran, was appointed to lead the German Reich Commission for Physical Exercise. Sport became subsumed to the Nazis' propaganda aims and *Heil Hitler*, the greeting at sporting events. Von Tschammer knew little about mountaineering, but recognized the value of Himalayan expeditions in demonstrating German national prowess and heroism, and was supportive when Willi Merkl proposed a new Nanga Parbat expedition for 1934. This made things much easier than in 1932 when Welzenbach had been denied leave; in 1934 von Tschammer insisted on him being available for what he called a great national task.

Paul Bauer also wanted to go to Kangchenjunga in 1934, but Merkl had got ahead of him, so he again deferred his plans. Bauer did, however, get an important role within von Tschammer's state sports organization. The DÖAV did not fit the Nazis' idea of centralization, being highly federal and covering Germany and Austria, but, although von Tschammer disliked its democratic character, he did not want to impose changes on the DÖAV. Instead, Bauer was placed in charge of a new organization, the 'Hiking and Mountaineering Section of the Reich Commission for Physical Exercise'. The DÖAV continued to exist and kept its autonomy, but had a more National Socialist character under the leadership of Fritz Rigele, a good climber. Rigele was also a confirmed anti-Semite and the brother-in-law of Hermann Göring, who had an interest in mountaineering and had an alpine hut named after him, although by 1943 he was so obese he had to be carried by mule to visit it. There were also many within the DÖAV who were strongly anti-Nazi and resisted the state's interference.

At the 1933 annual meeting of the DÖAV Bauer set out his vision for climbing: 'For us, who live within the National Socialist world of thought, ... everything should turn to the state ... there can be no creation, no activity ... which is not related to the state.... For outsiders, the strong organizational ties between sport ... and the state may not be readily understandable.'[2] Whilst many saw alpinism as an essentially individualistic if not anarchic activity, Bauer maintained it had always been directed to a common goal benefiting the whole people. He continued:

> what is new ... is that ... the people and the state are completely fused into one. ... For us Germans, the salvation of the German state is equal to the salvation of every individual.... In the midst of

> a different *zeitgeist*, in the midst of a bourgeoisie oriented towards enjoyment and easy living, we, misunderstood and laughed at by the public, have written the defiant fight against wild forces of nature on our flag, a fight that was apparently pointless, a fight that was made only for the sake of its inner spiritual content.[3]

Bauer contrasted climbers' noble struggle with what the Nazis viewed as the decadence of the Weimar Republic. Bauer believed his generation had the task of reshaping the German people, and 'a very important part of this falls on us mountaineers. Just as ... the German landscape would not be perfect if we did not have the Alps, nor can German people of the future be fully trained if we mountaineers do not give them what we have worked out: the calm prudence combined with that defiant and bold will to fight.'[4]

Bauer's vision is a frightening one: the philosophy of his Kangchenjunga teams – resilience, determination and the submission of the individual to a collective goal – is extended to the whole German nation. It is made even more menacing by the references to the will to fight. Maybe Bauer's world-view was an inevitable consequence of his war experience: when young impressionable men are sent away to fight and come through the nightmare of war thanks to these qualities, it is unsurprising that they hold them up as worthy in peacetime.

Rivals on the *Conte Verde*

Whilst not all German climbers agreed with Bauer, these types of nationalist sentiment were prominent in the publicity around the 1934 Nanga Parbat expedition. Merkl was not necessarily a Nazi supporter, but he had understood what the regime was looking for and 'caved in to Nazi pressures',[5] which eventually contributed to some catastrophic errors of judgement on the mountain. Even Merkl's team selection became highly political, with a great deal of discussion around two half-Jewish scientists he wanted to include in the research team. Von Tschammer got involved, as indeed did Hitler's deputy Rudolf Hess. Eventually one of the scientists was included, but not the other, who was found to have been been a

Communist supporter. For the climbing team, Bechtold, Merkl and Aschenbrenner were returning, and there was also Willo Welzenbach and Alfred Drexel, who had made hard new climbs together in the Alps. While most of Welzenbach's climbing partners had played support roles, Drexel was often in the lead. There was no one from either of Bauer's Kangchenjunga expeditions: the rivalry between the two groups was too great for that.

Three climbers who could strengthen Merkl's team were Hermann Hoerlin, Erwin Schneider and Uli Wieland, all of whom had been with Dyhrenfurth on Kangchenjunga in 1930. Given the value of Himalayan experience, they found themselves invited on both expeditions. The ambitious Schneider feared that Dyhrenfurth's team would get no financial backing in Nazi Germany, writing to Hoerlin that 'the accident of [Dyhrenfurth's] birth means he will no longer be able to win a flower pot in the Third Reich.'[6] In the summer of 1933 Schneider met the Dyhrenfurths to discuss their plans and see how their team was developing. Firmly in the anti-Nazi, anti-Bauer camp, Schneider learnt that, since Dyhrenfurth was now a Swiss citizen, 'our beloved friend Bauer can no longer spoil his fun'.[7] Dyhrenfurth was in discussion with potential sponsors and team members from around the world. With the Nazis having come to power a few months before, Dyhrenfurth told Schneider that 'everybody is speaking very badly about Germany, especially the English'. He had been asked whether there would be any Germans on the expedition. Hettie asked whether Hoerlin, Schneider and Wieland were Nazis or members of the paramilitary SA, because she wanted to avoid difficult political discussions.

Schneider believed that Merkl's expedition would be better financed, but he had negative feedback on Merkl's leadership on Nanga Parbat in 1932 and wrote to Hoerlin that 'we know Dyhrenfurth well, he is nobody's fool, we can surely influence him and get along well. None of this is certain with respect to Merkl! Merkl, although he is certainly a nice guy, is vain, conceited and stubborn.'[8] Wieland hesitated, but joined Merkl's team after being personally called by von Tschammer. Hoerlin turned down both invitations, worried about the leadership of

Merkl, the increasing nationalist tone of the Nanga Parbat expedition, and the organizational shortcomings of Dyhrenfurth, but Schneider joined Wieland in accepting Merkl's offer, as did another Austrian friend, Dr Willi Bernard.

As Schneider suspected, finance was a challenge for Dyhrenfurth: his solution was to make a film. This was not unprecedented – a documentary had been made on the 1930 Kangchenjunga expedition – but in 1934 there was more at stake: a Berlin film company run by a former government minister, Gottfried Treviranus, was the main source of finance for the expedition. Treviranus's company had developed a new sound process and needed a feature film to showcase it, which required a much larger film team than a documentary. A new company was created to make the film and a director appointed. By the time the final contract was signed, there was a seemingly impossibly short time to prepare, but the experience of the Dyhrenfurths allowed them to get the equipment together very quickly. Few of the 1930 team remained. However, they recruited others, including German Hans Ertl, a colourful character with an impressive climbing record, who later became known as 'Hitler's photographer'.

On 13 April 1934 Dyhrenfurth's team made it onto the ship the *Conte Verde* in Venice, which was also carrying most of the Nanga Parbat team. German newspapers played up the rivalry, writing about a 'race to the Himalayas' and an 'exciting fight for the 8,000ers'.[9] Interest in the Nanga Parbat expedition in Germany was so great that Merkl appointed a press secretary, music critic Dr Willi Schmid. Whilst doubtless there was friendly rivalry, any antagonism seems to be an invention of the nationalist newspapers. The teams got on well during the voyage, playing quoits on the deck. Dyhrenfurth's team worked on their plans, studying the four 8,000ers around the Baltoro Glacier. Rejecting K2 as too difficult, they decided to try Hidden Peak, at 8,068 metres the second highest mountain in the Karakoram. Once this had been climbed, they hoped to move on and bag another 8,000er. Given that no 8,000-metre peak had ever been climbed, the assumption that they would succeed on two seems hopelessly optimistic.

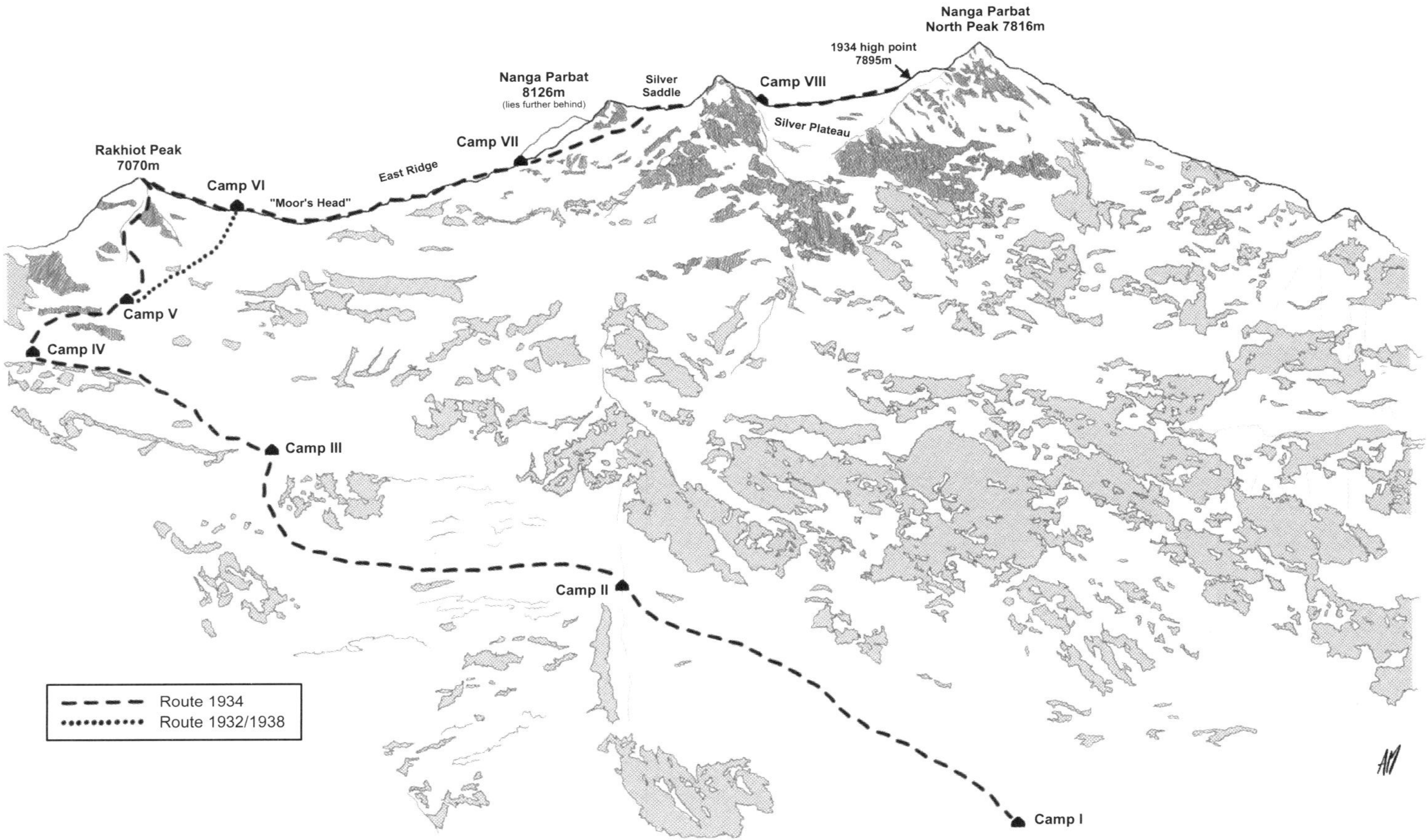
Nanga Parbat
North Peak 7816m
1934 high point
7895m
Camp VIII
Silver Plateau
Silver
Saddle
Nanga Parbat
8126m
(lies further behind)
Camp VII
East Ridge
"Moor's Head"
Camp VI
Rakhiot Peak
7070m
Camp V
Camp IV
Camp III
Camp II
Camp I
Route 1934
Route 1932/1938

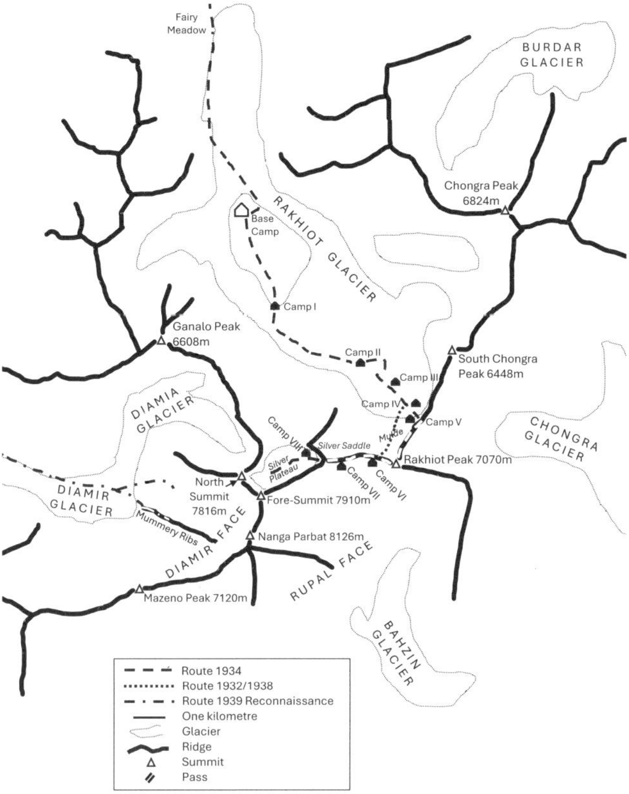

Nanga Parbat Rakhiot Face route.

Nanga Parbat map.

Merkl's team were also hoping to climb the first 8,000er. After the problems with local porters in 1932, Merkl decided to use Sherpas above Base Camp. He went to Darjeeling to confirm the final choice of thirty-five high-altitude porters, including some who had performed so well on Everest in 1933. Dyhrenfurth's team had too precarious a financial situation to hire Sherpas. When they arrived in Bombay, the first payment of 70,000 Swiss francs due from the Berlin film company had still not arrived. It was the start of a series of money worries which plagued the Dyhrenfurths throughout the expedition and brought the family close to financial ruin. With bills to pay for hotels and transport, Dyhrenfurth was in a tight corner, firing off an angry telegram to the film company and then using his charm with the local bank director to get an interim loan. This allowed them to go to Kashmir, but there they learnt that their most experienced climber, Marcel Kurz, had been injured in a riding accident and had to return to Europe. Whilst Merkl's team left for Nanga Parbat, the Dyhrenfurths had to stay behind in Srinagar, as guarantors for their creditors, with no sign of money from Berlin. When the first instalment did arrive, the Dyhrenfurths went on to Skardu. From there it was five days' march to the start of the 63-km-long Baltoro Glacier. When they came to the first large snowfields, the porters sank in the snow and asked for mountain boots, but Dyhrenfurth had brought these only for the forty-five high-altitude porters; the reaction of the others was to go on strike. Dyhrenfurth dismissed the 'mutineers' and continued with a smaller group of sixty porters, who shuttled the loads up the glacier, arriving at the foot of Hidden Peak nearly a month later than originally planned.

The Night of the Long Knives hits both expeditions

At the end of June the notorious 'Night of the Long Knives' completely stopped the flow of money to Dyhrenfurth's expedition. The paramilitaries of the SA supported the Nazis but had their own command structure and leadership under Ernst Röhm. By the time Hitler gained power, the SA was 2 million strong. By the end of 1933 this had swelled to 3 million. During the Weimar Republic the SA made a nuisance of themselves by breaking up Communist meetings. Of course once the latter had been banned, the SA were deprived of this 'pleasure'. The ever-growing number of SA groups caused trouble on the streets, spending their evenings drinking, attacking passers-by and confronting the police if they were called to help. Röhm saw the National Socialist revolution as incomplete and wanted to merge the SA into the army. Hitler wanted to avoid seeming a threat to his industrialist backers and the leadership of the army, who were ambivalent towards the Nazis but viewed the SA as an undisciplined rabble. Hitler saw Röhm as a threat to his authority, and in the summer of 1934 he decided to act, unleashing a purge in which Heinrich Himmler's SS carried out the extrajudicial

The route on Rakhiot Glacier beyond Camp II on Nanga Parbat in 1934.

killing of Röhm and other SA leaders, taking the opportunity to get rid of other internal enemies, including conservative politicians from the Weimar era like former Chancellor Schleicher. Also among the targets was Gottfried Treviranus, a former minister in the Brüning cabinet and one of the main owners of the film company backing Dyhrenfurth's expedition. When the Gestapo arrived to arrest him, he was playing tennis and they did not recognize him, allowing him to escape and reach the Netherlands. But his company folded, leaving the Dyhrenfurths with a large financial shortfall.

By a strange twist of fate, the Night of the Long Knives also impacted the Nanga Parbat expedition: their press officer Willi

Schmid was arrested by the SS and shot without investigation. The Nazis had no grudge with Schmid, who was a victim of mistaken identity, the SS combining extreme cruelty with incompetence. For Schmid's wife and three children, all of this was desperately irrelevant. Newspapers described Schmid's death as a tragic accident and Hitler's deputy Rudolf Hess visited Schmid's widow Kate to apologize, assuring her that 'not a shadow of guilt' would fall on her husband. Kate, who herself had Jewish ancestry, was comforted by the fact that Hess seemed genuinely apologetic, writing that 'when he left, he could not utter a sound. He simply bent for a long time – ever so deeply – over my hand'.[10] Kate had a good relationship with Willi Merkl and assured him that she would continue the work of press secretary. The contact person for the expedition at the DÖAV was a man who had been close to accepting Merkl's invitation to Nanga Parbat, Hermann Hoerlin. Hoerlin, who had been receiving letters about the expedition from his friends Schneider and Wieland, was asked to go to Munich to assist Kate. The two became close and would eventually marry and emigrate to the USA to escape the Nazi persecution due to Kate's Jewish ancestry.

By the time the bloodletting of the Night of the Long Knives took place, the Germans had been on Nanga Parbat for over a month. On 6 June, Welzenbach and Alfred Drexel descended from Camp III to try to improve the track to Camp II. When they came back a blizzard was raging; Drexel was the last to arrive, very tired and complaining of severe headaches. That night he didn't sleep at all and was delirious. Initially he refused advice to go down, before descending in the afternoon, arriving in Camp II a bit blue in the face and breathing heavily, but otherwise not giving serious concern. Bechtold and Drexel lay in the tent and chatted; everything seeming quite normal; but in the evening Drexel developed a bad cough, before falling into a broken and feverish sleep. In the morning his condition worsened sharply and Bechtold sent for help. Drexel lost consciousness, visibly sinking from life. The expedition doctor Willy Bernard arrived and diagnosed pneumonia, although acute mountain sickness seems more likely. Realizing that oxygen might save Drexel, Bernard sent two

Sherpas down to fetch the equipment from Base Camp, but by the time they returned during the night Drexel had died.

They carried his body back down to Base Camp, where the whole team assembled for his burial. Although they were united in grief, Merkl's decision to photograph Drexel's body wrapped in a Nazi flag to send to the German newspapers brought tensions within the team to a head. The three Austrians, Schneider, Aschenbrenner and Dr Willi Bernard, saw it as lacking respect and refused to take off their hats when the funeral was being filmed. The strong-willed Schneider was most vocal, telling Bechtold and Müllritter to put the cameras away or he would knock them out of their hands. There was a furious row, with Merkl telling Schneider to leave the expedition and go home, before eventually calming down.

Welzenbach wrote in a letter home that Schneider had 'merely said what most of us were thinking'.[11] Whether and how actively the other climbers supported or opposed the Nazi Party is not clear in all cases. Welzenbach was an officer in the SA, but had only joined after the Nazis came to power, apparently to protect his job with Munich City. Previously he was an active member of the Bavarian People's Party, a centre-right party, opposed to the Nazis. Welzenbach wrote that in Drexel 'we lost an effective mainstay in the battle against Willy's delusions of grandeur and persecution mania.'[12]

There was never any doubt that the expedition would continue: too much financial and political capital was invested in its success. At the graveside Merkl spoke of how they would 'gladly ... continue the struggle with the iron determination of our dead friend' and referred to 'a soldier's burial'.[13] Nevertheless, after Drexel's death there was a strange hiatus in the team's push on the mountain; although porters restarted operations a few days later, the German climbers initially stayed down in Base Camp. The weather was perfect, but the team worked on making a great sarcophagus to commemorate Drexel. A snowstorm on Burzil Pass had delayed the supply of tsampa, the Tibetan flour which was the staple food of the Sherpas. Welzenbach felt that this should not delay their departure since other food was available, but Merkl wasn't willing to be flexible. As time was lost, frustrations increased. Welzenbach wrote in a letter home that 'Merkl is increasingly trying to act like a dictator who tolerates no comments. He really seems to believe that a stern and uncompromising attitude serves to establish his authority and to suppress the inferiority complex which he obviously feels.'[14]

Merkl was angry with Schneider and with Aschenbrenner, who he felt was influenced by his fellow Austrian. He remarked to Müllritter that 'It is a beastly thing that we have those two [Austrians] with us. We should not have taken them.'[15] Some of the German participants felt that the two Austrians were dodging work by always being the first off in the morning, leaving others to follow on in the heat of the day with the porters; although it was the Austrians who were doing most of the route-making. One evening in Base Camp, when the Austrians weren't around, Bechtold asked how it would be perceived back home if the Austrians were the first to reach the summit – the implication being that a successful ascent would not provide the desired propaganda effect for the Third Reich if it was made by Austrians.

Even when the tsampa arrived, Welzenbach wrote to his family that 'the departure of the first group was originally planned for today. However, Merkl and Bechtold can't drag themselves away from Base Camp and won't follow us until tomorrow. Thus, our advance will be delayed once again.'[16] Trust had broken down between the old climbing partners Merkl and Welzenbach, who concluded his letter: 'you will be wondering why I am telling you all of this. Well, because I don't want to entrust it to my diary. You never know whose hands diaries will fall into. For example, Merkl seized [Drexel's] diaries immediately.'[17] It has been speculated that tension between Merkl and his team was linked to his feeling of inferiority due to a more modest social background. Welzenbach's letters provide some support for this, but there were probably a variety of factors involved, including the pressure from the Nazi authorities to succeed. Finally, on 22 June, six European climbers and fourteen porters left Base Camp, to the sound of music on their gramophone, the departing climbers singing along. Nine of them would never return.

Albert Höcht, Günter Dyhrenfurth, Hettie Dyhrenfurth and Hans Ertl after returning from their climb on Sia Kangri in 1934.

The final attempt

A day later Dyhrenfurth's expedition established Base Camp on the huge Baltoro Glacier and split into groups to explore the approaches to Hidden Peak. André Roch and Dyhrenfurth went up a fantastically broken glacier basin but concluded there was no viable route up Hidden Peak from there. A better option seemed to be a huge rock and ice spur leading to snow fields, which could be followed to the summit pyramid. Hans Ertl and Roch managed to reach 6,300 metres on this spur, and were convinced that, equipped with fixed ropes, the route was safe for porters. The porters watched with amazement and horror as the two Europeans climbed the insecure brittle rocks and soft snow. No amount of coaxing, pressing or financial inducement would persuade them to carry loads on it.

Dyhrenfurth's team realized that attempting an 8,000er was out of the question, but once the filming was complete and the weather had improved they planned to tackle Sia Kangri and Baltoro Kangri, two 7,000-metre mountains on either side of the 6,300-metre Conway Saddle. The Dyhrenfurths, Ertl and Albert Höcht attempted Sia Kangri, starting from a snow cave. Ertl and Höcht broke the trail, with Günter Oskar following at a very slow and steady pace, keen to lead his wife above 7,000 metres, a female altitude record. Hettie was suffering badly from the altitude but kept plugging away until the mist suddenly cleared and they saw Ertl's team on the summit ridge. The Dyhrenfurths caught up, and in the last section Ertl and Höcht let them be the first on top. For Günter Oskar it was another 7,000-metre peak; for Hettie, a world female altitude record. Nine days later Ertl and Höcht also climbed Baltoro Kangri. When a tired Hettie Dyhrenfurth got back down she was excited to see the mail sack with news from Europe and about her children. Inside there was also a newspaper that told in a few lines of a terrible tragedy that had unfolded on Nanga Parbat. As she remembered the time spent together on the *Conte Verde*, tears ran down her face and the concerned porters surrounded her, trying to understand what was wrong.

A month and a half earlier Merkl's team had left Base Camp later than planned and were caught in sweltering midday heat on the glacier. The snow bridges over the crevasses softened and the porters sank up to their hips. They continued the next morning to Camp III, before easy angled slopes led to Camp IV, the base for operations on the upper part of the mountain. Several of the team climbed Chongra Peak for acclimatization, getting a great view of Nanga Parbat, which in Bechtold's flowery prose was 'shining unveiled like a Castle of the Holy Grail ... at this sight, we all pressed the hand of Willy Merkl, as if to show him our faith.'[18] This sort of writing helped to build the myth of Nanga Parbat as Germany's 'Mountain of Destiny'. In reality, the team had significant doubts about Merkl's leadership. Welzenbach wrote home about Merkl that 'I fear that we will have a row sooner or later. At all events we have drifted further and further apart mentally during the course of the expedition.'[19] Welzenbach was a friend and climbing partner of Merkl, but it was

Merkl's old schoolfriend Bechtold who was starting to have more and more influence over him. Welzenbach saw the weakness in Merkl's plan to reach the summit with a 'large and cumbersome' group, which required lots of porters. Welzenbach believed 'you can't hope to take a party of ten to twelve up an 8,000-metre peak. The result is that nobody gets to the top. But ... Willy always knows best ... [and] is awfully capricious ... today he says one thing, tomorrow another.... I am pinning all my hopes on Schneider and Aschenbrenner who with their driving enthusiasm will perhaps help us yet to achieve success.'[20] Paul Bauer had proved an effective strong leader, but, unlike Merkl, he had a united team who had confidence in his decision-making.

The next obstacle to reaching the East Ridge of Nanga Parbat was Rakhiot Peak. In 1932 they made a tricky traverse around its foot and up through the *Mulde* to reach the East Ridge, but this had significant avalanche danger, and in 1934 Aschenbrenner championed an alternative passing over Rakhiot Peak. This meant one camp fewer was needed, but it was a challenge to create a safe route for the porters. Aschenbrenner, Schneider and Welzenbach tackled the ice slope leading to Rakhiot Peak. In the Alps top-level climbers would have climbed a slope like this directly, but here they had to spend time driving in ice pitons, fixing rope ladders and creating a zigzag line of steps for the porters. It took two days, with Welzenbach doing a lot of the work despite a severe cough, leaving the rest of the team in awe of his physical strength and resistance.

On 4 July, with the weather settled and hopes high, Merkl, Bechtold, Wieland, Welzenbach, Aschenbrenner and Schneider headed up with a group of porters to establish Camp VI and attempt the summit. The two Austrians, Aschenbrenner and Schneider, went in front to make the final section of the route across Rakhiot Peak, with the others following, each supervising two or three porters. The rocks were icy, but thanks to the fixed ropes the porters were able to pass safely, even though some had never been on such difficult terrain before. They made Camp VI in a small niche on the East Ridge, which swept up ahead to the twin peaks of the Silver Saddle.

The last rays of the evening sun made the saddle glow: they had named it in similar conditions in 1932.

The Europeans slept well, but in the morning three of the porters reported sick, leaving them seriously short of manpower. Wieland and Welzenbach headed along the ridge towards a dark rock tower which they had named the 'Moor's Head', reflecting the period's racial prejudices, after which the ridge dropped to a col. They placed Camp VII at 7,200 metres on a broad snow terrace. Despite the promising progress, tensions remained, and during an argument Schneider told Merkl that 'we [Schneider and Aschenbrenner] have made the route up here, now we are turning back. You can go to the summit on your own from here.'[21] The lure of the summit meant that things were patched up enough for them to carry on the next morning, but two of the Sherpas were suffering from mountain sickness and Bechtold volunteered to supervise their descent to Camp IV. He was disappointed to miss out on the first summit attempt but sure he would be up again within four or five days. The remaining team was now sixteen men, five Europeans and eleven Sherpas. Bechtold shook hands with each man and wished them to 'Macht es gut!' As he descended, he saw Aschenbrenner, Schneider and Welzenbach arrive at the Silver Saddle, three black dots against the snow, with Merkl following and Wieland still at the camp organizing the porters.

On the Silver Plateau

Aschenbrenner and Schneider had made rapid progress, cutting steps up the steep slopes to the Silver Saddle, where they waited for the others on the rocks of the East Peak, smoking cigarettes, borrowed from the Sherpas because the expedition doctor had forbidden smoking on the mountain. Before the others reached the top of Silver Saddle, the Austrians set off again, skirting the broad snow field beyond it, which they had named the Silver Plateau.

Uli Wieland leading the way up the East Ridge of Nanga Parbat towards the so-called Moor's Head in 1934, with the Silver Saddle behind.

At 12.30 p.m. they saw Welzenbach appear on the Silver Saddle and yodelled to him. Welzenbach waited for the others, as the Austrians carried on across the plateau. It was laborious due to the wind-blown ridges in the snow, but they went nearly as far as the fore-summit. The true summit seemed very close, but they couldn't go on to it because Merkl had ordered that the whole team reach the top together. Merkl's order, perhaps motivated by what would maximize the propaganda benefit, perhaps by his own personal ambition or perhaps because he did not want the Austrians to make it to the top before the Reich Germans, not only cost them the summit but created a lethal trap for the team and their Sherpas. At around 2 p.m. Merkl, Wieland and the porters appeared on the Silver Saddle. The Austrians started to doubt whether the full group would follow them higher and decided to wait. When they saw the porters setting up camp near the Silver Saddle, Schneider went back to persuade them to come higher. Aschenbrenner waited an hour and a half, but the wind was increasing in strength and he got very cold and descended. On this afternoon the two Austrians were within reach of the summit, and possibly could have made it if they had pushed on rather than waiting for the others.

At the camp, the wind continued to increase in violence, but there were blue skies above and they still expected to go to the summit in the morning. They lay in the tents listening to the wind reach hurricane force. The tent occupied by Merkl, Welzenbach and Wieland was blown down and they lay inside the collapsed tent until the morning, before managing to refix it with ropes. In Aschenbrenner and Schneider's tent fine snow dust got through every crack and the walls rattled incessantly. Headaches prevented them sleeping much.

That day Bechtold had had a trying descent from Camp VII, with the sick porters often wanting to sit in the snow. His powers of persuasion were stretched to the limit to get the porters down the fixed ropes. Camp V was heavily snowed up, and Bechtold realized that the snow must have been falling there whilst the ridge above was in the sun. Driving snow covered the tracks. With night approaching, Bechtold went ahead to get help from Camp IV. He kept shouting and eventually got an answer. Then the clouds parted, and he saw his teammates Willi Bernard and Peter Müllritter coming to help him bring the porters safely into camp. Bechtold was sure the summit would be reached the next day.

His confidence was shared by those up at Camp VIII. Excited by the prospect of being one of the first men to climb an 8,000er, Schneider was the first out of his sleeping bag in the morning, preparing a light rucksack for the summit climb, but the blizzard was so violent that they had to stay in the camp that day. Snow was blown wildly across the plateau, making it almost dark until mid-morning, but they felt well sheltered in the tents, and with food for five or six days they believed they could wait out the storm. During the day the hurricane kept getting more severe, and after a night with no sign of an improvement the summit was clearly out of the question and they couldn't stay much longer where they were.

Wieland came to the Austrians' tent to discuss the position and they agreed to descend immediately to Camp IV. Merkl asked the Austrians to go ahead with three porters to make the track. They had trouble getting the porters to leave the warmth of their sleeping bags and prepare. Whilst Aschenbrenner roped up with the porters, Schneider discussed with Merkl, Welzenbach and Wieland what equipment to leave behind at Camp VIII for another attempt. The three Germans seemed to be in good health and the Austrians set off sure their teammates would follow not far behind. By the time the first group reached the Silver Saddle the wind was so violent that a rubber mattress was torn off the back of a porter. They had to exercise a lot of care on the descent down the steep slope on the other side. Schneider led, with Aschenbrenner bringing up the rear as anchor man. Pasang Norbu was going very well, but Nima Dorje, who had carried to 8,350 metres on Everest the year before, and Pinzo Nurbu were struggling. Some 100 metres below the Saddle, Nima Dorje was blown from his steps; Pasang Norbu and Aschenbrenner managed with difficulty to hold him on the rope, but the sleeping bag he had been carrying disappeared. To save weight, they had only been carrying two two-man sleeping bags, one for the porters and one for the two Austrians.

What happened when they got close to Camp VII is highly controversial and had tragic consequences. Aschenbrenner's diary entry says that 'in the raging snowstorm we could not see a dozen yards, and often missed the way. In order to save the porters from these exhausting detours, we took off the rope on the easy ground before Camp VII. We impressed on them that they should follow immediately in our track, to which they agreed absolutely.'[22] Schneider's account does not mention the rope being taken off, and simply says 'we lost sight of our three porters near the tent of Camp VII.'[23] Jonathan Neale's book *Tigers of the Snow*, based on interviews in 2000 with many Sherpas, including the last survivor of the expedition, Ang Tsering, says that the Austrians left the Sherpas on their skis, but his endnotes explain that there are reasons to doubt they had skis. The Austrians used skis lower down, but it seems unlikely they took them past Camp V, above which there was a steep ice face on Rakhiot Peak. What is not in doubt is that the two strongest members of the team separated from the three Sherpas, two of whom, Aschenbrenner said, 'were going very badly'. They could not know the consequences of this action, but as things turned out it looked like they prioritized getting down themselves without worrying enough about others. The Austrians justified that choice as due to the lost sleeping bag, which, Aschenbrenner wrote, created an 'imperious necessity of reaching Camp V ... if we did not wish to be frozen to death'.[24] Things did indeed go badly for those left in the open.

The Austrians were very tired but kept going: on the ascent back up to Camp VI Aschenbrenner had to stop every 30 metres. At one point the clouds parted and they saw the main group coming down from the Silver Saddle. They did not think about stopping at Camp VI, which was deeply snowed in. When they reached the fixed ropes on the ice slope they were able to descend quickly to Camp V, where there were provisions and sleeping bags, but after eating and resting they continued the descent to Camp IV, arriving at 7 p.m. Bechtold,

Bernard and Müllritter had been waiting in Camp IV for two days and were astonished to see Aschenbrenner's and Schneider's ice-encrusted figures appear in the doorway of their tent.

The day after Bechtold had got down it had snowed heavily. Müllritter and Bernard tried to reach Camp V with two Sherpas, but had to give up after floundering in deep, bottomless fresh snow. The next morning they saw their teammates descending from the Silver Saddle through a short gap in the clouds. As the storm raged, the team at Camp IV started worrying about those above, before the unexpected arrival of the Austrians. No one else arrived at Camp IV that evening. They hoped their teammates in the storm above had been able to reach the relative safety of Camp V, but knew that if they were still on the far side of the Rakhiot Peak in Camp VI or VII their position would be very serious. The next day they made another attempt to reach Camp V, but once again were driven back by deep snow, the blizzard filling their tracks almost as soon as they made them. At one point the clouds parted and they could see a large party still descending from the Silver Saddle. They were shocked that the others had got no further. Behind the main party was a lone man moving slowly, who then sat down in the snow. Then the clouds closed in, and they could see no more, leaving them desperately worried.

The second party

Whilst the group led by the Austrians moved quickly down from the Silver Saddle, the rest of the party, including Merkl, Welzenbach, Wieland and eight Sherpas, were much slower. The night in the collapsed tent probably took a lot out of the three Germans and they were not as well acclimatized as the Austrians, who had done most of the route-making lower down. Whatever the reason, some way below the Saddle they made the catastrophic decision to bivouac. They only had three two-man sleeping bags for eleven men during what must have been a terrible night. Welzenbach slept without a sleeping bag on the snow and one of the Sherpas, Nima Nurbu, died. Both Merkl and Wieland suffered frostbite.

Despite his night in the open, Welzenbach was the strongest of the Germans in the morning and fixed a rope to his ice axe to help the Sherpas descend towards Camp VII. However, three of them, Gay-Lay, Ang Tsering and Dakshi, felt ill and decided to spend a second night at the bivouac. The other four Sherpas, Nima Tashi, Kitar, Da Tundu and Pasang Kikuli, waited by Camp VII for Merkl and Welzenbach for more than an hour. Uli Wieland had already fallen behind and died. There was not enough space for all of them in Camp VII, so the Germans told the Sherpas to continue to Camp VI, but, sinking up to their chests in snow and with the blizzard raging, they instead had to spend a night in a snow cave. The next morning they carried on and crossed Rakhiot Peak, where they met Pasang Norbu, Nima Dorje and Pinzo Nurbu, the three porters who had been left behind by Aschenbrenner and Schneider, and who had lost their way in the blizzard. Pinzo Nurbu was the younger brother of one of the men who caught them up, Da Tundu. They went on together, the storm so furious that both Nima Dorje and Nima Tashi died, their strength giving out whilst descending the fixed ropes on the steep ice face of Rakhiot Peak. Kitar, Pasang Kikuli, Pasang Norbu and Pinzo Nurbu made it as far as Camp V, but just before reaching it Pinzo Nurbu collapsed and died. Da Tundu, who had been roped to the two men who had died on the fixed ropes, untied and came down to join the other three, finding his brother dead. Despite the horrific descent, with two nights in the open and the death of three of their comrades, including the brother of one of them, the four remaining Sherpas managed to continue the descent towards Camp IV, an amazing feat of endurance.

At Camp IV a further half-metre of snow had fallen. It was again a stormy day with huge snow plumes blown horizontally off Rakhiot Peak. At midday the Germans saw seven or eight men descending the ice wall. They started to prepare tea and food, and Doctor Bernard got ready to treat the climbers, before going to meet the descending men. To their dismay, only four figures were coming down from Camp V, leaving behind them a trench as high as a man. Assuming the Europeans were stronger, they expected Merkl,

The exhausted Pasang Kikuli being brought into Camp IV on Nanga Parbat after the disastrous retreat from the storm in 1934.

Welzenbach, Wieland and one porter, but as they got closer they realized it was actually Kitar, Pasang Norbu, Pasang Kikuli and Da Tundu. Near the bottom, Pasang Kikuli fell down a serac wall and injured his back.

All of them were exhausted and had frostbite; Pasang Norbu had lost his sunglasses and was snow-blind. The Germans gave them soup and they worked all night massaging the Sherpas' hands and feet and rubbing them with snow under instruction from Doctor Bernard. Kitar had the worst frostbite, with terribly swollen hands. Pasang Kikuli was in great pain, having injured his back in the fall. It was not until midnight that Kitar was able to tell the Europeans what had happened. In the morning the blizzard still raged; the four porters had high temperatures and needed to be taken down to Base Camp. Ideally, the doctor would have gone down with the sick porters, but with seven men still potentially alive up on the mountain they felt Bernard should stay at Camp IV. Bechtold escorted the sick men with medicines and instructions for their treatment. Kitar had the most difficulty because he could not hold an ice axe in his frostbitten hands. Those at Base Camp waved excitedly when they saw Bechtold approaching, expecting him to bring news of a successful summit climb. When they saw the exhausted and frostbitten Sherpas, they realized that things had gone very differently.

Up at Camp IV the weather had improved a little, and Aschenbrenner, Schneider, Müllritter and three Sherpas finally made it to Camp V, going without loads and taking six hours. They found the body of Pinzo Nurbu, lying roped up in the snow. The other two dead men, Nima Tashi and Nima Dorje, were hanging off the fixed ropes above, but an attempt by Aschenbrenner and Schneider to recover their bodies was driven back by a blizzard. Müllritter dug a grave for Pinzo Nurbu in the snow, and then they all returned to Camp IV. Convinced that no one could have survived further up, they decided to evacuate the mountain to avoid further risk, but to their shock the next morning they saw three men descending the ridge from Camp VII. Halfway along, before the rise up to the Moor's Head, one of them stepped forwarded and waved and there was a faint a cry for help on the wind. Knowing there were still people alive up above, Aschenbrenner, Bernard and Schneider passed an anxious night.

The men left on the mountain

The man they had seen waving was Ang Tsering, an extremely strong and experienced Sherpa, who had carried to Camp VI on Everest in 1933. At the start of the retreat he had waited behind in the highest bivouac with Dakshi and Gaylay, when the others had continued towards Camp VII. He was suffering from snow blindness, but knew this would pass after a day or so. By contrast,

Dakshi, a fellow native of the village of Thame in the Everest region of Nepal, was in a bad way physically and simply couldn't go on. Gaylay was in reasonable shape at this stage and probably waited with the other two out of solidarity.

In the morning Ang Tsering had recovered his sight, but Dakshi was too weak to move and so Ang Tsering and Gaylay left him behind. They probably rationalized this by saying that they were going for help, knowing that Dakshi was going to die and that they had to give themselves a chance. Ang Tsering was the stronger of the pair and soon pulled ahead. Not far above Camp VII he came across the body of Uli Wieland, who had died 30 metres away from the tent, perhaps not realizing he was so close. In the tent, Ang Tsering found Merkl and Welzenbach still alive, having spent two nights there, but without the strength to clear the snow filling the tent. Welzenbach's feet were shaking uncontrollably, and Ang Tsering had the impression he was close to death. The day before he had written a note, hoping a porter would take it down:

> To the Sahibs between Camps VI and VII, in particular the Doctor Sahib. We have lain here since yesterday, when Uli got lost on the way. We are both ill. An attempt to reach Camp VI failed due to general exhaustion. I, Willo, have probably got bronchitis, angina and influenza. Bara Sahib [Merkl] has a feeling of general exhaustion, and frost-bitten feet and hands. We have neither of us eaten a hot meal for six days and have drunk almost nothing. Please help us soon here in Camp VII. Willo and Willy.[25]

The pair had not understood the situation and thought that Camp VI was occupied, and that climbers including Doctor Bernard had been able to come up from below. Welzenbach and Merkl had survived a long storm before in the Alps, but doing so at over 7,000 metres, where the body deteriorates with every day that passes, is much harder. Ang Tsering realized that to survive they had to keep going down. He was worried that Camp IV would be stripped, removing any chance of support and supplies. Welzenbach was too sick to move and was doomed, so Ang Tsering proposed to

Merkl going down together, but Merkl refused, unwilling to leave Welzenbach alive. Ang Tsering also needed to wait for Gaylay, who eventually arrived.

Although at least Ang Tsering, and possibly also Gaylay, could have got down, the four men stayed at Camp VII for the rest of that day and the following night, the Germans in the tent and the Sherpas outside in the snow. The next day Ang Tsering again suggested to Merkl going down. The weather was a little better, and they could see Müllritter, Aschenbrenner and Schneider coming up from Camp IV. This gave Merkl hope that a rescue was on its way, which unfortunately made him want to stay put. Again, Ang Tsering and Gaylay waited outside the tent. At 5 p.m. Merkl came out to say Welzenbach had died, but it was too late in the day to set off down, so they spent yet another night in Camp VII, Merkl in the tent with Welzenbach's body, the two Sherpas out in the snow.

The next morning they finally set off, Merkl moving very slowly due to his frostbitten hands and feet and only able to walk leaning on two ice axes. They saw climbers below and Ang Tsering waved and shouted. They nearly made it to Camp VI but found the climb back up to the Moor's Head too hard; overtaken by nightfall, they spent another night in the open. They hadn't eaten or drunk for several days, although they kept sucking ice. That night Ang Tsering lay awake thinking their chances of surviving were disappearing and worrying that Camp IV might be stripped and the mountain abandoned. He resolved to send Gaylay for help, with him following more slowly with Merkl, and in the morning proposed this to Gaylay. Gaylay's English was better; he talked to Merkl and told Ang Tsering to go down for help, while he stayed with the expedition leader.

Ang Tsering continued past Moor's Head, and traversed across the face of Rakhiot Peak, moving slowly and frequently stopping to shout for help. He believed he had received a reply, although he was mistaken; no one had come up to Camp V that day. Although his feet were badly frostbitten, he could still handle the fixed ropes on the steep ice face, but he couldn't get past the body of Nima

Ang Tsering (on the left) returning to Base Camp after the terrible storm on Nanga Parbat in 1934. Fritz Bechtold is on the right.

Dorje, who was frozen rigid and tangled in the ropes. His face was so frozen that Ang Tsering could not tell who it was. He lost a lot of time, unable to bear the thought of having to pass directly over the body, before he saw a second parallel rope and managed to tie into this until he was past the dead man. At Camp V he looked for food but found none, although he did find a camera and decided he ought to take it down. By the time he left Camp V it was dark. Ang Tsering kept losing his way and the large camera made it difficult for him to keep his balance. He fell and slid, finishing just on the edge of a crevasse. Abandoning the camera, he continued, and finally the men at Camp IV heard his shouts and came to meet him with tea and rum.

Learning that there were still two men alive on the mountain, Schneider and Aschenbrenner wanted to make another rescue attempt. The next morning the men at Camp IV heard cries from the ridge and the two Austrians tried both that day and the next to reach Camp V, but were defeated by enormous masses of fresh snow. On 16 July most of them descended to Base Camp, taking the exhausted Ang Tsering, who had eaten nothing but ice for nine days. Ang Tsering lost some toes due to frostbite, but recovered and returned to work as a porter. He died in 2002, just a few months before his hundredth birthday.

A final unsuccessful attempt was made to reach Camp V, but, with the weather still bad and no sound from above, those at Camp IV were sure that Merkl and Gaylay must be dead. When the team with Ang Tsersing arrived at Base Camp and reported that Merkl and Gaylay had still been alive two days earlier, Bechtold and a team of porters headed up again. Above Camp II they met the team coming down from Camp IV, looking exhausted and worn. Aschenbrenner was wearing wide felt shoes because his feet had been frostbitten in the rescue attempts; Bernard's hair had turned grey with the anxiety. They sat in the snow and looked upwards, thinking of their friends who they knew were dead. Despite the tragedy, tensions at Base Camp were not calmed, and Schneider and Aschenbrenner continued to be angry with Merkl, calling him a coward and a philistine. Then they returned to Europe to face the consequences.

NINE

Arguments and defeats

There was a great deal of publicity about the tragic accidents in Germany. The climbers' deaths were portrayed as heroic sacrifices for the glory of the nation. Public interest in Himalayan climbing had originally been limited, gradually growing after the two Kangchenjunga expeditions, but now it exploded with nearly ten times as many news stories about Nanga Parbat in 1934 as two years earlier. While the team was still in India, new reports were largely factual, but after the return to Germany the focus on the more emotive aspects increased. The National Socialist *NS-Kurier* wrote that the men who returned to Germany 'had to endure hardships and privations, they had to fight hard and suffer, but they are not defeated yet. They will continue to fight and struggle and win.'[1] After returning, Fritz Bechtold wrote that 'the ideals created by the sacrificial death of our comrades who have stayed [on the mountain] must be carried forward by German youth.'[2] In Third Reich Germany, references to heroism and sacrifice had a wide appeal, and mirrored the Nazi propaganda message that 'the war dead had not died in vain and that the younger generation had a heroic mission to fulfil to redeem them and the German nation'.[3] There was a battle to control the narrative of the expedition between the Nazi-sympathizing Bechtold's idealized version of events, where even better than success was for climbers to lay down their lives 'to be a way and a light for the young hearts of those that come after',[4] and Erwin Schneider, who wanted to be honest about the arguments at Base Camp and the shortcomings in Merkl's leadership. Kate Schmid, widow of the murdered Nanga Parbat press secretary, who had taken on his role, tried to mediate between Bechtold and Schneider, but it was exhausting work.

British reaction to the tragedy was supportive, with the *Alpine Journal* praising Merkl's 'desperate gallantry' and contending that 'survivors and victims were ... worthy of his leadership'.[5] Frank Smythe wrote to *The Times* paying tribute to Wieland, with whom he had climbed on Kangchenjunga in 1930, as well as Merkl and Welzenbach, but also emphasizing the terrible loss of the Sherpas. Privately some of the British climbers, who personally knew the Sherpas who had died, were more critical. Smythe felt that the expedition was too large and cumbrous and this led to the disaster. More selfishly, he realized that when the British returned to Everest they would have to re-establish the Sherpas' confidence that if they carried to the top camp they would be able to get down again safely. It is not certain that his fears were justified: Tenzing Norgay, who was trying to break into work as a climbing Sherpa, heard about the disaster on Nanga Parbat, but was further inspired by 'the stories of Sherpa heroism'.[6]

By the mid-1930s a lot of Himalayan experience had been accumulated and leading climbers felt the time was ripe to succeed on one of the big mountains. Despite the tragedy on Nanga Parbat, Schneider was keen to lead another expedition to finish the job. Smythe felt the same way about Everest, and with no prospect of another official expedition started planning to enter Tibet illegally in 1935. With only local porters, he wanted to establish seven camps on the North Face before going to the summit alone. He only shelved the plan because Tibet unexpectedly authorized an official expedition.

Paul Bauer was also still hoping to make his much-postponed return to Kangchenjunga, but the British authorities would only allow one German expedition in 1935, so this plan put him in conflict with Schneider, who was supported by the DÖAV. Bauer's superior, Reich sports leader von Tschammer, was crucial to winning this conflict and Bauer lobbied him hard. Bauer attacked the actions of

Schneider and Aschenbrenner in a letter to von Tschammer, writing that the Nanga Parbat expedition had received 'an extraordinary amount of justified criticism', with the events 'astonishing all mountaineers'. Bauer floated the possibility of an official investigation; he considered incomprehensible how the pair 'left their porters behind in the blizzard ... to certain death'.[7] Bauer's criticisms are not totally without merit: the decision to separate from the three Sherpas arguably caused the death of two of the men. The Austrians' fear of being caught out without equipment was genuine, but they should still have stayed with the porters, two of whom were unwell. Aschenbrenner and Schneider are certainly not the only climbers whose misjudgement led to the death of porters. George Mallory's misreading of conditions on the North Col in 1922 led to seven porters being killed in an avalanche. Bauer himself had persisted in the 1931 attempt on Kangchenjunga despite the very difficult conditions, leading to a fatal accident. Bauer suggested that the Austrians rushed ahead to save their own skins, but they probably imagined that the porters would be caught up by Merkl's group shortly after they separated. Bauer also accused the Austrians of not waiting for Merkl, Wieland and Welzenbach, saying that 'it is a fixed rule that in confusing weather the team has to stay together', that Schneider and Aschenbrenner had run away, and that it was 'very dangerous if people with such dubious attitudes'[8] are now seen as heroes. This accusation is much less valid: it was agreed that the Austrians should go ahead, and the Germans were very experienced climbers.

Bauer and Bechtold became friends and close collaborators, but Bauer felt the need to defend himself against accusations from Schneider and Aschenbrenner. In another letter to van Tschammer, Bauer set out the history of his rivalry with Welzenbach, whose support for the centre-right Bavarian People's Party Bauer contrasted with his own political stance, saying that he 'always felt like an old soldier', consistently pursuing a nationalist line within the AAVM. For Bauer's supporters, 'Adolf Hitler was the man we protected in 1923',[9] referring to the Beer Hall Putsch. From a twenty-first-century perspective it seems strange that political differences were so important in a mountaineering rivalry, though according to historian Richard Evans Germany between the wars experienced 'a politicization of whole areas of life'.[10] There were also differences in political outlook among British climbers – Younghusband campaigned for the Tories, whereas Mallory was a socialist – but these rarely had such a big role in mountaineering discussions as they did in Germany.

Bauer told von Tschammer that the great peaks of the Himalayas required far more than 'ambition and striving for records'. What was required instead was 'a spirit that loves difficulties for their own sake'[11] and that does not ask whether overcoming them will lead to personal success. Bauer contrasted the Nanga Parbat expedition with his own to Kangchenjunga, where he picked people he had known for years, saying that Welzenbach and Merkl gathered stars. The British Everest climbers generally saw the merits of Bauer's model. Ruttledge pointed out that the Bavarians on Kangchenjunga were organized as 'a small company, each member of which knows the others really well and is aware of their potential contribution'.[12]

Bauer said that Schneider and Aschenbrenner, and their associates Hoerlin and Schneider, didn't understand that climbing was a 'national matter'. He accused Merkl of working with wealthy foreign climbers, and Schneider and Hoerlin of participating in the 1930 expedition of 'the Jew Dyhrenfurth', and not even having 'the courage to raise the German flag [on the summit of Jongsong Peak], but hoisting the "Swabian" and "Tyrolean flags"!'[13] Bauer's statement is clearly antisemitic, albeit one made in a private letter to his boss, a senior Nazi official. There had been mutual personal animosity between Hoerlin and Bauer since 1928, when Bauer had offhandedly rejected Hoerlin's inquiry about joining the first Kangchenjunga expedition. Hoerlin was a board member in the DÖAV and a prominent opponent of its Nazification, but was becoming frustrated about meetings where 'one group sits there in their brown SA uniforms ... others in black SS uniforms. Many are totally pig-headed.'[14]

Prompted by Bauer, von Tschammer held a 'court of honour' in the spring of 1935 to assess whether Schneider and Aschenbrenner were guilty of deserting the rest of the expedition on Nanga Parbat. No inappropriate actions were proven, but it was decided they could no longer take part in German expeditions. Their case was a side issue in the more fundamental battle for control of German mountaineering. The DÖAV leadership, and particularly the chairman for foreign expeditions Philipp Borchers, remained supportive of Schneider, and even broached the idea of a purely Austrian Nanga Parbat expedition. Bauer had issued an official order that all planned foreign expeditions had to be sent for consideration to his Office for Hiking and Mountaineering, but he would have had no say over an Austrian expedition, although it would have been hard to finance. An alternative plan for a joint expedition revealed the irreconcilable differences between Bauer and the DÖAV, who disagreed about the choice of leader and selection criteria for members. Both sides planned their own expeditions, whilst continuing the discussions about a joint one. With Nanga Parbat now seen as the German 'Mountain of Destiny', great prestige would come from the first ascent, and a successful DÖAV expedition could help it maintain independence from the Nazi authorities.

For Bauer the controversy was between the 'parliamentary' principles of the DÖAV and his idea of working strictly according to *Führerprinzip* (Führer principles), meaning the leader had complete authority and could demand absolute obedience. This required the leader to choose a team of people he could fully trust. Bauer saw team spirit, unconditional camaraderie and voluntary submission to a common goal as core German values, which allowed them to achieve more in mountaineering than other nations. The British tended to favour a more parliamentary leadership model, but still spent a lot of time arguing about what type of leader would prove most effective. When they returned to Everest, this was once again a major topic of debate.

The British return to Everest

These internal political battles cost German mountaineers two years, during which their competitors were active. After the 1933 failure, the British hoped to return to Everest in 1935. However, the Tibetans replied that

> the guardian deities of the mountain take great exception to such attempts and in their anger they render the weather very rough, and the after-effects are very bad. Moreover, it is obvious that [the climbers] will not be able to reach the summit ... such attempts only work undesirably on the temper of the gods and the guardian deities ... we ask the British Government to withdraw the proposal for another expedition for the present.[15]

The British Political Officer in Sikkim discussed the objections with senior monks close to the Dalai Lama. The real obstacle was the extremely influential Kalon Lama, 'a most charming and friendly old gentleman, but [one who has] ... never been out of Tibet and is imbued with all the prejudices of the monks.'[16] Another senior monk suggested that in four years' time the view might be more favourable. In 1935, though, permission unexpectedly arrived. There was no time to organize a full expedition that year, so a small reconnaissance team was sent under the leadership of Eric Shipton. The goals were to test the conditions in the post-monsoon period and assess possible candidates for a full attempt in 1936.

In 1933 Shipton had returned from Everest by an unexplored route with Lawrence Wager, awakening an enthusiasm for lightweight exploration. They both relished the freedom from the tensions, jealousy and arguments of a big team, with Wager summarizing their philosophy as 'Own councils. Patience. No uppishness about efficiency. Truthfulness ... a game of skill keeping on good terms.'[17] In 1934 Shipton and Bill Tilman, who had first climbed together in Kenya, managed to pass through the Rishi Ganga Gorge to the base of Nanda Devi, which had previously proved inaccessible despite many attempts. It was a totally different style of expedition to Everest, with a team of the two Britons and three Sherpas living off the land as much as possible. Although paid employees, the Sherpas worked as part of a single harmonious team. Shipton greatly preferred this type of journey and on Everest had had 'a mighty longing to detach myself from the big and cumbersome organization which for some reason had been thought to be necessary ... and to wander with a small, self-contained party through the labyrinth of unexplored valleys, forming our plans to suit the circumstances.'[18] These were understandable and attractive aspirations, but they probably meant that Shipton, despite being perhaps the finest British climber of his generation, lacked the single-minded obsessiveness needed to succeed on the very highest mountains.

Shipton presented the results of the lightweight Nanda Devi expedition, which had cost only £287, at the Royal Geographical Society to rapturous applause. The Mount Everest Committee realized that Shipton could make a reconnaissance of Everest for a fraction of the cost of a full expedition. Rejecting the extravagance of earlier expeditions, he worked with a nutritionist on a diet of 4,000 calories a day, with all required nutrients and using local food where possible. Shipton later admitted that, compared to the extravagance of early expeditions, 'in 1935 I went rather too far the other way',[19] but it did keep costs low.

On their way to the North Col, Shipton's team discovered the remains of Maurice Wilson, a Briton without significant climbing experience, who had believed that he could climb Everest through fasting and prayer. In 1934 he managed to recruit three Sherpas and enter Tibet disguised as a monk. Wilson expected to find the steps and fixed ropes from Ruttledge's expedition, but of course they had been swept away or buried. When his attempt to reach the North Col failed, the Sherpas begged him to retreat, but Wilson stayed camped below the North Col, hoping to make another attempt. Shipton's team found him lying in the snow with the tattered remains of a tent nearby.

The 1933 route to the North Col was no longer feasible, so Shipton went further right, before making a long traverse to the Col. Heavy monsoon conditions prevented climbing further up, and after four days they descended, finding a massive avalanche had removed 2 metres of snow from the slope they had traversed. Realizing their ascent route had actually been extremely dangerous, they decided it was not reasonable to return to the North Col that year. Instead, they climbed twenty-six other peaks over 6,000 metres in the Rongbuk Valley, nearly all first ascents. They also visited a col to look at the southern side of Everest. Shipton was keen to see if there was a feasible route from Nepal if access became possible, and concluded that it 'did not look impossible, and I should very much like to have the opportunity one day of exploring it'.[20] For Shipton's team it had been a highly enjoyable expedition, but maybe not one which progressed the goal of climbing Everest. Smythe thought that Shipton had climbed peaks and enjoyed himself instead of doing 'his job properly'.[21] Shipton wrote later that he 'hoped that the achievements of the 1935 expedition ... would convince the Establishment of the virtues of a light, mobile party. In this I was sadly disappointed.'[22] The 1936 expedition returned to a heavyweight style and the pre-monsoon period.

The last mountain attempted was 7,540-metre Changtse. Shipton, Bill Tilman and Edmund Wigram attempted the North-East Ridge but had to turn back because of dangerous snow conditions at 7,000 metres. I was part of a team attempting the same mountain fifty-five years later. We had made two trips up the long East Rongbuk Glacier to the foot of the North Col, where we placed our final camp below the 900-metre East Face of Changtse. We fixed ropes on the steeper bottom half, expecting the upper part to be more straightforward. On our planned summit day, we awoke to the strongest wind I've ever encountered. It came in gusts, which we could hear booming over the North Col before we felt them, knowing that seconds later the tent would be shaken by a wind strong enough to lift us in the air. Attempting the summit was out of the question, so we stayed put, hoping that conditions might improve. After an equally windy night, a strange calm settled in the early hours, and we were blessed with a perfectly calm and sunny morning. We climbed the fixed ropes to the top of a gully in the middle of the face, arriving at 12.30 p.m., confident of being able to climb the final 400 metres to the summit. The angle was less steep and we continued upwards unroped. I was only able to manage ten or fifteen paces before stopping, panting with lungs desperately gasping for what little oxygen was in the thin air, but gradually we gained height. The North Col was below us, and we were looking across the North Face of Everest, the scene of so much climbing history. Kangchenjunga, tinted yellow by 125 kilometres of distance, was now also in view. But, as often happens on the adjacent slope to the North Col, as we gained height snow conditions worsened. Whilst lower down we had firm snow, which the teeth of our crampons bit into reassuringly, we were now climbing up a hard breakable crust with soft powder underneath. When the crust held it was tiring but not impossible to shuffle forwards on the hard surface, but when the crust broke it was necessary to make a big, lung-sapping step out of the deep soft hole in which the foot had sunk. These were classic wind-slab avalanche conditions and very dangerous. So, having reached a couple of hundred metres higher than Shipton's team, we had to turn back for the same reason. I felt the emotional numbness of altitude – neither satisfaction at having got so high, nor great disappointment – despite being within grasp of one of the fifty highest mountains in the world.

The German Himalayan Foundation

In 1936 Paul Bauer, Fritz Bechtold and Karl Wien planned an expedition to Nanga Parbat. Wien travelled to Britain to negotiate with the authorities and meet Bauer's mountaineering contacts, including Kenneth Mason, who in 1932 had been appointed as the first ever Professor of Geography at Oxford, a quite unexpected change of career for a man who had not previously even set foot inside a university. Mason liked life in India, but funding cuts to the Survey of India and the challenges of a young family made a move back to Britain attractive. In 1931 he had been transferred to Burma (Myanmar) to work under fellow surveyor Henry Morshead, a veteran of the 1921 and 1922 Everest expeditions. Like Mason, Morshead was sad to be so far from the Himalayas, and when Mason arrived asked him whether he was 'punished and exiled like me, for being too keen?'[23] In Burma a rebellion was under way, and this restricted surveying activities and may have been the cause of Morshead's murder. He had ridden out into the jungle and his horse returned alone with a bloodstained saddle. Mason was one of those who found the body, guided by vultures circling overhead. Not long after he received a letter from Arthur Hinks of the RGS, who suggested applying for the newly created chair of Geography at Oxford. Although friends told him there was no chance that the university would appoint 'a brutal and licentious soldier',[24] he was selected, and when Wien visited had settled down to academic life.

The visit to Britain was productive – neither the Nazi regime nor the catastrophic 1934 Nanga Parbat expedition seemed to have diminished British faith in German climbing, and Wien reported back to Bauer that the British were prepared to 'support and promote [our] endeavours. We have the opportunity to really take the lead in the conquest of the Himalayas, and it became quite clear that the expeditions you led were groundbreaking.... We have to take this chance! Besides their own teams, the English are thinking practically only of the Germans.'[25] Despite this openness to German expeditions, the India Office was irritated that both Borchers and the DÖAV, on the one hand, and Bauer and Wien, on the other, were trying to get permission for Nanga Parbat. The British Foreign Office had already denied permission to an American expedition to Nanga Parbat, as they believed the Germans should have priority, but they informed the German embassy that the expedition could not happen in 1936 because a French team had a long-standing request to attempt Hidden Peak. The British authorities did not want pressure on agriculture from too many porters being away from their fields in the summer. Strutt and Mason made it clear to Bauer that the chances of obtaining a permit for Nanga Parbat or Kangchenjunga in 1937 were very good. Given the way in which the 1934 expedition had been publicized as a heroic enterprise, von Tschammer insisted the target should be Nanga Parbat.

To organize and fund expeditions according to Bauer's model, a new body was created, the 'German Himalayan Foundation'. It was separate from existing clubs and, in theory, open to funding any

The German 1936 Sikkim team: Karlo Wien, Günther Hepp, Paul Bauer, Adolf Göttner.

mountaineer who met its principles. In practice, the link between the Foundation and Bauer's Office for Hiking and Mountaineering was obvious, and the creation of the Foundation allowed Bauer to prevail over his rivals in the DÖAV. Von Tschammer was one of the three founders, with Bauer and Bechtold, but he had no mountaineering experience, meaning Bauer and his associates made all the decisions with von Tschammer only formally signing off. In the competition to organize foreign expeditions, the small and tightly organized Himalayan Foundation had a huge advantage over the decentralized and supranational DÖAV, which had to work with the Foundation if it wanted to be involved at all.

With Nanga Parbat unavailable for 1936, Bauer decided to lead a team to attempt some of the fantastic lower mountains close to Kangchenjunga. They wanted to see what could be achieved by a small and highly mobile party, and to prepare for Nanga Parbat in 1937. As well as Bauer and Wien, the team included a doctor, Günther Hepp, and 22-year-old Adolf Göttner. They made a series of attempts and first ascents of the peaks lying around the Zemu Glacier, including the 6,888-metre Siniolchu, which Bauer described as of 'beauty and steepness that perhaps no other peak in the world can compete with'.[26] Near the end of the expedition Wien and two porters headed off to survey an unexplored area south of Siniolchu. After crossing to an unknown glacier in zero visibility they spent two days under incessant heavy rain, before forcing their way through the thick undergrowth of deep-cut ravines to arrive at the nearest hamlet, the last food having long since been eaten. It was the sort of daring crossing of unexplored terrain that exemplified the adventurous style favoured by Shipton and Tilman; very different from large expeditions trying to make their way on high peaks through the slow grind of attrition.

We are beginning to look ridiculous

A couple of months earlier Everest had been attempted by a much larger British team, with very experienced climbers like Frank Smythe, Eric Shipton and Percy Wyn Harris, as well as three men who had gone to Everest first on the 1935 reconnaissance, but not Bill Tilman, who had had trouble acclimatizing. There were also a couple of new rising stars, including Peter Oliver, a serving army officer on the North-West frontier, who had made the second ascent of the 7,000-metre Trisul. It was a strong team, but the reappointment of Hugh Ruttledge as leader was a comedy of errors. After the failure of the 1933 attempt, the younger climbers were frustrated at the way expeditions were organized, feeling the Mount Everest Committee was out of touch with real climbing problems, and wondering why the RGS was still involved, since Everest was now purely a mountaineering challenge. Even the Alpine Club members on the Committee were seen as 'largely ... people who had not been near a serious climb for years'.[27] Although well liked, Ruttledge was emblematic of the Committee's approach: effectively a non-climber and incapable of understanding the climbing challenges. Even if they would not have liked an authoritarian leader in the style of Paul Bauer, the younger climbers would have preferred someone who could lead from the front, and thought that 'if there is really no man on the North Col capable of deputizing for the leader, the mountain might as well be handed over to the Germans or the Americans at once.'[28]

Ruttledge was originally supported by his friend, the influential Tom Longstaff. However, Longstaff changed his mind when he learnt that Ruttledge was thinking of dropping some of the younger members of the 1933 team and, worse, that he was 'absolutely convinced that if you can get hold of a good type of soldier who is a good mountaineer, you have the best material for Everest'.[29] Given that several in the team felt that the time lost due to the mistake of the soldiers Birnie and Boustead in setting up Camp V had cost them the summit in 1933, Longstaff was dismayed. Ruttledge also thought that modern British rock climbers were 'just gymnasts; bad travellers; a mutual admiration society, disliking outsiders and hating discipline'.[30] Longstaff felt he could no longer support him, and Ruttledge wrote to the Committee in 1934 resigning. At that time the debate was hypothetical, since there was no immediate prospect of Tibet giving permission.

An alternative was Colin Crawford, who had been on the 1922 and 1933 expeditions but was only six years younger than Ruttledge and had not been high on either expedition. There was a confused and unseemly tussle between supporters of Crawford and Ruttledge on the Mount Everest Committee, with various other alternatives suggested, but all proved unavailable or unsuitable for one reason or another. In 1935 Ruttledge wrote to Geoffrey Winthrop Young, still one of the most respected figures in British mountaineering, giving his perspective that 'even an ideal Everest party would be difficult to handle' because it would consist of 'men accustomed to lead and individualist by nature'. In 1933 'one section [of the team] heartily despised another ... and entertained a rooted hostility to soldiers'. Ruttledge observed that 'many of us ... think that the Bauer Kangchenjunga team was a model', and some 'believe that a section of us resembled it. I wish I could agree, but I observed ... dissensions, jealousies, criticism, even amongst our best men.' Ruttledge could never hope to command the influence exerted by Bauer. He felt supported during the 1933 expedition, but after returning there was a groundswell of complaints, with 'the severity of criticism [varying] ... inversely with the efficiency of its authors on the mountain'.[31] Ruttledge withdrew his resignation after Smythe spoke very strongly in his favour, and he eventually retained the leadership. The events caused a lot of tension between him and Crawford, who was asked to resign from the Committee. Longstaff called the arguments 'a gangster melodrama', and half the Committee ended up resigning. The manoeuvring and tensions on the British side were not much more dignified than those between the likes of Bauer, Dyhrenfurth and Welzenbach in Germany, although there was much less of an explicit political dimension to them.

Smythe might have seemed an obvious leadership candidate himself, but he was seen as a 'difficult' character and the more diplomatic Ruttledge was preferred. This suited Smythe, as it meant he was effectively in charge on the mountain whilst not having responsibility for all the complications of leadership. In 1936 Edwin Kempson felt Smythe was able to dominate Ruttledge, 'throw his weight around' and be very dogmatic.[32] Ruttledge, who was given a free hand in team selection, reflected carefully on whether 'men who had criticized ... could give of their best under me again'.[33] He invited some of the critics, but not all of them accepted. Smythe was involved in the assessment of some potential new team members in the Alps in 1935, a process which led to the best rock climber of the day, Colin Kirkus, once again being excluded. When Longstaff showed the list of members to George Finch, he said he thought the climbing strength was too low, but this proved academic because the weather meant the 1936 team never had a chance.

They reached the North Col earlier than in 1933 and by mid-May nearly one hundred porters had carried loads to establish Camp IV there. The senior climbers worked out a strategic plan, which foresaw three camps above the Col, with Smythe strongly believing a very high camp was needed to allow time for the difficult crossing of the Norton Couloir, where he wanted to put ropes to protect a retreat, and the summit pyramid. Three years earlier Smythe had spent three nights at 8,350 metres without oxygen, and had not suffered great ill effects, so he believed it was feasible to camp very high. After Everest was finally climbed using oxygen in 1953, many came to believe that it was not possible without. Smythe, though, was ambivalent as to whether oxygen was necessary, and turned back in 1933 because of the lack of time and the difficulty of the solo climbing, rather than the thinness of the air. Despite the army of porters, a large, experienced team and better equipment than ever before, the 1936 expedition did not get much further than the North Col. Conditions on the North Ridge were difficult, with 60 cm of fresh snow; even if they had set up Camp V, the traverse across the slabs of the North Face would have been impossible. When more snow fell, Smythe ordered a retreat back to Camp III. For him the descent was 'a big responsibility – 41 men's lives ... the snow held except in one place, there was a nasty "whump" as the snow split',[34] but the windslab avalanche did not come away and they made it down safely.

An unusual combination of heavy snowfall and relatively high temperatures created enormous avalanche risk on the slope to the North Col, and the usual winds across the North Face blowing snow clear were absent. Worryingly, the monsoon was already forming off the coast of Ceylon, much earlier than normal. They invited the Sirdar Nursang – a man who had been on far more expeditions than any of the British – into the mess tent to discuss the situation over a glass of Navy rum. He told them:

> I can't understand the way things are going this year: you have the most competent mountaineering party I have seen, and by far the best porters ... they will carry anywhere you like, and go to the summit if you want them to. But Everest is not willing. She has lured us on with false encouragement, and now closes the door. Always hitherto we have been beaten by wind and cold, never by this warmth and vile snow ... we shan't get up unless the north wind comes.[35]

A few days later, a strong north-west wind started blowing snow off the North Face and they felt renewed hope. They had another try to reach the Col, but the weather turned again with more heavy snowfall, and the 1935 traverse route was obviously far too dangerous. In desperation, Smythe tried straight up the steep ice above. He was disconsolate and wrote off their chances of reaching the Col again that year. That evening in Camp III arguments raged, some saying they had already risked too much and others that they were too cautious. According to Jack Longland, Smythe taunted his teammates with cowardice, causing Wyn Harris and Shipton to make another attempt against their better judgement. They found deceptive but very dangerous wind-slab avalanche conditions. About halfway up Shipton started traversing left, with Wyn Harris belayed on the lower lip of a crevasse. Shipton had almost reached the end of the rope and Wyn Harris was starting to follow when, with a breaking sound, the whole slope on which Shipton was standing started 'to move slowly down like a descending escalator'[36] towards an ice cliff 60 metres below. Wyn Harris managed to dive back into the crevasse, ram his axe into the snow and twist the rope around it. Shipton continued to slide helplessly as the slab started to break up into great blocks, but when the rope came tight it neither broke nor left Shipton buried under the snow. Wyn Harris apparently never forgave Smythe for having pushed them to try.

The frustration of the climbers boiled over, with Shipton attempting Changtse, the peak he had turned back on in 1935 due to avalanche conditions, with the same result again. Smythe and Wyn Harris wanted to attempt Everest by approaching the North Col from the other, western, side and found a feasible way with less avalanche risk, but were not able to overcome the final steep section before bad weather set in. They noted it could be an escape route for a group trapped on the Col by avalanche danger on the normal eastern side. An important but grim discovery was made by Frank Smythe when he was scanning the North Face with a telescope. He saw a shape that he believed was a body in the area where Mallory and Irvine could have fallen to. He wrote to Edward Norton about it, but said 'it's not to be written about, as the press would make an unpleasant sensation'.[37] The letter was only discovered by Smythe's son Tony many years later, after Mallory's body had already been found in the area.

There was a lot of criticism at the end of the expedition, with George Finch telling the *Morning Post* that 'we are beginning to look ridiculous' and raising the spectre of competition from the Germans or others, adding 'unless we put up a better show it will be difficult to argue we are justified in keeping Mount Everest to ourselves.'[38] He suggested that future expeditions should be led by climbers, that there be an age limit of 35 and no objection to strong characters in the team.

Nanda Devi

The French expedition to Hidden Peak, which had prevented the Germans from going to Nanga Parbat in 1936, also failed due to bad weather, but another expedition that year did achieve a notable success, even though still not the first ascent of an 8,000er. Unconstrained by the metric system, a British–American team led by Bill Tilman reached the highest mountain yet climbed, the 7,816-metre Nanda Devi. The expedition was conceived by four young Americans, including Arthur Emmons, who had been part of a team which climbed the 7,556-metre Minya Konka in China. One of the Americans, Charlie Houston, had met Frank Smythe's nemesis, Thomas Graham Brown, and the young Americans ended up teaming up with four experienced Britons: Graham Brown, Noel Odell (the last man to see Mallory and Irvine), Cambridge graduate Peter Lloyd and Bill Tilman, who was elected as leader. Odell had been selected for the 1933 Everest team, but had declined to participate for business reasons and was then not considered for 1936; Tilman had been on the 1935 reconnaissance but had not acclimatized well and was not selected for Everest in 1936; Lloyd was also a rejected candidate for Everest – so they all had something to prove.

The British–American team were not able to get permission for their original goal of Kangchenjunga and so switched to Nanda

H.W. Tilman on Nanda Devi in 1936.

Devi. Tilman's team followed the route he had discovered with Shipton to the base of the mountain two years earlier. They then established camps, the highest being a bivouac at 7,130 metres, where they installed Odell and Houston to attempt the summit. The rest of the team were in a camp 500 metres further down, when they heard Odell's familiar yodel from above. At first they thought Odell was announcing a successful summit climb, but then they made out the message 'Charlie is killed'. Thinking Houston was dead, a group led by Tilman started climbing up to the higher camp as fast as possible. When they arrived they realized that they had misheard Odell's shout: he had in fact said that Houston, who had eaten some beef from a punctured can and had severe food poisoning, was ill. It was left to Tilman and Odell to climb to the summit. Shipton admitted to a 'pang of envy' about his climbing partner Tilman bagging

Nanda Devi, a mountain he loved, whilst he wasted his time 'on that ridiculous Everest business',[39] but he was magnanimous enough to call Odell and Tilman's climb 'the finest ... ever performed in the Himalayas'.[40]

The following year Shipton teamed up with Tilman again, for an expedition which fitted much better their developing taste for mountain exploration. Instead of siege climbing a single high mountain with a large team, the pair wanted to explore a large unknown region of the Karakoram – the title of Shipton's book about it was *Blank on the Map*. Their goals were as much about surveying and exploring as they were about climbing, Shipton recruited Michael Spender, a cartographer who was on the 1935 Everest reconnaissance, and geologist John Auden. Both had brothers who were famous poets, Stephen Spender and W.H. Auden, which made it a cultured team – something that Shipton appreciated, even if the gruff and iconoclastic Tilman did not.

The politicization of mountaineering was explored in a successful play by W.H. Auden and Christopher Isherwood which premiered in London in 1936: *The Ascent of F6*. It tells of a climber, Michael Ransom, who is persuaded to attempt the first ascent of a fictional mountain, F6, which lies on the border of the British Empire and another competing empire, which is also attempting the mountain from the other side. The people of the imaginary country where F6 lies are in a state of rebellion, but believe that whoever first reaches the summit will rule for a thousand years. Ransom dreams of climbing F6, but he does not like doing it for reasons of political propaganda and national prestige. The plot explores many of the themes of 1930s climbing, with national rivalries, the use of climbing to project power on restive imperial subjects, press barons willing to finance struggling climbers and a general public distracted from the country's economic problems by stories of heroic ascents. Even the contrast between the British and German climbing styles is satirized, with the rival nation's team 'hammering the whole south face full of pitons and hauling each other up like sacks'.[41] Ransom goes ahead with the climb, but a number of his friends are lost along the way, and he dies after reaching the summit. The play was a topic of conversation on the Karakoram expedition, with Shipton saying that 'the idea of a race to seize a summit ... reminded him of all he hated about the massive, siege-style Everest expeditions'.[42]

The summer of 1936 also saw the infamous Berlin Olympic Games, awarded before the Nazis came to power. The International Olympic Committee discussed moving the venue on account of the regime's antisemitic policies, but the Germans gave assurances that Jewish athletes would be able to compete. It's easy to forget that British views of Nazi Germany in the mid-1930s were ambivalent: although Hitler's regime had taken actions in contravention of the Treaty of Versailles, like the reintroduction of conscription and remilitarization of the Rhineland, the Western Allies' reaction was muted. When the Treaty of Versailles was signed in 1919, most Britons wanted to see Germany severely punished for its aggression in the First World War, but by the 1930s opinion had shifted, with many believing German complaints about the harshness of the treaty were justified. Mallory's university friend John Maynard Keynes wrote that the Treaty contained 'nothing to make the defeated central empires into good neighbours'.[43] British newspapers regularly reported disapprovingly on the Nazis' persecution of the Jews, but this did not lead to a general conclusion that the whole regime was far beyond the pale, which encouraged the policy of appeasement.

The Berlin Games brought an unexpected recognition for the Dyhrenfurths in the form of an Olympic medal. Alpinism had been introduced in the very first modern Games but, because of disagreements about selection criteria, it was not awarded until 1924, when it was given to the 1922 Everest team. The 1936 International Olympic Committee met in Berlin three days before the official opening and decided unanimously to give the gold medal for alpinism to the Dyhrenfurths, representing Switzerland, for their various ascents in the Himalayas. Whilst a case could have been made for other candidates, the Nazis were on a charm offensive. There was even a temporary suspension of visible antisemitism during the Olympics, with storm troopers told to give up seats on public transport to Jewish women, but no one in Germany doubted this was a temporary truce in the Nazis' war of persecution: the antisemitic thugs of the SA used the slogan 'When the Olympic Games are over, we will beat the Jews to a pulp.'[44] News of the award took over a week to reach the Dyhrenfurths in Switzerland, by which time the Games were halfway through. Hettie's Jewish origins were well known, and she had no desire to receive her medal under the gaze of the Nazi leadership, so Günter Oskar flew alone to Berlin to accept the two medals.

A few months earlier Hettie had undertaken a lecture tour in the USA: it proved a big success, filling halls, colleges and universities, and she even met President Roosevelt. Hettie liked the attention she got in America and the fact that it was for her achievements in her own right rather than as the wife of a famous professor. The USA was an attractive alternative to Europe's grim economic outlook and the ugly antisemitism of Nazi Germany. The Dyhrenfurths' 17-year-old son Norman was interested in film-making and worked as a camera assistant for Hans Ertl, who had been on their Hidden Peak expedition. Ertl was a rising star, working for Leni Riefenstahl, the actress and film director greatly admired by Hitler. For Norman it was exciting to be working on a commercial that Riefenstahl was making for the Winter Olympic Games in Garmisch-Partenkirchen, but he also got first-hand experience of how Nazi rule was affecting life in Germany. One evening they were having dinner in a bar after filming, when the door flew open and a group of stormtroopers noisily entered. 'Beer! Heil Hitler! What's there to eat?' they shouted and gave the Nazi salute. Everyone returned the salute except Dyhrenfurth, and the SA men came to their table and asked why he refused to give the 'German greeting'. Intimidated, but defiant, the young Dyhrenfurth pulled out his Swiss passport This saved the situation. However, Nazi investigators later found out that he wasn't 'of Aryan descent' and he was sent back to Switzerland. In the end, Norman and his two siblings emigrated to the USA, but only after the family, still burdened by the debts of the 1934 expedition, had saved enough money to pay for the crossing.

TEN

When the watches stopped

After their successful Sikkim expedition, Paul Bauer and Karl Wien planned an attempt on Nanga Parbat for 1937, with Wien leading. Bauer would not be participating, as he was still hoping to climb his dream mountain, Kangchenjunga, in 1938, but knowing the 'problem of Nanga Parbat' needed to be solved first. The scale of the compensation debts incurred for the victims of the 1934 expedition meant that a solid financial backing for the new venture was crucial. The biggest financial problem was getting foreign currency, needed for many expenses in India, but closely controlled by the authorities due to Germany's difficult foreign-exchange position. The Himalayan Foundation pushed official bodies for sponsorship, including the Reich Education Ministry and the Aviation Ministry. The Nazi regime had been transforming the country, and expedition members were considered ambassadors of the 'new Germany' who should show the supposed characteristics of the German people: readiness to fight, toughness, comradeship and team spirit. They believed they were fulfilling the 'legacy' of the dead mountaineers of 1934, and succeeding would become a heroic deed, providing a role model for the German youth of camaraderie which lasted beyond death. Nanga Parbat had come to be seen as a 'German mountain'.

Selection was based on Bauer's principles, with a willingness to devote 100 per cent to team effort and accept a quasi-military discipline being more important than exceptional climbing ability, meaning that some top-performing alpine climbers were ignored.

There was a strong contingent from the AAVM, including Wien, Göttner and Hepp from the 1936 Sikkim expedition, as well as Hans Hartmann and Martin Pfeffer. Pfeffer, an architect born in 1908, had first come across the AAVM climbers at a mountain hut in Austria during Christmas 1927. Heavy snowstorms kept everyone in the hut, except Eugen Allwein and his partner. Pfeffer decided he wanted to be part of this elite group and got accepted thanks to his determination and climbing skill. In 1932, climbing with one of the most charismatic members of the club, Leo Maduschka, he was caught in a storm in the Dolomites. During a night of rain and icy storms, Maduschka died; Pfeffer, for his part, exhibited an iron will and survived. Maduschka's application of Nietzsche's philosophy to climbing made him an iconic figure among young German climbers. A book of his writings was published posthumously. Climbing in the Himalayas was a dream for Pfeffer, who had married only a few months before the expedition.

Hans Hartmann hesitated a long time before accepting the invitation for Nanga Parbat. Frostbite had claimed parts of his feet in the Alps, which had caused him problems on Kangchenjunga in 1931. In 1937 very few understood or approved of his decision to go: he had a wife and children and would have to interrupt his academic work, but the pull of the mountain was strong. He repeatedly read the diary of polar explorers Robert Falcon Scott and Alfred Wegener, both lost on their expeditions. He remembered the critical moments on Kangchenjunga with 'Bauer, whose iron will still caused his eyes to shine, when above Camp X his heart nearly gave out'.[1] The fact that his great friend Karl Wien was leading was decisive. Also in the team were Peter Müllritter, the only veteran of the 1934 team, and Ulrich Luft, who was going to perform high-altitude physiological studies together with Hartmann.

The idea of making a film was considered, as it could provide revenue for future expeditions, but it also increased the volume of equipment required. One cameraman who applied to join was Hans Ertl, but with his vagabond style he was not the type of character the Himalayan Foundation wanted, being neither an academic nor one likely to accept the discipline of the Bauer model. He was also a notorious womanizer. Nevertheless he was well connected: he had made a film with Leni Riefenstahl about the Berlin Olympics and had supporters in the Ministry of Propaganda. The Himalayan Foundation prevaricated, not wanting to take Ertl, but fearful of snubbing the Ministry.

After a stand-off, another factor allowed Bauer to reject Ertl: an affair with Hettie Dyhrenfurth during the 1934 Hidden Peak expedition. On the approach march the pair were separated from the others in the rearguard and became lovers. Ertl wrote that 'the coming days and nights passed like in a dream ... We both knew that this week would be the happiest of the whole expedition for us – and perhaps one of the most beautiful and light-hearted of our whole life!'[2] When they rejoined the others, Ertl felt the breach of trust had to be admitted to avoid tensions, and asked to talk to Günter Oskar. Ertl wrote that 'my giant opponent, who was almost a head taller than me, stepped in front of me and grabbed me by both shoulders, like a boxer who is getting ready to give his battered opponent the knockout punch', but instead of delivering a punch Dyhrenfurth calmly said 'something like this can happen, my young friend!' He explained they had been in an open marriage for nearly twenty years. He and Ertl shook hands and became firm friends. However, under the 1935 Nuremberg laws sexual relations with a Jew were illegal; hence, with this 'racial shame' hanging over him, the Ministry of Propaganda dropped their support for Ertl.

Ertl took his rejection badly, writing to Dyhrenfurth that Bauer chose the members of his expeditions 'just as arbitrarily as before ... focusing exclusively on his clubmates from the AAVM even if they are only average climbers'.[3] He listed the participants dismissively, saying that Adolf Göttner was the best climber and the only non-academic, but had been taken as a trail-breaking machine. He described Hans Hartmann as an invalid who had left his toes on Kangchenjunga. Ertl finished by saying that he hoped he would go on an expedition with Dyhrenfurth again one day – something that never happened.

After the success of German athletes at the 1936 Olympics, public expectations were high: many expected the first ascent of an 8,000er to show the supposed physical superiority of the German people and the reinvigorated *Reich*. The participants felt similar optimism, buoyed by extensive publicity, with the *Volkischer Beobachter* reporting that 'the hopes for success made the memory of earlier blows of fate recede' as the 'daring and thoughtful pioneers departed, devoted, not least to the global reputation of Germany'.[4]

At Base Camp Wien's team met the British liaison officer attached to the expedition, Lieutenant Dermot Smart of the 4th Gurkha Rifles. In the latter part of May it snowed every day, slowing progress up the Rakhiot Glacier, but in early June the weather was more stable, and they moved to Camp IV at the foot of the Rakhiot Peak. Their plan was for six Europeans and eight Sherpas to go up together from Camp V, with two of the Europeans and four Sherpas returning from Camp VI or VII. The remaining four Europeans and four Sherpas would cross the Silver Saddle and place Camp VIII, from where the two strongest climbers would make a dash for the summit, with the retreat being covered by the others. It was a plan aimed at correcting Merkl's mistakes by having a gradually reducing team as they got higher, leaving support in place for the summit team.

A first attempt to reach Camp V was driven back by bad weather. The supply chain kept working below and they had what they needed to finish the climb, apart from the required two weeks of good weather. Hartmann wrote that the mountain's 'main defensive weapons are cold and snow, and she is using them this year earlier and more aggressively than in 1932 and 1934'.[5] They were worried that Camp IV was not altogether safe from avalanches, and decided to move it 50 metres higher up to what was judged a safer spot, digging deep pits for the tents to protect them from storms. On 12 June Hartmann's team woke to clear weather, so they broke the trail to the first rocks of Rakhiot Peak. As they descended they saw Wien, Smart and a large team of Sherpas heading up to Camp IV, which they had to expand to accommodate the larger number of residents.

Camp II on Nanga Parbat, 1937.

Four Balti porters were sick, and it was agreed that they should go back down to Base Camp as soon as possible with Smart. The next day the weather was uncertain, so they rested, and had coffee with gingerbread and songs accompanied by the mouth organ to celebrate the departure of Lieutenant Smart. He was 26 years old and had been with the British Army in India for a few years at the time of the Nanga Parbat expedition. He had been due to go down to Base Camp to fetch the mail, but when the sick porters needed to descend he offered to go earlier with them, something that saved his life. Since some of the sick porters needed to get to a lower altitude quickly, Smart forced the pace, reaching Base Camp in one day. On 14 June the Germans woke to sunshine and decided to take loads up to a big glacier terrace, to make the move up to Camp V the following day easier. Hans Hartmann got far ahead of his companions, writing in his diary that his performance that day was 'almost miraculous'. He wondered whether it was because he was in a good mood, remembering his son's second birthday that day. Martin

Pfeffer wrote in his diary, 'How fortunate I am, to have the chance of looking at all this beauty.'[6]

The greatest tragedy

A week later Paul Bauer chanced to be in his office on a Sunday, when he got a telephone call from a journalist telling him that seven climbers and nine porters had been killed in an avalanche on Nanga Parbat – news so dreadful that Bauer at first struggled to comprehend it. Three days after Smart came down, Uli Luft had set off from Base Camp with five porters, bringing the mailbag and supplies. After passing a night at Camp II, they reached Camp III before 10 a.m. The Balti porters had headaches, so Luft suggested they paused and made tea whilst he went ahead, eager to see his teammates. The old track was faintly visible, but when he reached the foot of the ridge coming down from Rakhiot Peak where Camp IV had been built a week earlier, he could find no trace of it. Instead, he saw the remains of a huge ice avalanche: 300 metres above, an enormous serac had broken off and strewn massive ice blocks across a wide slope below. His worst fears were confirmed by the porters arriving, who agreed they were at the exact spot where Camp IV had stood.

They started to search in the debris, but the avalanche had happened days before and the ice blocks were frozen into a rigid mass. They found the rucksacks of Hartmann, Hepp and Müllritter, but the tents were in a deep pit and they had no chance of reaching them without tools. Luft hurried down to Base Camp to get help, arriving after dark. Smart, worried at seeing someone approaching with a lantern, rushed out into the rainy night to meet Luft, who told him the terrible news. They agreed that the avalanche must have happened on the night of the 14th; this was confirmed later from the climbers' diaries. Smart immediately sent off runners to ask for men and shovels and bring the news to the outside world.

Bauer realized that they needed to help with the terrible burden which had fallen on Luft and the scientist Professor Troll, the only surviving members of the expedition. Bauer faintly hoped that some climbers might be alive at the higher camps and knew of cases in the Alps of people being dug out alive many days after being trapped by avalanches, but when he calculated the quickest time he could reach Base Camp it was a depressingly long twenty-four days, even if he travelled to India by air. He made plans to leave all the same, together with Fritz Bechtold and Karl von Kraus, a doctor and veteran of the 1929 Kangchenjunga expedition.

The events received a good deal of publicity in the British Empire, the tragedy touching a nerve with the public. *The Times* wrote that 'the British public know the terrible risks that British climbers have faced on Everest; know too, what it means when men are killed who have taken up in the nation's name the challenge of unscaled mountains. Out of such knowledge ... British sympathy goes out today to the relatives of the Nanga Parbat climbers and to the German nation.'[7] Similar articles appeared in the Indian newspapers, with the *Statesman of Calcutta* saying, 'all Germans will respond to the call of Nanga Parbat, to which German mountaineers may be said to have a claim appreciated by everybody'. They asked of the tragedy, 'dare we call it a waste of valuable lives?' And answered that 'when men cease risking their lives for things that have not been done before, humanity will be on the down grade.'[8]

Bauer spent the next days glued to the telephone trying to organize a relief expedition. Kenneth Mason, a friend since the 1929 Kangchenjunga expedition, asked the British and Indian authorities for permission for the Germans to enter India. Just before leaving, they heard that the RAF would fly them to Gilgit, much closer to the mountain than possible with commercial flights: Bauer was enormously grateful for the support. From Gilgit they went on horseback the 40 miles to the Rakhiot Valley. When they met Uli Luft, he simply said 'I'm so glad you've come.' The calls to the British in India had been answered, with various officers coming from the surrounding area with men and equipment. Luft and Smart had already tried to go up with a team of porters with shovels, but the route through the icefall had been cut by seracs falling on the previous track. By the time Bauer and his companions arrived, the chances of discovering anyone alive were extremely low. It was not easy to find a way up the glacier, which had been changed significantly by the summer heat and was more dangerous. The new arrivals were also insufficiently acclimatized. Bauer fell ill with malaria. It was only on 15 July that Luft, Bechtold and Kraus finally arrived at the scene of the disaster with a team of porters. Since Luft had stood there alone four weeks earlier, another avalanche had descended, and a metre of fresh snow had buried all traces of the camp.

They started digging trenches across the avalanche traces and probing with iron rods, but it was slow work with fresh snow lying over huge blocks of ice. Four days of digging yielded no results, but in a final attempt before abandoning the search they dug 3-metre-deep pits and one yielded an ice axe marked H.C. 114, meaning it belonged to the Sherpa with the registration 114 on the Himalayan Club list. Digging further down, they discovered the body of Sherpa Pasang Norbu, lying peacefully in his sleeping bag, confirming their suspicions that the avalanche had hit during the night. Pasang Norbu was one of the Sherpas who had survived the desperate retreat from Nanga Parbat in 1934, suffering terrible frostbite. He had also been on the 1936 British Everest expedition and had been assigned duties low on the mountain to avoid further damage to his hands, but he had 'escaped the boredom' of Base Camp and carried loads to the North Col. We only have second-hand evidence of the motivations of men like Pasang Norbu, but it appears he had a genuine enthusiasm for climbing, which went beyond merely being a job. If this was part of his motivation to return to high dangerous mountains again and again, it eventually cost him his life, as well as that of his brother Mingma Tsersing and another seven Sherpas killed in the avalanche.

The Sirdar Nursang, who had first worked with Bauer back in 1929, said that for religious reasons the Sherpas preferred to leave the bodies where they were. The Germans were now able to guess the positions of the other tents, and late in the afternoon they found the corner of one and extracted a rucksack marked H.H., meaning this was where Hartmann, Pfeffer and Hepp lay. They also found a second tent before stopping digging for the day. The next morning they were surprised by the arrival of Paul Bauer, who had made a quick recovery from his bout of malaria and come up the mountain with more porters. They had just uncovered the body of Pfeffer, lying peacefully in his sleeping bag, his leather helmet making him look like a medieval knight. Beside him was Hartmann, whose watch had stopped at 12.20. Later it started again, so it must have been stopped by the cold, meaning the avalanche must have struck sometime earlier. Each body took lung-sapping work to dig clear. They discovered the diaries of the dead climbers and read them to try to understand what had happened. In another pit they found the tent containing Wien and Pert Fankhauser, but by now the rescue team were very weak after the exertions of digging. Bauer himself was unable to dig, and Luft and Kraus had to rest after every blow of the pick.

It was cloudy and snowing when they buried Wien and Fankhauser in a common grave, placing crossed ice axes and a rope, and flying the German flag from an avalanche probe. The third tent containing Göttner and Müllritter was under a big block of ice and impossible to access.[9] Bechtold, who had had to descend to Base Camp due to illness, watched anxiously for the return of the searchers, feeling horribly like he was reliving his experience in 1934, waiting for men trapped up on the mountain. He decided to go and help with Smart, who went above Base Camp again despite orders from his superiors forbidding him to do so. For Bauer, it was to Smart's 'honour that he ... did on this occasion what so many brave soldiers have said and done before when they obeyed the voice of their hearts, albeit in defiance of military orders.'[10] Bauer wrote this in the 1950s, and seemed to have a different attitude to military discipline than during his first Himalayan expeditions when he talked about the leader's need for absolute authority. The Prussian military tradition of unquestioning obedience is often viewed as a factor in facilitating the Nazi atrocities in the Second World War. Post-war, it was seen as correct to disobey orders which conflicted with a soldier's conscience. By contrast, British military tradition already encouraged officers to exercise judgement rather than blindly

Paul Bauer on Nanga Parbat, 1938.

follow orders, an attitude strengthened by the disastrous outcome of the Battle of the Somme when British troops had been told to obey by instinct without thinking and had been mown down by German machine guns. This subtler approach to discipline was also reflected in the attitude to leadership in British mountaineering expeditions. Before Smart and Bechtold left Base Camp they saw others coming down, bringing diaries, films and personal belongings to give to the dead men's loved ones.

Bauer concluded that a freak set of circumstances had caused the disaster: a large block of ice had 'calved' off a serac and slid across 400 metres of nearly level ground, picking up a mass of soft snow and coming to rest on top of the camp. The very cold weather before the accident made the powdery snow act like ball bearings, causing the mass of ice to travel so far. Wien and his team of very experienced climbers hadn't made any obvious mistake, and had even moved the camp from another site which they considered more dangerous days before the accident. The avalanche could not have been predicted; the fact that everyone was in the camp that day was due to an unfortunate chain of circumstances. Erwin Schneider, embittered at being banned from Himalayan expeditions, was less charitable, writing to Hermann Hoerlin that he could not understand why the camp was set up in the path of potential avalanches, and that 'those who are religiously inclined could interpret [the accident] as poetic justice.'[11]

The initial reaction of the British press was overwhelmingly sympathetic. The *Alpine Journal* agreed with Bauer's analysis, Strutt writing that 'no atom of blame can be adjudged to leader or individual, the party was a victim to the limitless powers of the great Himalaya.'[12] Strutt was friendly with Bauer and viewed accidents from German climbing activity in the Alps much more severely. Francis Younghusband wrote the introduction to the English translation of Bauer's book about the expedition. Despite being published in 1938, with the clouds of war on the horizon, Younghusband was supportive of Bauer's message of nationalism and sacrifice, writing that those who died on Nanga Parbat 'did love mountains. But they loved their country more. And it was to show the world that Germany still produced men that they ... [pitted] themselves against some of the monarchs of the Himalayas.'[13] Others were more critical of the accident, the *Yorkshire Post* writing of 'signs that young Nazi climbers are courting danger with fanatical zeal, almost as though they were ready to welcome death in the cause of national glory'.[14]

Help from the skies

As the survivors and rescuers of the 1937 tragedy sat around the campfire before leaving Nanga Parbat Base Camp, they resolved to return the next year to finish the job of climbing the mountain which had claimed the lives of so many of their friends. Bauer's plan had always been to return to Kangchenjunga; but if the tragedies of 1934 and 1937 were to be painted as heroic sacrifices to achieve a greater goal, it was first necessary to succeed on Nanga Parbat. As in 1934, the Nazi propogandists painted the tragedy as an example to German youth. Von Tschammer wrote an introduction to the expedition book, where he said the climbers required 'every ounce of will-power, courage and self-sacrifice'.[15]

With this heightened public interest, Bauer could no longer choose only from the tight-knit circle of the AAVM. There were many applicants for the 1938 expedition, some with only limited climbing experience. In Nazi Germany's complex web of political structures, Bauer was under pressure to accept candidates sponsored by different bodies. An SS member unknown within climbing circles, Hermann Raditschnigg, tried to force his acceptance by having a prominent SS general promote his candidature to von Tschammer. Bauer had autonomy in choosing team members, but things were complicated because the SS was interested in having responsibility for sport within the Third Reich, threatening von Tschammer's own position. Fortunately for Bauer, von Tschammer bought into his concept that not only climbing skills were decisive, but also personal characteristics like companionship and selfless obedience to the leader. Bauer stressed the parallels between this and the military philosophy of the country's Nazi leaders.

Bauer may have been making such arguments opportunistically to maintain control over recruitment, but for practical reasons he could not choose only from the AAVM in 1938: many of those with Himalayan experience had been killed in the 1937 tragedy. Fritz Bechtold was again part of the team, as was Uli Luft, the only survivor from 1937. Another with Himalayan experience was Ludwig Schmaderer, who had been to Sikkim on a private expedition.

Austrian Mathias Rebitsch had established his credentials with an attempt on the North Face of the Eiger in Switzerland, by the mid-1930s a magnet for ambitious young German, Austrian and Italian climbers, encouraged by Hitler's promise of a Gold Medal for the first ascent. The first serious attempts in 1935 and 1936 led to the deaths of all six climbers involved. Rebitsch and Ludwig Vörg failed due to bad weather after spending 100 hours on the Eiger, but were the first to retreat unharmed. Vörg wanted to attempt the Eiger again in 1938, but Rebitsch preferred to go to Nanga Parbat. If the unhealthy climate of reckless romanticism in late 1930s Germany meant that the deaths on Nanga Parbat in 1934 and 1937 only led more candidates to try again, the same was not true of the Sherpas. Nursang was again acting as Sirdar for Bauer, but when Tilman saw him in Darjeeling he was 'having some difficulty in persuading men with the memory of so many dead comrades fresh in their minds, to go again to that unlucky mountain. [His] forcible appeals reminded [Tilman] of the exhortation of Frederick the Great to his wavering troops: 'Come on you unmentionable offscourings of scoundrels. Do you want to live for ever?''[16]

The 1938 Nanga Parbat expedition was the first ever to have air support with the Aero Club of Germany, providing a specially adapted Junkers Ju 52 piloted by Alexander Thoenes, a member of Bauer's 1929 Kangchenjunga expedition. They planned to drop loads on the glacier near Camp IV and on the Silver Plateau. This could avoid a significant part of the load-carrying burden of previous expeditions, but Bauer was not confident it was feasible and organized an alternative supply chain with porters. Whilst most of the team went to India by sea, Thoenes flew the Ju 52 from Germany to Srinagar.

For Bechtold, on his fourth visit to Nanga Parbat, every turn of the path to Base Camp brought back memories, including the grave of Alfred Drexel, who died next to him four years previously. For Uli Luft, the sole survivor of 1937, it was also an emotional experience, particularly passing the spot where he saluted the others for the last time with 'Auf Wiedersehen im Lager IV!' Route-making up the Rakhiot Glacier was supported by the plane, a swastika painted on its side, which dropped loads so close to Camp IV that the occupants ran for cover for fear of being hit. It proved more difficult than they expected to recover all the loads in the deep snow, but they had fresh fruit as a result.

Grim discoveries

When Stephan Zuck, Luft and Bechtold tackled the ice wall of the Rakhiot Peak, Zuck suddenly shouted that there was a dead man hanging above from an old rope. It was one of the Sherpas who died in 1934. Although the face was quite well preserved, Bechtold was unable to tell if it was Nima Dorje or Nima Tashi. They decided to recover and bury him the next day. The Germans wanted to avoid the porters knowing about it, because they were sure it would make them unwilling to go further. They sent a letter down to Bauer explaining the 'tricky situation'. Early the next morning he arrived with Rebitsch and said he wanted to consider the possibility of avoiding Rakhiot Peak altogether and instead going through the ice basin of the *Mulde*, the route followed in 1932. Luft and Zuck went up to recover the Sherpa from the fixed ropes and buried him in a deep crevasse. After exploring the route via the *Mulde* with Rebitsch, Bauer announced he was determined to go that way.

Rebitsch and Hans-Herbert Ruths managed to pass the *Mulde*, before climbing deep unconsolidated snow to reach the East Ridge between the 1934 Camp VI and the Moor's Head. The following day, Bauer, Bechtold, Luft and Zuck, each accompanied by a Sherpa, set off to establish Camp VI on the ridge. Bechtold thought how happy Merkl, Welzenbach and Wieland would have been to see a new team coming up the route on which they had lost their lives. Together with a porter, Bauer headed along the ridge, but when he reached the Moor's Head rock tower he hung back rather than continuing. He had seen two boots half-embedded in the ice; immediately suspecting what this might mean, he called for Zuck to take the porters back. As Zuck passed Bechtold, he told him, 'There are two dead people by the Moor's Head, probably porters.'

Luft and Bechtold went up to join Bauer at the Moor's Head, under which the bodies were lying on top of each other, with a foam rubber mat between them. The face of the upper body was perfectly preserved, bleached straw yellow by the sun, as if mummified. They stood in silence with their heads bared in respect. Bechtold tried to remember the 1934 porters to identify the visible man, but couldn't, although the clothing was clearly a Sherpa's. They could not see the lower body, but Bechtold noticed the boots, gaiters and trousers of a European expedition member and realized it could only be Willy Merkl. This meant that the Sherpa was Gay Lay, who had stayed with Merkl whilst Ang Tsering went down to try to get help.

They dug a pit in the snow to bury Gay Lay and worked at freeing Merkl from the snow. Bit by bit they managed to free his face, seemingly unharmed by the four years in the snow. The emotion of seeing his childhood friend was overwhelming for Bechtold, who bent over the body in tears, his chest cramped in pain. Inside Merkl's pocket Luft found a sealed and undelivered letter from Willo Welzenbach, written when he and Merkl were terribly sick in Camp VII. The desperate appeal for help was never heard: Welzenbach had died in Camp VII and Merkl had struggled on with Gay Lay and Ang Tsering to the spot where they found him. They buried Merkl next to Gay Lay and then trudged back in silence to where Zuck had made the camp.[17]

In the following days two attempts to reach the Silver Saddle were driven back by storms, the highest point reached being 7,300 metres, by Ruths and Rebitsch. The original plan was for two lightly laden climbers to go straight from Camp VI to the Silver Saddle and build a bivouac there, supplied by plane. But if the weather did not allow a drop, the two bivouacking climbers would be in a tight spot. Not wishing to repeat the mistakes of 1934, they wanted to place a camp below the Saddle. They were well placed for a summit attempt, but with many porters ill the Germans started to worry about the lack of material coming up from below. The plane could not help them in that section, because it would have been impossible to drop loads on the narrow East Ridge. They felt in good shape and wanted to wait for better weather, but a red parachute was laid out in the snow at Camp V, the agreed sign for everyone to descend. Expecting to be back a few days later, they carefully stocked the tents and supplies in an ice cave before descending to meet Bauer, who had ordered a retreat because of bad weather and lack of porter manpower. Attempts to go back up were driven back by the weather and the expedition was abandoned.

Bauer's approach on Nanga Parbat in 1938 was rather cautious and far from the do-or-die fanaticism that some British climbers associated with Germans. He was disillusioned with the route from the Rakhiot Valley, which was technically not difficult but very long and indirect. This was the fourth failed German attempt this way. Wondering about the alternative of the steeper but more direct Diamir Face, attempted by Albert Mummery in 1895, Bauer sent Uli Luft and Stefan Zuck to the Diamir Valley to survey and take pictures of potential routes at the end of the 1938 expedition. It was decided to make a full reconnaissance in 1939, and then for Luft to lead a team to attempt the climb in 1940, something which never happened due to the outbreak of war.

Although the 1938 attempt did not create a narrative of heroic sacrifices, as had happened in 1934 and 1937, it still featured prominently in propaganda communications. Schoolchildren were asked to pray for Bauer's team, and a 1938 radio play about the earlier tragedies addressed them saying, 'German youth ... [has heard] of the deeds and sacrifices of your comrades [and vows we] will preserve the legacy of the fallen ... like a holy flame. Nanga Parbat team ... we greet you in the spirit of the dead, whose flag you have taken up again.'[18]

Trying light

German disillusionment with the repeated failures on Nanga Parbat was mirrored by the British reaction to the unsuccessful Everest expeditions, particularly in 1936, when a large experienced team had been unable to get above the North Col due to bad weather, whilst Tilman had succeeded with a much smaller and cheaper team on Nanda Devi. When permission was received to attempt Everest again in 1938, the Committee did not want to make a public appeal for funds in a period of austerity and with public interest in Everest declining. Raymond Greene summed up the attitude of many climbers: 'too much has been said in the past about the spiritual and mystical significance of climbing Everest and its possible effects on British prestige.'[19] This was the opposite of the mood in Germany, where the national and spiritual importance of climbing 'special' mountains like Nanga Parbat and the Eiger was being emphasized ever more. The different attitudes stemmed in part from the propaganda goals of the Third Reich, and partly because a younger generation of Britons had moved past the jingoism and nationalism of the First World War. In Germany the wound to the national psyche of the defeat and its aftermath was still open, even for the younger generation. In the introduction to Bauer's book about the 1937 Nanga Parbat expedition, Francis Younghusband and the translator compared what they saw as 'fundamentally different' British and German attitudes to climbing. The translator quoted Jack Longland, who said it was a pity that 'mountaineering has ever been acclaimed as more, or deeper than ... the most satisfying of sports', and continued that any loftier conception is sheer hypocrisy. Younghusband explained that the Germans 'undertook the enterprise with great seriousness' and saw it as having a greater significance.[20]

The Everest Committee was short of money and struggling to get newspaper and book deals, so when Tom Longstaff offered to personally cover the shortfall in funding, but set conditions, they had little choice but to accept. Longstaff had been on the 1922 expedition, but did not like big teams, felt there should be no advance publicity and wanted either Shipton or Tilman to lead. A small-scale team was planned and the leadership offered to Tilman, who accepted providing organization and choice of personnel were entirely in his hands. This doesn't mean that he wanted to be an authoritarian leader. On the contrary, he felt somewhat in awe of the experience of Shipton, Smythe and Odell, but he was keen to maintain a lightweight approach, writing that:

> everyday life is sufficiently cluttered up with complicated gadgets without our wishing to introduce them into such an essentially simple thing as mountaineering ... We want more simplicity not less – small parties equipped with bare essentials, not large, over-organized, over-fed, over-equipped expeditions.[21]

Tilman had been at Berkhamsted School with Frank Smythe and even played cricket against him, but, whereas Smythe just escaped going to the First World War, Tilman was a few years older and went. Like Paul Bauer, his life was shaped by this experience, and even though he did not have the bitterness of defeat he had the same sense of needing to find a direction in life to come to terms with the horrific but powerful experience of the war. Tilman starts his first book by explaining that 'to those who went to the War straight from school and survived it, the problem of what to do afterwards was peculiarly difficult'.[22] A few months after returning from the trenches, Tilman set off to start a coffee planation in colonial British East Africa, where ex-servicemen were given plots of land. In Kenya, he eventually met Eric Shipton, nearly ten years younger but a much more experienced mountaineer. Shipton took the almost novice Tilman up the first ascent of a difficult new route on Mount Kenya. The pair went on some great mountain explorations together, but were very different characters: Shipton sociable and friendly, Tilman notoriously gruff and reserved. Shipton recounts that, after spending seven months continuously together addressing each other as Shipton and Tilman, he suggested to Tilman that he called him Eric. Tilman hung his head and muttered, 'it sounds so damned silly'.[23]

For Everest in 1938 Tilman had a very experienced team, but not necessarily a contented one. Frank Smythe was feeling deeply unhappy in his marriage and wrote to Francis Younghusband that 'I was vaguely hoping that I should leave my bones on the mountain because life seemed entirely pointless and futile.'[24] Younghusband, by then in his mid-seventies, had become a mentor for Smythe, who spent a lot of time at the Younghusbands' house, where he met Nona Miller, who was to be his partner for the rest of his life after his marriage broke up. Tilman and Smythe were wary of each other, but

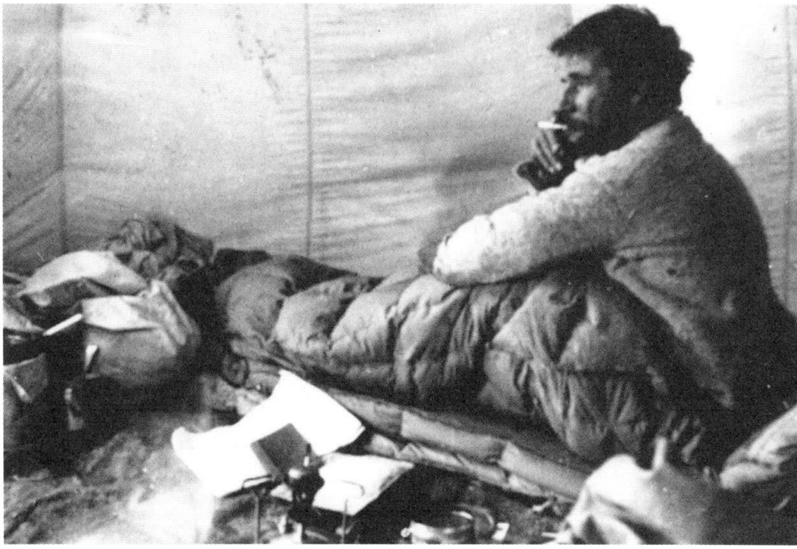

Tilman smoking in a sleeping bag in a tent during the 1938 Everest expedition.

Tilman still saw Shipton and Smythe as a likely summit pair. Also in the team was Noel Odell, returning to the mountain fourteen years after he saw Mallory and Irvine for the last time. The Sherpa team included Tenzing Norgay, who had already been a porter in 1935 and 1936 and who would become world famous. Tilman followed the frugal and functional approach to food that he and Shipton had used on their joint expeditions. Shipton was aligned with the approach and found things 'much better than the awful turmoil of a large expedition',[25] but not all the team was happy with what his Nanda Devi companion Charlie Houston had called Tilman's 'starvation tactics'. After returning, Odell commented that 'we did what we did on the mountain not because of our meagre rationing but in spite of it', and advised that in future there should be 'a compromise between the lavishness of some earlier expeditions and the frugality of this year's enterprise'.[26]

Determined to avoid the failure of 1936, caused by the early onset of the monsoon, they reached the Rongbuk Valley ten days earlier than any previous team. Everest was black and quite free of snow, but it was far too cold and windy to start the climb. They crossed into the more hospitable Kharta Valley to recover from various illnesses picked up crossing the windy plateau of Tibet. When they returned to the Rongbuk Valley they were shocked to find Everest now white with snow. Despite this, they didn't believe the monsoon had started and tackled the route to the North Col.

Which way to the North Col?

The lower slopes were in good condition, but higher up Peter Oliver was caught in an avalanche, although fortunately he was held on the rope. That evening a storm started and during the night they could hear avalanches roaring off the mountains around them. An alternative was to reach the North Col from the other, western side, which had less avalanche risk. It was agreed that Shipton and Smythe should go with all available porters on the week-long journey back down the East Rongbuk Glacier to Base Camp, and then back up the main Rongbuk Glacier to the other side of the Col. When it dawned fine the next day, they changed their minds and managed to reach the Col from the eastern side, finding the apex of a tent from 1936 just visible above the snow. They were dismayed to see that Norton's traverse across the sloping rocks of the North Face was white with snow, which they felt would make it impossibly difficult. As the weather changed, they kept debating the best approach to the North Col.

A party under Tilman occupied Camp IV on the Col, but that night 30 centimetres of snow convinced them that the monsoon was already under way. They had plentiful supplies, and decided to explore the North Ridge towards the planned site of Camp V. The 'tireless' Tenzing and Tilman turned back at 7,500 metres, because there was little to be gained from occupying Camp V in those conditions. That evening it started to snow again, so they abandoned Camp IV.

On 1 June there was a change in the weather, with low clouds and a strong west wind. Shipton and Smythe engaged all porters to move loads to the western side of the North Col, and the rest of the team followed. Large quantities of snow were being blown off the North Face, giving a chance of an attempt on the summit. The same wind created avalanche conditions on the east side of the Col, which was abandoned altogether. The way to the western side went over the cone of 'the father and mother of all avalanches',[27] probably created a few days earlier. This meant the first 150 metres of the route was bare ice and they had to cut steps. After the ice, they had 250 metres of steep snow to reach the Col, finding their camp from a few days earlier still intact.

The slopes to Camp V were much easier than before, with snow hard enough that a strong kick from the edge of the boot was enough to provide a footing, but the good snow ended and the final section to the site of Camp V was more trying. Shipton, Smythe and seven porters camped there, whilst Tilman and Peter Lloyd descended to the North Col with the rest of the porters. That evening Tilman wrote in his diary: 'Frank and Eric going well – think they may do it.'[28] It proved to be over-optimistic. Two days later, Shipton, Smythe and seven Sherpas climbed steep, snow-covered rocks to place Camp VI at 8,300 metres, too low to give them a realistic chance of the summit. The British pair stayed in the camp, determined to try to explore further, but gave up in thigh-deep powder snow. Shipton noted that, 'had it simply been a matter of ploughing a way through many feet of soft snow, we might somehow have contrived ... by working continuously in ... shifts for a week, to force a way ... to the top',[29] but in those conditions the rocks of the Yellow Band were excessively dangerous.

Tilman and Lloyd went up to the top camp, where they met Shipton and Smythe, who told them about the bad snow conditions. Tilman and Lloyd still wanted to explore a route to the Second Step. On the way to Camp VI, Lloyd was in the lead using oxygen and arrived thirty minutes before the others, a performance that made the British a bit more positive on the merits of oxygen, although Tilman was still opposed on grounds of sporting ethics. Their objective was to reach the North-East Ridge, which meant climbing

Frank Smythe at the highest point reached on Everest in 1938.

a 15-metre rock wall, but despite several attempts to go up or round it they had to turn back. Even if they had been able to get to the ridge, it was too far to the summit to have a realistic chance. The descent was made troublesome first by a blizzard and then by the need to lower and carry one of the porters, who was seriously ill, paralysed down his right side.

The 1938 British attempt at least proved that it was possible for a relatively small group to get high enough on Everest to make a summit attempt. That they didn't make a serious one was for the usual reason of bad weather and the onset of the monsoon. Tilman felt they had proved that 'a small party run on modest lines is as likely to achieve success as a large, expensively run party'. He noted that, based on the approach of several other expeditions in 1938, such 'saner methods ... are already in vogue', but was critical of the use of the aircraft on Nanga Parbat, pointing out that once you started dropping stores on the mountain 'the [next] logical step ... is to drop men as near to the summit as convenient. It will probably be quicker and safer to climb there in the end, but we must move with the times, and the end which is certainly not mountaineering justifies the means.'[30] Tilman felt that success depended on getting lucky with the weather and recommended that the Committee ask permission from the Tibetan government for expeditions in 1940, 1941 and 1942. It was clear by the time the team returned to Britain that a war was likely to start sooner rather than later. These expeditions never took place.

ELEVEN

The gathering storm

After the Germans, the next biggest threat to Britain's primacy in Himalayan mountaineering was the Americans. As Tilman's team was turning back on Everest in 1938, an American team, led by his Nanda Devi teammate Charlie Houston, was making a very strong attempt on the world's second highest mountain, K2. Houston and Paul Petzoldt reached 7,900 metres, but felt that carrying on would have been 'gambling on good weather ... unjustifiable and ... very poor mountaineering'.[1] The following year Fritz Wiessner led another American attempt. One of the pioneers of the VIth grade in the Alps in the early 1920s, Wiessner had become a US citizen after emigrating from Germany. He had Himalayan experience from Merkl's first Nanga Parbat expedition and was probably America's leading climber at that time. But Wiessner was not successful in assembling a strong team, the difficult economic climate forcing him to focus on climbers who could cover their own costs, including two students in their early twenties and the wealthy but overweight Dudley Wolfe, all with limited mountaineering experience. Wiessner's deputy Tony Cromwell had done more climbing, but only with guides and did not expect to go high on K2.

They did have a strong group of Sherpas, led by the very experienced Sirdar Pasang Kikuli. Wiessner led all the way on K2, with limited support from the other Americans, meaning inefficient stocking of the lower camps. When Wiessner went down to Base Camp, progress ground to a halt. A rift opened between Wiessner

A weary Fritz Wiessner on the return march from the 1939 K2 expedition after the fatal accident.

and the rest of the team, with only Wolfe and the Sherpas remaining with him high on the mountain, isolated from the others below. Wiessner attempted the summit with the Sherpa Pasang Dawa Lama from Camp IX at just under 8,000 metres. They avoided today's standard route up a snow gully to the 'Bottleneck' traverse, instead climbing more difficult rocks on the left. Wiessner was a superb rock climber, but it still took nine hours to reach the top of the rocks at 8,370 metres. With only a 240-metre snow slope to the summit, Wiessner was keen to carry on through the night, but Pasang Dawa Lama stopped paying out the rope and Wiessner had to turn back. Although he regretted stopping when the summit was so close, he never criticized his partner for the decision. During the descent, darkness overtook them, and Pasang Dawa Lama lost both the sets of crampons he was carrying.

They made another attempt, but it proved too difficult without crampons. The other Sherpas had stopped ferrying loads up the mountain and seemed to assume there had been an accident, with everyone above dead. Some of Wiessner's teammates had set off home, and Sherpas were sent up to clear the camps. When Wiessner and Pasang Dawa Lama went down to Camp VIII to collect supplies, they found a shocking scene: no one had come up from below for a long time, leaving Dudley Wolfe alone and, having run out of matches, unable to cook or melt ice for drinks. Together with Wolfe, they carried on down to Camp VII, expecting it to be well stocked, but instead it was even worse, with collapsed tents and no sleeping mattresses. Wiessner was still hoping to make another attempt; the next morning he left Wolfe at Camp VII and descended further with Pasang Dawa Lama to pick up supplies, but they passed camp after camp, finding little food and no sleeping bags, until they reached Base Camp utterly exhausted.

Wiessner was furious and accused Cromwell of abandoning and trying to murder them. Cromwell retorted that it was Wiessner who had abandoned Wolfe on the mountain. Three Sherpas climbed back to Camp VII, where they found Wolfe still alive, but apathetic and covered in excrement. He was not interested in the letters they had brought and refused to go down, saying they should return the following day to fetch him. After a day blocked by a storm at Camp VI, the three Sherpas, Pasang Kikuli, Pasang Kitar and Phinsoo, went up again to rescue Wolfe or, if they couldn't persuade him to come, to get a chit from him confirming they had done their best. A storm lasting several days came in, and none of them were ever seen again, rescue attempts being driven back by storms and Wiessner's exhaustion. Pasang Kikuli was a very experienced high-altitude porter and survivor of the storm on Nanga Parbat in 1934, which left him with bad frostbite. He left a widow and two young children.

The arguments about who was to blame for this tragedy were as bitter as on Nanga Parbat in 1934, not helped by the onset of war. Although a US citizen, Wiessner still had a pronounced German accent, and the report of the US Consulate General for Calcutta said that some of the conflicts might have been due to someone with 'a large share of German bluntness ... a national characteristic ... [and] ... like every German ... very forceful in giving commands',[2] leading Americans. It did not help when Wiessner told the *New York Times* that on big mountains, as in war, one must expect casualties. Despite his attitude to risk, the critique of Wiessner's leadership style could in part be based on a national stereotype, an easy trap to fall into in the late 1930s, although Kauffman and Putnam, who wrote a book about the tragedy and knew Wiessner well, referred to him as having been 'reared in the school of absolute obedience to authority that characterizes much of the Teutonic ethos: the leader leads, and the troops obey, whatever the situation'.[3] But if Wiessner had succeeded it would have been as an American, not as a German: he was later disappointed at not being able to fight for America in the Second World War. Wiessner was one of the closest to climbing an 8,000-metre peak before the war. Apart from the British Everest expeditions, Pasang Dawa Lama and Wiessner were the only climbers to go above 8,000 metres before 1950.

The murder wall

British views of German climbing in the second half of the 1930s were largely shaped by events on two mountains, Nanga Parbat and the Eiger, whose North Face was nicknamed the *Mordwand*, or Murder Wall, as a macabre pun on its German name (*Nordwand*). The first attempt in 1935 had resulted in the deaths of two Munich climbers. In 1936 a pair of Bavarian soldiers, Toni Kurz and Andreas Hinterstoisser, and two members of the Austrian Nazi Legion, Willy Angerer and Edi Rainer, had started separately, but then combined their efforts. Hinterstoisser overcame a key traverse, which still bears his name, but they did not leave a rope on it to safeguard their retreat. When bad weather came, they had to abseil to the foot of the face but were hit by an avalanche. Only Kurz survived this. However, he died from exposure within reach of his rescuers. Edward Strutt was outraged, describing the route as 'an obsession for the mentally-deranged'. His report on accidents in 1936 discussed the 'suicidal follies of the *Eigerwand*. Never perhaps in the entire history of mountaineering has a more deliberate attempt been made to combine extreme danger with the hope of that notoriety.'[4]

He was particularly critical of an article in the German magazine *Der Bergsteiger*, referring to the heroes of the *Eigerwand*, mirroring propaganda messages about the deaths on Nanga Parbat.

Switzerland, where the Eiger is situated, was shocked by these events, especially since Swiss mountain guides had taken personal risks in attempting a rescue. Comments made to the Swiss press described the climb as being possible, but depending 90 per cent on luck, with 'technical development, a fanatical disregard of death, staying powers and bodily toughness ... of mere secondary importance. The ... climb lies completely outside the pale of mountaineering, belonging far more to a degenerate form of the Children's Crusade of the Middle Ages.'[5] The canton of Berne issued a ban on climbing the North Face, but it was found not to be legally enforceable and was repealed. Strutt's analysis of the 1936 accident noted that 'the Teutonic Press ... considers that harsh criticism of the insane deed has been meted out by the Swiss and European newspapers.'[6]

In the summer of 1938, when the Germans were failing again on Nanga Parbat, the Eiger North Face was finally climbed. In July, Munich climbers Ludwig Vörg and Anderl Heckmair made their attempt. They were financially supported by the Nazi authorities as employees of the Sonthofen National Socialist Order Castle, one of three special training centres modelled on the crusader-era Teutonic Orders, created by Robert Ley of the German Labour Front to develop future Nazi leaders. Heckmair and Vörg were not Nazis, but being employed by the Order Castle meant they could buy modern climbing equipment and had financial security. Heckmair had never had a job previously.

Austrians Fritz Kasparek and Heinrich Harrer were also at the foot of the Eiger. Harrer was born in 1912. His links to the Nazi Party are controversial; some believe he was a committed supporter, who had a Nazi pennant in his rucksack on the Eiger. The two teams started the climb separately, with the Austrians initially ahead, and the Germans hesitating about the weather. Vörg and Heckmair were able to catch up, helped by their state-of-the-art equipment, including twelve-point crampons, with two added points at the front of the existing ten below the foot, giving better grip on steep ice. Kasparek only had ten-pointers and Harrer had no crampons at all. They continued independently, but Heckmair, the strongest climber, was often in the lead. After they were hit by an avalanche, the two teams joined and finished the climb together, after difficult bivouacs, bad weather and many avalanches.

There was huge press coverage in Germany, the previously unknown climbers hailed as national heroes. The climb took place five months after the annexation of Austria by Germany in the *Anschluss*. Hitler was born in Austria, which he had long desired to include in a 'Greater German Reich'. By the 1930s there were many Nazi supporters in Austria, including several leading alpinists. The Party was banned in Austria, but the Nazis carried out terrorist attacks, including the assassination of Chancellor Dollfuss. Hitler put pressure on his successor Kurt Schuschnigg, who agreed to a series of demands, including appointing Austrian Nazi Arthur Seyss-Inquart as Minister of Public Security with full control over the police. When Schuschnigg started to organize a referendum, expected to support Austria's continued independence, Hitler demanded Seyss-Inquart be appointed chancellor and threatened an invasion, which took place on 12 March 1938. At least part of the public seemed to give a genuinely warm greeting to the troops.

Hitler toured the country personally and decided to incorporate Austria into a Greater Germany immediately. Seyss-Inquart was only chancellor for two days. He was a keen mountaineer; when the DÖAV became the DAV (Deutsche Alpenverein) following the *Anschluss*, he was made its leader. The obstacle of the DÖAV being a multi-country organization was removed, and its full Nazification could take place, with Bauer's Reich Office for Hiking and Mountaineering merged into the DAV. In compensation for his loss of leadership of this organization, Bauer was appointed as a deputy to Seyss-Inquart, but the merger suited neither the DAV nor Bauer. Bauer did not get on well with Seyss-Inquart, who as *Reichskommissar* of the occupied Netherlands during the Second

World War oversaw a reign of terror, including the deportation of Dutch Jews to the concentration camps, for which he was tried at Nuremberg and executed.

The ascent of the North Face of the Eiger by a joint Austrian-German team was presented as a victory for the 'Greater German Reich'. Congratulatory telegrams arrived from leading Nazis, including Robert Ley and Seyss-Inquart, and the climbers were personally received by Hitler. In the book about the climb by the Nazi publishing house, Harrer wrote that they had climbed the North Face 'beyond the summit to our Führer',[7] although he later claimed this was ghostwritten.

Bauer's struggle to control team selection

The appeal of sending the climbers who had 'conquered' the Eiger on an expedition to Nanga Parbat, 'Germany's Mountain of Destiny', was obvious, but led to disputes. Realizing it would be the perfect symbol of a 'tough education system', training future Nazi leaders to conquer nature, an expedition from the Sonthofen Order Castle was planned, with Heckmair and Vörg in the team. Since the Himalayan Foundation was created, Bauer had had to submit his proposed teams for approval by von Tschammer, who had always trusted Bauer's judgement, but von Tschammer was indirectly a subordinate of Robert Ley and keen to support the ambitions of the Order Castles. Bauer pointed out to von Tschammer that 'It is not possible to weigh and evaluate mountaineering achievements. We know who the best short-distance runner is, but there is no concept of the best mountaineer',[8] setting out the qualities he looked for when choosing climbers, such as discipline and self-sacrifice. Bauer felt climbers needed an academic education to possess these attributes and avoided 'mountain vagabond' climbers like Heckmair, who had spent most of his childhood in orphanages. The vagabonds did not have careers and tried to climb full time, taking casual work when necessary. The four Eiger climbers did not conform to Bauer's principles, but his influence over foreign expeditions was dwindling since the *Anschluss*. He was still responsible for overseas expeditions within DAV, but there was less benefit from his strong relationship with von Tschammer, and a bitter dispute over the composition of the 1939 Nanga Parbat team occurred.

Heckmair and Vörg had made their collaboration with Order Castle dependent on carrying out a Himalayan expedition, and were already choosing participants and buying equipment when suddenly all preparations had to be stopped. In his autobiography, Heckmair wrote that the final decision was made by Hitler himself. Ley sent him to meet Hitler at a Christmas party in Munich's Löwenbräukeller beer hall for the *alten Kämpfer*, literally old fighters, the earliest members of the Nazi Party. Heckmair describes the SS Men taking him to Hitler. After the climber explained his request to carry out the expedition, Hitler replied: 'I need you for quite a different task', making it clear the question was closed.[9] Heckmair drove back to Sonthofen depressed, because he would not be going to Nanga Parbat and it was clear from Hitler's speech to the *alten Kämpfer* that Germany was heading for a new war. Events proved as bad as Heckmair feared. Both he and Vörg refused to join the SS and found themselves conscripted as ordinary soldiers due to 'political unreliability'. Vörg died on the first day of the Russian campaign, whereas Heckmair survived, despite experiencing horrific fighting near Moscow in the winter of 1941–2. There are doubts whether the meeting between Heckmair and Hitler actually took place, but other sources confirmed that the dispute between von Tschammer and Bauer had been settled by Hitler, who saw the propaganda value of climbing Nanga Parbat.

With the dispute resolved, plans were made for a 1939 reconnaissance, prior to a full attempt the following year. Bauer's trusted collaborator Peter Aufschnaiter was leading the reconnaissance, but did not have many good candidates in the AAVM. One AAVM member recruited was Lutz Chicken, a medical student from the German-speaking South Tyrol, which was lost by the Austro-Hungarian Empire to Italy in the First World War. Significant efforts were made to Italianize it, particularly after the Fascists came to power in 1922. Growing up in a predominately

German-speaking region of Italy during this Fascist oppression, Chicken naturally felt affinity for the German language and culture, and was in sympathy with the anti-Italian movement, cultivated in secret by meetings of friends and families. With the suppression of German culture, National Socialist ideas were attractive for South Tyrolian youth, and negative aspects of the Nazi regime seemed far away. When Chicken moved to Munich to study medicine, he joined the Hitler Youth, providing medical care at camps. In January 1939 Chicken went to the Himalayan Foundation's office to borrow maps for Easter ski tours in the Alps and met Aufschnaiter, who invited him to Nanga Parbat. The request took Chicken by surprise, and at first he wondered whether Aufschnaiter was serious, but he was a good candidate, with solid climbing credentials, speaking English well, and with nearly complete medical training could serve as the expedition doctor. Chicken drove to Bolzano to get his parents' approval and inform his girlfriend he would be away for six months. Events were such that his absence turned out to be much longer.

Heinrich Harrer, an ambitious and driven man with more than 400 climbs in the Dolomites under his belt, had applied to go on the expedition at the suggestion of Heckmair. Harrer's motivation for climbing the Eiger North Face was to become famous and possibly lead to his goimg to the Himalayas, but Bauer did not see sensational routes as a criterion for selection. Like Heckmair and Vörg, Harrer was not close to Bauer, but at least he was a graduate, which for Bauer was important. In 1933 Harrer had joined the SA, which was banned and operated underground in Austria. In April 1938, only a few weeks after the *Anschluss*, Harrer transferred to the SS. As a 'glorious victor' over the North Wall of the Eiger, Harrer met SS head Heinrich Himmler, who asked if he would like to join Ernst Schäfer's zoological expedition to Tibet, which hoped to prove the Nazis' pseudo-scientific theories that the Germans descended from a superior Aryan race by showing genetic links between the Germans and the Tibetans. Harrer turned down this invitation, still hoping to go to Nanga Parbat.

On Christmas Eve 1938 Harrer married Charlotte, the daughter of Polar explorer Alfred von Wegener. As a member of the SS getting married, Harrer was required to undergo special checks at the behest of the SS Race and Settlement Office, including verifying that both bride and groom were of pure Aryan ancestry back to at least 1800. Harrer asked for these checks to be accelerated because of his possible participation in the Nanga Parbat expedition. When a spokesman for Seyss-Inquart wrote to Bauer pointing out the level of political support for Harrer's candidacy, Bauer realized he could not block his participation and invited him to join. The final member of the team was Hans Lobenhoffer, a soldier in a mountain regiment.

To India under the clouds of war

The team had been constructed artificially and did not gel naturally: Aufschnaiter was much older than the others and demanded strict discipline. They had still not received visas when they sailed for India, and it was not certain they would get them, given the increasingly tense political situation in Europe. Following the *Anschluss*, Hitler aimed to seize Sudentenland, an area of Czechoslovakia with a significant German-speaking population. The area's annexation was agreed by the Allies at the Munich Agreement in September 1938, with British prime minister Neville Chamberlain famously returning to London hailing the agreement as 'peace for our time'. At the time of the Munich crisis, Aufschnaiter was staying with Kenneth Mason in Oxford to discuss his plans for 1939 and 1940. The terrible pogrom of *Kristallnacht* in November 1938 made clear to even those who had wanted to give the Nazis the benefit of doubt that they were not a civilized regime that could be dealt with. Within a few months it was obvious that Hitler's expansionist ambitions wouldn't be satisfied by what had been agreed in Munich. In March 1939 Hitler invaded further parts of Czechoslovakia and demanded the return of the free city of Danzig (Gdansk) and the corridor of Polish land which separated East Prussia from the rest of Germany. Britain and France decided that Hitler could not be trusted, and guaranteed the independence of Poland, committing them to go to war if Poland was attacked. Many started to think war was inevitable.

In this climate Mason knew that Aufschnaiter might have problems and wrote to the India Office, saying he had advised the Austrian to delay his departure. Aufschnaiter wrote to Mason asking if the political situation prejudiced his chances of getting a visa; Mason replied that he thought not, but that 'we were all pretty disgusted at the way the Munich agreement had been cast aside'.[10] Aufschnaiter replied explaining that, in the interests of time, the Germans had set off, but would turn back at Port Said in Egypt if they were not allowed to enter India. Aufschnaiter's decision annoyed the India Office, but after a flurry of telegrams they issued the relevant paperwork. German expeditions were becoming a matter of concern to the British authorities. A note from the India Office to the Secretary of State said that 'In the present state of international affairs it is obviously necessary to be vigilant in regard to the activities of German expeditions ... We have always maintained friendly relations with Dr Bauer ... and Aufschnaiter is a friend of Mason and apparently not a Nazi.'[11] In fact, Aufschnaiter was a member of the Nazi Party, but the British were probably right in concluding that the expedition was not 'mischievous' and that, if the Nazis took a keen interest in it, this was not because of plans for espionage, but merely on account of the glory and prestige in a possible ascent of Nanga Parbat.

From a Base Camp in the Diamir Valley, Aufschnaiter's team first explored the rock ribs in the middle of the face, attempted by Mummery in 1895. Lobenhoffer and Chicken climbed to the top of the second rib, where they were very puzzled to find a 25-centimetre-long piece of wood, seemingly brought by Mummery as fuel forty-four years earlier. The way ahead over the third rib looked feasible, but the next day they saw a huge avalanche from the hanging glacier on the right which swept the ribs. Their tent at the foot of the first rib was at a safe distance but was still covered in snow dust. Aufschnaiter had agreed with Bauer not to take any risks and ruled out any further attempts via the ribs.

Instead, they looked at routes on the broad face below the North Summit, reaching 6,000 metres on steep ground with loose rocks. Given the difficulties, Aufschnaiter decided to postpone further attempts, but noted that the huge avalanches which crashed down from the hanging glaciers to the side did not cross the planned route itself, meaning it could be a viable way. The second part of their plan was to attempt the 7,781-metre Rakaposhi, but permission was denied. They returned to the Diamir Valley, where Harrer and Lobenhoffer went higher up the face below the North Summit. They had to traverse on bare ice for several pitches and climb treacherous rocks, before reaching a rock ridge. They had difficulty in finding a place for their tent and were troubled by falling stones. Harrer felt that the rock above them looked difficult rather than impossible, but they did not go further and halted their exploration of Nanga Parbat. The Diamir Face had a big advantage over the Rakhiot one: height could be gained quickly by a steep and direct route. Aufschnaiter judged that a team of experienced technical climbers would prefer this route, but would have to do a lot of load-carrying themselves, since porters would be unlikely to work on such steep exposed ground. At the end of July they left the Diamir Valley for good, with Chicken and Aufschnaiter visiting the Political Officer for Gilgit to discuss plans for the 1940 expedition.

On 22 August they all met up in Srinagar, the capital of Kashmir, where they hoped to spend a few days, but news from Europe forced them to head directly towards the coast. They had left Germany at a time of political crisis, but were confident peace would reign during the expedition and that return would not be difficult. In the Diamir Valley mail arrived with a long delay, preventing them understanding how the situation was evolving in real time. By August 1939 tension in Europe was very high, negotiations between the British and French and the Soviet Union about a security pact had broken down, and the Soviets had started discussions with Germany, which led to the Molotov–Ribbentrop Pact. Aufschnaiter's team now understood the imminent danger of war, and the risk of being blocked in India, and immediately set off for Karachi. There they hoped to get back

Below the Diamir Face of Nanga Parbat during the 1939 reconnaissance.

to Europe on a German ship, but it was ordered not to approach the Indian coast.

In Karachi they tried and failed to get on flights to Germany or onto boats stopping at Persian ports. Aware that the secret police were watching them, Harrer, Lobenhoffer and Chicken attempted to reach the Persian border overland. Aufschnaiter did not expect the escape to be successful and stayed with the equipment and photographs. His younger teammates shook off the man shadowing them and escaped in a ramshackle taxi in the direction of the autonomous principality of Lasbela, but after a night in the desert they awoke to find themselves surrounded by soldiers, who arrested them and took them back to Karachi. The same day Germany invaded Poland, making war inevitable, and two days later Britain declared war on Germany. A few minutes later twenty-five armed Indian soldiers marched into the restaurant where the four climbers were sitting and took them off to an already prepared prison camp. A fortnight later they were transferred to a large internment camp near Bombay. After the freedom of the mountains, it was depressing to find themselves behind barbed wire, although they did not imagine they would have to wait for years to regain their freedom.

With war inevitable, British climbers knew their freedom to explore mountains was likely to be restricted and took the chance to make trips in the summer of 1939. In the final weeks before war, Frank Smythe went on a prolific alpine climbing tour with his friend and Everest 1936 teammate Jim Gavin. Smythe's experience of seeing his former classmates dying in 1918 had left him anti-war, and he asked Gavin, a serving soldier, about the views of British officers. Gavin confirmed that even those too young to remember the last war had no illusions that war was 'an unpleasant and bloody business'. Before their final climb, the Innominata Ridge on Mont Blanc, they met a group of German climbers who were 'all ardent Nazis', but who Smythe felt on a personal level were decent people. Smythe saw it as 'one of the greatest tragedies the world has seen that a political ideology ... should imbue such men with its vicious principles'.[12] They climbed the route at the same time as the young Germans, who were friendly 'despite the poison assiduously pumped into them for years'. Smythe's position of being positive towards individual Germans whilst negative to the Nazi regime is probably typical of British climbers, who were generally educated people with an international outlook. A few days after Smythe and Gavin returned to

England, Europe was at war. The same summer Eric Shipton was on a long exploratory expedition in the Karakoram. His team had a small battery-powered radio for use only to get time signals to fix their position by the stars for surveying purposes. At the beginning of October one of the team broke the rule not to use the radio 'for frivolous purposes, and was punished by the appalling discovery that the war had begun'.[13]

Internment

Fired by nationalism, the young Nanga Parbat climbers regretted missing the chance to fight for Germany. Chicken reflected afterwards that internment quite likely saved his life, and he was probably right: the onset of war not only stopped any Himalayan climbing for nearly ten years; it also cost the lives of many of the climbers of the 1930s. Rolf von Chlingensperg, of the 1938 Nanga Parbat expedition, died when a U-Boat he was on was sunk by the Royal Navy in 1945. His teammate Stefan Zuck had died on service for the Luftwaffe four years earlier. The four members of the Nanga Parbat expedition were 'safely' in British custody in India. In 1941 they were moved to a camp north-east of Bombay. Lobenhoffer and Harrer escaped by jumping off a moving truck, but they were immediately recaptured. The camp was unbearably hot, and after a hunger strike the authorities moved them to the cooler Himalayan foothills at Dehra Dun, which some of the internees noticed was only 120 miles from the Tibetan border. Again, Lobenhoffer escaped during the move and was recaptured, but claimed that as an army officer he should be treated as a prisoner of war and was transferred to Canada.

Aufschnaiter and Harrer made several failed escape attempts. Harrer also approached Lutz Chicken to join, but Chicken turned him down. He had been depressed after his original internment, but then resolved to develop his medical skills in the camp hospital and work on his doctoral thesis. Previous escape attempts had always failed, and an attempt would mean his permission to work in the camp hospital being revoked. Chicken returned to Europe in November 1946 and completed his medical studies. In 1944 Aufschnaiter and Harrer finally succeeded in escaping and headed for Tibet. Aufschnaiter had studied Tibetan in the camp, and this proved crucial in overcoming various hurdles. Eventually he and Harrer made it to Tradun in Tibet, where they waited months without getting permission to go to Lhasa, before setting out anyway, only to be driven back by wolves. When permission finally arrived, it was winter and bitterly cold on the Tibetan Plateau. They were rewarded with views of Everest, and even got help from a relative of a porter from the 1931 Kangchenjunga expedition. There were two ways to Lhasa: one with many passes, meaning very cold conditions and snow; the other with many Khampas, the Tibetan bandits. They chose the second, surviving some narrow escapes before arriving in Lhasa in early 1946. Both men stayed for many years. Aufschnaiter informed the outside world of their whereabouts by getting a letter to his old friend Kenneth Mason, who was able to trace Aufschnaiter's mother and Harrer's wife in Germany to inform them they were alive and well: they had been 'missing' for over two years.

Not so lucky was Ludwig Schmaderer, a member of the 1938 Nanga Parbat team, who was interned with Herbert Paidar after making the first ascent of Tent Peak in Sikkim in 1939. They made several attempts to escape, before succeeding in 1945 and crossing a pass into Tibet, but were turned back by an official. Moving clandestinely through border areas of India to avoid being arrested, they looked for another route into Tibet. Negotiating to buy food was difficult and involved long discussions and high prices. As they entered the village of Tabo, close to the Tibetan border, Schmaderer went ahead to buy food, while Paidar followed with their donkey. When Paidar arrived, Schmaderer was already negotiating with the villagers, and they agreed that Paidar would camp beyond the village, whilst Schmaderer tried to strike a deal. But when he took money from his box to barter for food, he was attacked, killed and robbed by several locals. Fearing the same fate, Paidar let himself be rearrested by the Indians and returned to Dehra Dun.

TWELVE

War and delusion

Many climbers were killed in the war, and not only on the German side. One of the first to die was Norman Streatfeild, British liaison officer to the 1938 K2 expedition, who was killed at Dunkirk. Michael Spender, brother of the poet Stephen and a member of the 1935 Everest reconnaissance, was an RAF squadron leader, killed in a plane crash over Germany. Peter Oliver of the 1936 and 1938 Everest expeditions was killed in action in Burma, as was Dermot Smart, the British officer assigned to the tragic 1937 Nanga Parbat expedition.

Some prominent figures of 1930s climbing used their skills to serve their countries. Eric Shipton was appointed British Consul in Kashgar, Western China. How he got this post is a mysterious and complex story: many assume he was involved in intelligence work for the Foreign Office. Frank Smythe worked in the Canadian Rockies as a mountaineering instructor for the Lovat Scouts, an elite unit in the army. He died only four years after the end of the war from malaria at the tragically young age of 48. By the end of 1938 Tilman saw war as inevitable and curtailed his climbing plans for 1939 accordingly. He was still a reserve officer from the First World War, and volunteered for service, despite being 41 when war broke out, seeing action in France and the subsequent retreat to Dunkirk, then in North Africa and the Middle East. After 1943 he was in the special forces, parachuted behind enemy lines to fight with Albanian and Italian partisans; at one point he escaped the Germans by hiding

German mountain troops (*Gebirgsjäger*) on Elbrus, Soviet Union, 1942.

for three days on a cliff face. He was given the keys to the city of Belluno, which he helped save from destruction. Edward Norton and Geoffrey Bruce had followed distinguished military careers after participating in the 1920s Everest expeditions: among other wartime roles, Norton was acting governor of Hong Kong and Bruce led a force supporting the Chinese nationalists under Chiang Kai-Shek.

Like Tilman, Paul Bauer was still an army reservist with the rank of major; he joined the *Hochgebirgsjäger*, a specialist mountain division, participating in the Polish campaign, before his unit was transferred further east. In June 1941 Hitler invaded the Soviet Union, the largest military operation in history, and initially a spectacular success, with the Germans arriving close to both Moscow and Leningrad, before a Soviet counteroffensive in the winter of 1941–2. In 1942 Hitler launched an offensive in the south of the USSR, ordering a splitting of the Army Group South, with one part heading to Stalingrad (Volgograd), which became the scene of the deadliest battle in history and a key turning point in the war.

The other part headed to the Caucasus in the so-called Operation Edelweiss, and it was here that Bauer had a role to play. Before this German troops climbed Elbrus, the highest peak in the Caucasus, with the summiteers including Fritz Bechtold and Karl von Kraus. Leading Nazi Albert Speer considered it 'an adventure by a group of enthusiastic mountain climbers. All of us could sympathize with the impulse'; however, Hitler was furious and 'raged as if his entire plan of campaign had been ruined by this bit of sport', saying 'these crazy mountain climbers ... belong before a court-martial ... pursuing their idiotic hobbies in the midst of a war'.[1]

Hitler might have disapproved of climbing during war, but his propagandists continued to use the 1930s exploits of German climbers as an example of heroism and sacrifice to young Germans. A novel, *Der Kampf um den Nanga Parbat*, published in 1941 and aimed at young male readers, gave a fictionalized account of the 1934 expedition. When Drexel is dying in a tent with Fritz Bechtold, he asks his companion, 'Fritz! If I die now, promise me, the attack on the mountain it will continue yes? Don't let up – the summit – the summit – for Germany!'[2]

The German 2nd High Mountain Battalion, led by Bauer, had the objective of the Marukh Pass over the Caucasus. The soldiers were mainly volunteers, typically in their early twenties and without combat experience, but motivated, well trained and well equipped. When they took Soviet prisoners, they found them weak with hunger and poorly equipped, wearing summer uniforms while sheltering in crevasses during snowstorms; the elements caused as many Soviet deaths as German firepower. Despite the Marukh Pass being a strong defensive position with the Soviets well dug in, the Germans were successful, their assault described as 'a masterpiece of mountain warfare'.[3] The attack was conducted by two companies, personally led by Bauer and equipped with full mountaineering gear, including crampons, axes, pitons and rope ladders. During the night the Germans cut steps up the ice to reach the upper part of the glacier, which was not visible from the pass. Climbing across vertical rocks several of the soldiers fell and one died, but the others made it to the southern side of the ridge, from where they were at the rear of the Soviet troops defending the pass. In the morning the Germans attacked from up the valley, across the Marukh Glacier and from behind, completely surprising the Soviets, most of whom surrendered. It was a crushing victory for the Germans, who claimed to have killed 300 Soviet soldiers and lost only 7 men. Bauer led his soldiers in battle with the same professionalism, attention to detail and care for his subordinates that he showed on his expeditions. A member of his company wrote that when cases of frostbite began to appear, 'Major Bauer was everywhere to give the men advice and support.'[4]

Bauer's service in the war was as part of the regular army, not the Nazi structures like the SS, which were responsible for terrible atrocities. Many historians caution against accepting unquestioningly 'the myth of the clean Wehrmacht': the idea that the regular army was completely uninvolved and unaware of the Nazi war crimes as they conducted a 'normal war'. This was a belief consciously perpetuated by West Germany, the USA and its allies when the rearmament of Germany was seen as essential at the height of the Cold War. The reality is that many in the German army would have been aware of, and some were involved in, war crimes being committed in the conquered countries. Bauer apparently did not feel he had anything to be ashamed of during the war and was involved in mountain troop veterans' associations in the 1950s.

By 1943, defeat at Stalingrad had forced the Germans to retreat from the passes. In the fourth winter of the war Bauer fell ill with jaundice and malaria. The war was now hitting Germany more directly, and in 1944 Bauer's notary office was destroyed in an air raid. The offices of the Himalayan Foundation were also hit, with the loss of correspondence and photos. At the beginning of the war Bauer tried to stay in touch with his English friends, but as the conflict deepened this was no longer possible, and probably his friends had no desire for contact with him. Kenneth Mason preferred to help Jakub Bujak, the Polish climber who had made the first ascent of the 7,400-metre Nanda Devi East in July 1939. He was in the Polish Air Force, and after the defeat in Poland came to England to serve in the

RAF. Mason told him he could stay at his house, commenting to a friend that 'we are all in the same box until the huns are routed.'[5] When the war was nearly won, Mason wondered about the fate of his German friends. Despite his personal friendships with Bauer and Aufschnaiter, he wrote, 'how closely the German mentality ... during the last three or four years follows its pattern on ... the North Face of the Eiger; or even more so perhaps that of the failures on Nanga Parbat! It seems as though the avalanche has now gained control and that Germany is doomed.'[6] Later in the war Bauer ran a mountain warfare school in the Alps. He rebuilt his life in West Germany. Some members of his expeditions chose to leave, in different ways.

Escaping the bitterness of defeat

Karl von Kraus served as doctor in the Mountain Infantry and was taken prisoner by the Americans in 1945. With 8.5 million Germans being members of the Nazi Party, the denazification process was a daunting task, but made manageable by classifying people according to their level of involvement with the regime and the seriousness of their crimes. Kraus was held until 1948 in various camps, but he was then released and classified as a follower (*Mitläufer*), which allowed him to work as a doctor in Munich. Ten years later Kraus emigrated to Communist East Germany, a move welcomed by the authorities despite his Nazi background, given the massive flight of doctors from the East to the West. His situation became difficult when a West German radio station broadcast the story of his Nazi past, alleging that Kraus was not only a member of the SA, but also of the SS, and had even collaborated with the notorious Adolf Eichmann, who had been executed in Jerusalem only a few weeks earlier. Kraus vehemently denied the allegations, but the East German secret police, the Stasi, investigated his past, concerned that Kraus was a West German spy. There was plenty to find out: Kraus had been in the *Freikorps Oberland*, participated in Hitler's 1923 Putsch, was a member of the SA and later of the SS, although Kraus said these were honorary positions he couldn't refuse. Kraus died in 1968: it is hard to fathom his motivations for defecting to East Germany, beyond disillusionment at the way Germany had turned out. Maybe he simply felt he was 'on the losing side in history'.

It is easier to understand the choices of Uli Luft, the sole survivor of the tragedy in 1937 on Nanga Parbat. Luft was a doctor and had a fellowship in high-altitude physiology at the Aeromedical Research Institute of the Air Ministry, where he was supervised by Hans Hartmann until his death on Nanga Parbat. When war broke out, Luft's research became focused on questions of direct military application, such as the aerial supply of troops besieged on the Russian front. In this period the work of Luft and his colleagues became tainted by the horrific low pressure and freezing experiments carried out on prisoners at Dachau concentration camp. During the Battle of Britain the RAF had a significant advantage over the Luftwaffe, because their planes were able to fly at higher altitudes. The Germans were working on jet-powered aircraft. Two German doctors carried out research on the effect of low pressure and freezing on hundreds of mainly Jewish Dachau inmates, many of whom died. Luft's son asked him years later whether he knew about the experiments. He recounted that he had been at a conference in 1944 which was fairly normal, until 'the last paper of the day was presented. Dad said that armed SS men suddenly entered the room and announced that the next paper was top secret and that any violators of secrecy would be shot.'[7] When the Dachau experiments were described, only one person expressed indignation and disgust at the experiments. Luft, who had never been a member of the Nazi Party, did not speak up.

Another member of the 1938 Nanga Parbat team, Bruno Balke, had served in the Russian Campaign before his old university friend Luft offered him a job to set up a research laboratory in the Alps to study physical performance at altitude. At the end of the war Balke and Luft's knowledge about high-altitude physiology was of great interest to the USA, where they were brought under 'Operation Paperclip', a secret US government programme to smooth the entry of valuable Nazi scientists by rewriting their records and protecting them from prosecution for war crimes. It was seen as vital to recruit key German scientists, such as Wernher von Braun, the developer of the V2 rocket, to avoid them falling into Soviet hands. Both Luft and Balke had long and distinguished careers in the USA, including doing work relevant to manned space flight. Operation Paperclip allowed them to put the Nazi era behind them like a bad dream.

Bauer stayed in West Germany. In 1939 he had married Elisabeth Hüttenheim, whom he had met at the 1936 Winter Olympics, where she was in the German national ski team. They had two daughters, born in 1940 and 1943, who did not see much of their father because of the war. When he returned home they did not recognize him, which Bauer called 'the worst day of my life'. When denazification started, Bauer was scared of capture. He would sometimes abseil out of the first-floor window of their apartment to escape the searches carried out by the Americans in Bavaria in the first months after the war; however, he did eventually go through the denazification process. In 1949 Bauer and Elisabeth separated; two years later he fell in love with his housekeeper, Philippine Germann. The couple had two sons: Peter, born in 1951, and Michael, born in 1957. In 2024 my daughter Charlotte, her German boyfriend Johannes and I visited Michael at his home in the Bavarian countryside. Michael is a friendly and articulate man, who gave us a fascinating picture of growing up with a legendary figure in Himalayan climbing. When Bauer, who was already 60 when Michael was born, retired, he moved to the southern edge of Munich within sight of the mountains, where at least once a year the family would go hiking. Bauer was still very fit until late in life. Although the excursions were sometimes as long as twelve hours, he would bring nothing but a litre of white wine, a cigar and a few things to eat. These challenging tours put Philippine off the mountains, but Michael inherited his father's enthusiasm and did his military service in a mountain unit, the Hochgebirgsjägerzug. He made friends who were passionate mountaineers, but they teased Michael when he used his father's pre-war equipment, including old hemp ropes. Although not an extreme climber like his father, Michael went on to climb at a good level.

Paul Bauer fought for the future of the Himalayan Foundation, which was in a difficult financial position after the war, the currency reform of 1948 having nearly wiped out its assets. In 1951 the Bavarian office for reparation investigated whether it should be classified as a National Socialist Organization, because co-founder von Tschammer was a Nazi official, although the Foundation argued that he was acting as a private citizen. Another accusation was that Nazi Party membership was critical for selection on its expeditions. Bauer pointed out that on multiple occasions he had resisted pressure from senior Nazis to influence team composition. The old rivalry between Bauer and the DÖAV resurfaced, with some sections questioning whether Bauer should have any role. The Foundation was eventually accommodated within what was now called the DAV (since Austria was an independent country), with Bauer stepping back from management. He was also re-admitted to the British Alpine Club in 1953, sidestepping difficult questions, by apologizing 'for the lack of details. The times were so troublesome.'[8] Bauer's candidature was supported by Bill Tilman, on the grounds that he had willingly taken part in the denazification programme.

The most successful of all the pre-war Nanga Parbat climbers was Heinrich Harrer. After his escape to Tibet with Peter Aufschnaiter, Harrer returned to Austria only in 1952. His book about his experiences, *Seven Years in Tibet*, was a huge success, translated into fifty-three languages, selling more than 3 million copies and made into a film with Brad Pitt playing Harrer. His writing about Tibet and friendship with the Dalai Lama earned him an overwhelmingly positive image in Germany and internationally, but when Harrer was 84 journalist and film-maker Gerald Lehner confronted him with evidence of his involvement with the SA and the SS. Harrer always denied a strong commitment to Nazi ideology and described his roles in Nazi organizations as 'stupid mistakes'. Yet, according to some accounts, he boasted to fellow internees in India of having participated in setting fire to a synagogue in Graz during the *Kristallnacht* in 1938.

Harrer had fallen out badly with Aufschnaiter during their escape to Tibet together. They had never been close, always using the polite *Sie* form of address, and at times had bitter arguments, such as the December night in 1945 when they 'sat in a nomad tent and squabbled like fighting cocks until almost dawn, forgetting the cold'.[9] They had left Tibet separately, Aufschnaiter staying as long as possible, before the Chinese invasion drove him out. The news of the publication of *Seven Years in Tibet* came as a surprise to Aufschnaiter, who immediately realized that Harrer had scooped for himself a lucrative bestseller about their joint adventure. Aufschnaiter maintained a dignified silence in public, but he was deeply hurt, writing to Paul Bauer that 'the idea of going to Tibet, the idea of going to Lhasa, the route that successfully led to Lhasa and, furthermore, the perseverance, are all entirely my own. Harrer knows this.... When I hear that he is publishing a book without communicating to me, it does not surprise me. His strengths are his steadfastness and complete lack of scrupulousness.'[10] Aufschnaiter arrived in Nepal in 1952 and worked as a cartographer, eventually obtaining a Nepalese passport and spending most of the rest of his life there. He regularly visited Europe. Bauer's son Michael tells how Aufschnaiter would arrive at their house without notice, his luggage in a few plastic bags. Aufschnaiter never forgave the betrayal. When Harrer came to visit him in the hospital bed where he was dying of cancer, he'd turned away. Some of the other old enmities which had torn apart the pre-war German climbing community did calm down over time. When Bauer and Günter Oskar Dyhrenfurth both attended a Himalayan climbing conference in India in 1973, the former rivals sat together at dinner and exchanged old stories, and they did so despite Dyhrenfurth having manoeuvred to prevent Bauer's appointment as a vice president of the DAV in 1964.

The 8,000ers are finally overcome; nationalism isn't

After the many failed attempts on 8,000-metre peaks in the 1920s and 1930s, the luck of Himalayan mountaineers changed completely after the Second World War. Nepal now allowed expeditions, opening up three untouched 8,000-metre peaks entirely in Nepal as well as southern sides of five 8,000ers on its border, including Everest. In 1950 it wasn't a British or German team that was first to take advantage of this, but a French one. In 1943 Frank Smythe had written to the American *Alpine Journal* proposing a joint British–American Everest expedition and saying that he was 'against parochialism and international rivalry in mountaineering. The Germans introduced it both to the Alps and Himalayas and I hope post-war days will see this spirit dead.'[11] However, the French Annapurna expedition reverted to the 1930s nationalist model. Maurice Herzog's team made a rushed ascent of Annapurna just as the monsoon was breaking, but in reaching the summit he and Louis Lachenal suffered terrible frostbite. Many years later Herzog's daughter Félicité asked ironically whether 'the sacrifice of my father and of Louis Lachenal would restore a little of the national pride humiliated by the French defeat in 1940 and Vichy France?'[12]

Seeing mountaineering as helping national renewal was a return to the motivations of the Germans and British thirty years earlier, but there were some differences. The British Everest expeditions had been composed of upper-middle-class and upper-class men. Indeed, in Auden and Isherwood's satire on 1930s climbing, *The Ascent of F6*, these classes are setting an example to the lower-middle-class Mr and Mrs A, who 'follow the progress of this mountain mission ... let it inspire our lowly condition'.[13] The requirement to have British summit teams meant that the continental European guides they employed in the Alps were not invited to the Himalayas. For the French the situation was different: there were plenty of talented alpine guides who were French nationals, but there was still a class divide between the amateurs, like Herzog, who tended to come from the professional classes, and the guides, like Lachenal. Although the guides were the strongest climbers, Herzog was chosen as leader because he better fitted the profile that the French climbing establishment was looking for: based in Paris and a company director. Lachenal had made the second ascent of the North Face of the Eiger in 1947 – but he was anti-militarist and unlikely to promote a national revival narrative. For this, Herzog was much more suitable, having been in the Resistance, politically close to Charles de Gaulle and an alumnus of the prestigious *grande école*, HEC.

Two days before the team's departure from Paris they were asked to swear an oath of obedience to Herzog, very much in line with Bauer's leadership philosophy. Indeed, one of the guides, Gaston Rébuffat, noted that he found the oath depersonalizing and slightly 'Nazifying'. If Herzog and the French state, which provided one-third of the expedition's budget, wanted a triumph to raise the national mood, they were highly successful. French president Vincent Auriol awarded the *Légion d'honneur* to Herzog and Lachenal, saying they had 'shown the world a magnificent example of French solidarity. We know what France did during the Occupation, and how brave the French were in the Resistance ... now you have shown what the French are capable of in peacetime.'[14] Not everyone liked this explicit nationalism: the expedition contract prevented the team giving their own version of events for five years, but Lachenal then wrote an account less heroic than Herzog's official one. Some way below the top his feet were very cold, and, deciding 'I didn't owe my feet to French youth',[15] he asked what Herzog would do if he turned back. For Herzog, giving up was out of the question, writing with echoes of 1930s German climbing that 'we were consecrating an ideal, and no sacrifice was too great'.[16] Lachenal reckoned that Herzog would die if he continued alone, so, despite knowing he faced frostbite, he continued with him, not because of national prestige but out of solidarity with his partner. The arguments in the French climbing community have continued to this day, in part coloured by Herzog's right-wing views – he told his daughter he agreed with several of the far-right Jean-Marie Le Pen's ideas. There are rumours that before dying Lachenal admitted that they had not made it to the top, but recent analysis of the summit photos seems to show that they got close enough to the highest point for the ascent to be considered valid.

To the discomfort of some of his teammates – Rébuffat later wrote 'if only Herzog had lost his flags instead of his gloves, how happy I would have been'[17] – the French success and Herzog's classic book about it set a nationalist tone to Himalayan expeditions in the 1950s. Now that the French had shown that 8,000-metre peaks could be overcome, the leading mountaineering countries wanted to 'bag' first ascents, and within fourteen years all the 8,000-metre peaks had been climbed. Eric Shipton led a small team which explored the southern approach to Everest in 1951 and identified the first ascent route. He was selected to lead a full attempt the following year, but, to the surprise of the British, Nepal granted permission to the Swiss for 1952. The Mount Everest Committee, now renamed the Joint Himalayan Committee, was fearful that they would miss out on the first ascent and proposed a joint expedition with the Swiss. The Swiss pointed out that the British had blocked them from attempting Everest since 1926, but did open discussions about a joint team. They were not able to agree, and the Swiss team very nearly made it to the summit. The British were given permission for 1953.

Whilst the Swiss attempted Everest, a team led by Shipton failed on the much easier Cho Oyu, and questions started to be asked about his organization and planning. The modest Shipton did not push his own leadership credentials, practically suggesting it might be worth making a change. He had long ago fallen out of love with large Everest expeditions, disliked the 'greatly inflated publicity and ... keen international competition' around them and could not accept that the ascent was 'of high national importance'.[18] Shipton still looked likely to be made leader, but his view that 'if mountaineering has any value, ... it lies in the experience rather than in the result. If competition and above all nationalism are allowed to enter into it, it becomes debased and meaningless'[19] ran directly contrary to the establishment's overwhelming desire be the first to climb Everest. With the French given permission for 1954, it looked as if 1953 might be the last chance for the British. This focused minds, with Tom Bourdillon, who had been with Shipton in 1951 and 1952, writing to the Committee that 'to put it bluntly the expeditions have been based on the spare time efforts of people in London ... [which was not] an adequate basis for an expedition of this type.'[20]

The Committee wanted to impose John Hunt, who had been a candidate for the 1936 Everest expedition, as Shipton's deputy. After machinations similar to those around Ruttledge in 1936, the Committee proposed that Shipton share the leadership with Hunt. Shipton found this unacceptable and resigned. Hunt, a British Army colonel, 'developed a systematic plan for logistics of the summit "assault" using his background as a member of Field Marshall Montgomery's wartime planning staff'.[21] It was said that to Shipton an 'assault' sounded more like a criminal offence than a climb. There was a lot of implicit government support for the expedition, such as free transport to the Himalayas and loans of equipment and oxygen which became gifts. Hunt was diplomatic and managed to maintain the core of Shipton's planned team, including one very important veteran of the pre-war teams, Sherpa Tenzing, who had been on every Everest expedition since 1935. He also included two New Zealanders, Edmund Hillary and George Lowe, making it a Commonwealth team rather than a purely British one.

Neither of the pair who made it to the summit, Hillary and Tenzing, was British, but this did not stop the ascent being greeted in Britain with a wave of patriotic euphoria, reinforced by the coincidence of it happening at the same time as the coronation of Queen Elizabeth II. Despite the exuberant nationalism which greeted the ascent – *The Times* referred to it as a tribute of glory to the sovereign – it wasn't a simple imperial triumph. Following the Second World War, the British Empire started to be dismantled, with India granted its independence in 1947. As historian Peter H. Hansen has written, the ascent created 'conundrums ... rooted in the revision of sovereignty ... at this particular postcolonial moment at the height of the Cold War'.[22] Things were further complicated because Tenzing was claimed as a citizen by both India and Nepal, although he was actually born in Tibet. There were also arguments about which of the climbers reached the summit first: something normally unimportant to mountaineers, who see a roped pair as a single unit.

We cannot know to what extent the climbers privately approved of the nationalist tone to the post-expedition publicity, but they uncomplainingly supported the projection of the ascent as a British or Commonwealth triumph. This was a change from the 1930s, when, according to Isserman and Weaver, 'the strident nationalism of German mountaineering had, if anything, encouraged a countertendency in Great Britain, a reversion to Mallory's somewhat flippant "because-it-is-there" style of justification'.[23] Shipton, Smythe and Tilman, whilst all being patriotic, disliked the use of nationalism as a motivation for climbing. Tilman could have been an alternative experienced leader to Shipton, but was viewed as a maverick. His note in the *Himalayan Journal* defending lightweight expeditions in 1946 concluded: 'the virtues of simplicity and economy are not incompatible with a serious attempt upon Mount Everest, and I think it will be a retrograde step if we ever revert to the grandiose standards of earlier expeditions.'[24] This was clearly out of sync with the thinking of the post-war British climbing establishment, but Tilman's appetite to explore the Himalayas was undimmed: he attempted Rakaposhi in 1947, and when Nepal opened to foreigners was one of the first to visit. Ever restless, Tilman moved on from mountaineering to sailing, where his adventures were just as extraordinary. He bought a series of Bristol Channel Cutters and used them far beyond their intended range for voyages in remote seas, like those around Greenland and Patagonia. His famous advert in *The Times* went 'Hands wanted for long voyage in small boat. No pay, no prospects, not much pleasure.'[25] He was lost at sea in the South Atlantic, aged 79.

The German–Austrian expedition which climbed Nanga Parbat in 1953 was led by Willi Merkl's half-brother, Karl-Maria Herrligkoffer, a non-climber who hero-worshipped Merkl and wanted to complete his dream of climbing Germany's 'Mountain of Destiny'. Herrligkoffer's climbing leader was Peter Aschenbrenner, who had got close to the summit in 1934, before the disastrous retreat. The expedition was the subject of significant opposition from Paul Bauer, and Herrligkoffer was refused financial support by the DAV, which led to an unseemly battle in the German press. The summit was reached by Austrian Hermann Buhl, who climbed the final 1,000 metres alone against the wishes of Herrligkoffer, who shared his beloved half-brother's belief that if there couldn't be a team success it would be better not to succeed at all. Buhl paid tribute to the pioneers who had gone before him and lost their lives on Nanga Parbat, like Albert Mummery, Willo Welzenbach and Hans Hartmann, but he was clear that he made the final summit climb for himself rather than for some nationalist cause. As Buhl descended, he was met by Hans Ertl, who had been on Dyhrenfurth's 1934 Karakoram expedition. Ertl's family deny he was a Nazi, but his film work had brought him close to senior figures in the Third Reich, which initially stopped him working in post-war Germany. He emigrated to Bolivia, where he became a cattle farmer, but it wasn't a quiet life. His daughter Monika became a left-wing revolutionary and travelled to Hamburg to assassinate the Bolivian Consul responsible for cutting the hands off Che Guevara following his killing. She was later killed by the Bolivian security forces whilst planning the abduction of Nazi war criminal Klaus Barbie – the violence of war and conflict reverberating down through generations.

After the French and British national triumphs on Annapurna and Everest, the Italian expedition which climbed K2 has been described as 'a grossly nationalistic affair ... saving the wounded pride of a nation humiliated by fascism and wartime defeat'.[26] Like the ascents of Annapurna and Nanga Parbat, the expedition was marred by controversy and arguments. The greatest Italian climber of the day, Riccardo Cassin, was excluded from the team on spurious medical grounds; apparently the 57-year-old non-climbing leader Ardito Desio did not want a deputy who might be viewed as a rival. Desio made clear he wanted 'rigid discipline and a strong leader'.[27] Eventually Achille Compagnoni and Lino Lacedelli were poised to make their summit bid from a high camp, with young star climber Walter Bonatti and a local porter Amir Mahdi bringing oxygen up to support them, but the camp was deliberately moved from the planned site, seemingly with the intention of excluding Bonatti from the summit team. Bonatti and Mahdi couldn't find the camp and had to bivouac in the open, with the poorly equipped Mahdi suffering terrible frostbite. Compagnoni later falsely accused Bonatti of wanting to use the oxygen to make his own solo summit bid. Italy got its national triumph, the climbers were received by Pope Pius XII, but the collateral damage included the amputations suffered by Madhi, a diplomatic row between Italy and Pakistan and a defamation trial: it took Bonatti fifty years to clear his name.

Jack Longland called out the 'evil shadows of ... national rivalries and of the false doctrine that mountaineering achievement is a proper means of enhancing a nation's prestige', which hung heavily over 1930s mountaineering, and added that 'we are not clear of it even in the nineteen-fifties'.[28] But it was only interesting for climbers to keep feeding the nationalist publicity beast whilst it remained hungry, and after the ascents of Everest, K2, Nanga Parbat and Annapurna, public interest dipped significantly. In the USA the 1958 first ascent of 8,068-metre Hidden Peak by an American team was virtually ignored by the press: the *National Geographic* commissioned an article about the climb and then failed to publish it. In 1955 the British climbed Kangchenjunga, but not by the Bavarian route on the North-East Spur, which was only climbed twenty-two years later by an Indian team. They found a pair of crampons, which had been lost in 1929 by Peter Aufschnaiter when he had to jump off a ridge because Ernst Beigel had fallen off the other side. The British ascent of Kangchenjunga received far less attention than the 1953 Everest expedition, and historians Isserman and Weaver believed the climbers themselves 'seemed to have made a conscious decision to downplay the nationalist trappings of their endeavor'.[29]

By the time Himalayan climbing restarted in the 1950s, Mao's Communists had invaded Tibet; they did not allow Westerners to approach Everest until the 1980s. In 1960 a Chinese team resolved the puzzle of climbing the North Face, the key goal of British mountaineers for nearly twenty years. They followed the ridge route favoured by Mallory rather than Norton's traverse. Four climbers – Tibetan Gongbu and three Chinese, Wang Fuzhou, Liu Lianman and Qu Yinhua – overcame the Second Step after a desperate struggle lasting several hours, before Qu climbed on Liu's shoulders to a point where he could drive a piton in and pull over to the top. Liu was too exhausted to go on, but the other three made it to the summit, arriving after darkness and picking up Liu on the way down.

In 1975 the Chinese repeated their ascent and, knowing the difficulty of the Second Step, placed a metal ladder to overcome it, which has remained in place ever since. Conrad Anker, the American climber who found Mallory's body in 1999, twice tried to climb the Second Step without using this ladder, reasoning that 'if I could free-climb the Second Step and judge its difficulty, that would tell us a lot about whether Mallory and Irvine could have pulled it off in 1924, in hobnailed boots and tweed jackets.'[30] Anker (whose second attempt in 2007 was successful) wrote that the pitch was 'a lot harder than climbers were doing in Wales ... in the 1920s', but this is something of a red herring. The 1960 Chinese team overcame the Step without a ladder, using what are called combined tactics – that is, one climber standing on another's shoulders – and Mallory and Irvine could have used the same technique. Their lack of climbing hardware would have made this very risky because they would not have been able to get a solid belay, but this doesn't make it intrinsically more difficult. Jochen Hemmleb, probably the leading expert on the history of Everest's North Face, thinks that focusing on the technical difficulty of the Step is simplistic: several modern mountaineers have free-climbed it, finding different conditions and having different views on its difficulty.

The Chinese accounts display a form of nationalism different to the Germans and British, combining it with 'Communist propaganda and hyperbole', such as the climbers swearing 'a pledge to Chairman Mao and the Communist Party ... their eyes brimming with tears'.[31] We cannot always know in a totalitarian state how much events such as the Communist Party meeting held by the four climbers after overcoming the Second Step are embellished for propaganda purposes and how much they reflect the inner feelings of those involved. After my attempt on Changtse, I visited the Beijing home of one of the 1960 climbers. When he told me of his time on Everest thirty years earlier, I didn't feel he had just been performing some task for his country and party: the memory of a rich experience seemed deep and genuine.

It took climbing a few more decades to shake off this tendency to nationalism. Norman Dyhrenfurth was one of those who tried to combat it, organizing an international Everest expedition in 1971, following the model his father had used in the 1930s. It was not a success: climbers from different countries argued bitterly about the choice of route and who should be in the lead. Dyhrenfurth shared his father's love of the Himalayas, but wasn't necessarily wedded to the international model. He also led the 1963 American Everest ascent, which had exploited John F. Kennedy's desire to lead America to a new frontier to raise a record budget for the attempt. Although there was an awareness in an expedition press release that 'strident nationalism and jingo flag-waving have no place on the great peaks', it was also claimed that an American ascent would refute 'our detractors' taunt that we are a nation gone soft and gutless',[32] again viewing Himalayan climbing as a way to prove national vigour.

It was not a race and nobody won

The efforts by the British and the Germans to climb the world's highest mountains in the 1920s and 1930s are sometimes characterized as a 'race to the summits'. If it was a race, it was one that nobody won; but perhaps it was not a race at all. Both British and Germans were desperate to achieve their goals, but these were not exactly the same. Certain mountains came to be seen as exclusive goals of certain nations. For the Germans, the metric target of an 8,000-metre peak was everything, whereas the British were focused on Everest, and otherwise on the highest mountain yet climbed, whether over 8,000 metres or not – a 1938 British expedition chose 7,821-metre Masherbrum as its target because it was 5 metres higher than the previous highest mountain climbed, Nanda Devi. The Germans would have loved to attempt Everest, but never managed to overcome British obstructionism. Paul Bauer became the most successful pre-war German expedition leader by making friends with the British and choosing other targets. Race or no race, there was clearly a rivalry, but climbing was viewed as a gentlemanly sport where the participants were not supposed to admit to this. Statements in the British and German alpine journals were generally always supportive and generous about the other's expeditions, and British admiration for the Bavarian attempts on Kangchenjunga is repeated in private documents, Ruttledge calling them 'the most efficient party that ever visited the Himalayas'.[33]

British and German views of each other evolved between the wars, with the mutual animosity gradually dying down as the years passed. Britons felt sympathy for the suffering of Germans from hyperinflation and saw the terms of the Versailles Treaty as too harsh. When the Nazis came to power, views changed again, with many Britons appalled at the brutal and authoritarian regime. There was always a rivalry in mountaineering; as Robert Graves and Alan Hodge pointed out in their social history of the period, expeditions

> seemed like extra events in the Olympic Games ... and brought out the same unsporting instincts in patriotic sportsmen. It was a matter of great regret, for instance, that a German, poaching on what the British considered their territory, bagged [the famous lost Arabian city] Sheba; and of small regret when a German climbing expedition, intruding on the British Himalayan attempts, had no better success and more numerous casualties.[34]

The British view of German climbing as being driven by nationalism and characterized by fanatical and reckless risk-taking was not black and white: under Edward Strutt's editorship the *Alpine Journal* was highly negative on the Eiger but praised the German attempts on Kangchenjunga and Nanga Parbat. The negative view on German 1930s climbing was naturally consolidated following the horrors of the Second World War. Writing in 1957, Jack Longland contrasted the 'competent and undramatised achievement' of British Himalayan climbing with 'the German holocausts on Nanga Parbat, misguided in substituting national prestige for healthy mountaineering ambition'.[35] It was natural to see the 'German climbing excesses' coming from National Socialist ideas, even though some of the mindsets being criticized existed before the Nazis, and in people with very different political positions.

Wilfred Noyce, who played a key role in the first ascent of Everest in 1953, took this a step further in his essay 'Nietzsche and Modern Mountaineering', claiming that if Hitler was the political outcome of Nietzsche's doctrine of Superman, then the equivalent in physical activity were the 'conquerors of the Eiger Nordwand'. He discusses the Nietzschean theory that 'great suffering ... has produced all the elevation of humanity hitherto', and quotes from Bechtold and Bauer to show that 'nobody could accuse the modern continental climbers of shirking suffering. They seek it ... again and again.'[36] For Noyce, 'the element of risk was of course a "sine qua non" of German climbing between the wars, and linked curiously with the Nietzschean theory of the perfect man.'[37] His ideas were adopted by others, who referred to 'the flood of do-or-die Germans. Stimulated by nationalist ideology and inspired by Hitler–Nietzsche myths, they poured into the black, avalanching pit [of the Eiger North Face] from 1934 to 1938.'[38] Within a couple of decades of its first ascent, the Eiger North Face was being regularly climbed, and not viewed as an unjustifiably risky route for brainwashed fanatics. The connections between Nietzschean philosophy, Nazi ideology and extreme climbing are actually more nuanced than Noyce suggests. There was unjustified appropriation and distortion of some of Nietzsche's ideas by the Nazis, who took catchphrases like 'the blond beast' and the *Übermensch* out of context, but Hitler told Leni Riefenstahl that the philosopher, who was opposed to antisemitism and nationalism, was not his guide; it is not even certain Hitler read Nietzsche's books.

Many German climbers were inspired by Nietzsche's writing; whilst some just picked up on catchphrases, others clearly had a deeper understanding. Although Nietzsche loved mountain scenery and spent time in the Alps, he never did any climbing, but there is much in his writing which speaks to the spiritually minded climber. A famous example is in *Thus Spoke Zarathustra*: 'I am a wanderer and a mountaineer ... I stand now before my last summit ... I have to climb my most difficult path ... but a man of my sort does not avoid such an hour ... only now do you tread your path of greatness.'[39] Hans Hartmann, who died on Nanga Parbat in 1937, quoted Nietzsche when explaining his decision to join the expedition: 'There exists in the world a single path along which no one can go except you: whither does it lead? Do not ask, go along it.'[40] Hartmann's AAVM clubmate Leo Maduschka, a young Munich philosophy student, talented climber and writer, who died in a storm in the Dolomites, wrote an essay, 'Mountaineering as a Romantic Way of Life', which sets out the spiritual motivations for climbing. He noted that extreme climbers suffer from restlessness: 'no summit satisfies the longing, but each one shines brightly like the promised land.'[41] Nietzschean inspirations for climbing were not necessarily Nazi, nor limited to the 1930s. Dougal Haston, a leading British climber of the 1960s and 1970s and like Maduschka a philosophy student, was keen on the idea of an *Übermensch* who could create and impose his own law, even signing off his diary entries as 'Thus Spake DH'.[42]

German climbing of the 1930s was criticized for excessive risk-taking by 'fanatical climbers', but a significant level of risk is inherent in leading-edge Himalayan climbing. The criticism implies there is an acceptable level of risk to take, but this is highly subjective. In the 1920s, British climbers already tended to view the Germans as excessive risk-takers and used this as a benchmark of criticism. After the final attempt on Everest in 1922, which cost the lives of seven porters, Longstaff commented that Somervell was 'scornful of our refusing to countenance the German-alpine, forlorn-hope, success-at-any-cost, death doesn't matter, stunt'.[43] This was long before National Socialist-inspired climbers appeared; it is more likely Longstaff was thinking about the purist attitude to risk of someone like the Jewish Paul Preuss.

Wade Davis's magnificent *Into the Silence* places the story of the 1920s Everest expeditions in the context of the participants' First World War experience. He points out a divide between the older climbers, like Longstaff, 'who still considered climbing to be a sport of gentlemen, and those of the new generation, who

... had lived through a war that allowed them to walk with grace and commitment at the very edge of death. These were climbers prepared to do almost anything to succeed.'[44] Mallory and Somervell exemplified this new breed, but the same could be said of Paul Bauer or Willi Merkl. When Conrad Anker analysed the possibility that Mallory and Irvine had climbed the Second Step without a belay, he concluded that it 'would have been an utterly terrifying proposition in 1924',[45] but, given Mallory's insensitivity to risk, this would not necessarily have stopped them. Not everyone shares Davis's interpretation. British Everest climber Stephen Venables sees this as a big misconception and that Mallory and Irvine were

> by modern standards ... actually incredibly cautious ... [climbing] with immense skill on terrain where nowadays people routinely just clip into fixed ropes.... Mallory and Irvine made a mistake, ... they slipped and they died ... [but] that doesn't imply that they were hell-bent on some death-or-glory quest.[46]

When Frank Smythe participated in the recovery of the bodies of two young British climbers who had died in a risky attempt on Mont Blanc in 1934, he commented that it was 'symptomatic of the sort of do-or-die climbing which was arising on the Continent',[47] but Smythe himself arguably took do-or-die risks when making a name for himself with his first ascent of the nearby Route Major six years earlier. What seems too risky for one climber can seem faint-hearted to another. Smythe was referred to as an 'English coward' by his German teammates when he argued against carrying on after the fatal accident on the ice wall on Kangchenjunga in 1930, but six years later on Everest he was taunting his teammates with cowardice for turning back on the North Col.

All periods in the history of mountaineering have seen climbers willing to take what some felt were excessive risks in order to achieve burning ambitions. What made 1930s Germany unique was that such risk-taking was accepted and even actively encouraged by the authorities. Although they may not want to constrain liberties, governments tend to frown on activities which lead to fatal accidents. By contrast, the Nazis glorified deaths and encouraged risk-taking, creating a climate where it is hardly surprising that there were climbers – some but not all committed Nazis – who were willing to throw their lives away in desperate climbs to win glory.

Despite being called 'German Holocausts' by Longland, neither of the two terrible 1930s catastrophes on Nanga Parbat necessarily resulted from excessive, unreasonable risk-taking. The avalanche in 1937 which killed sixteen people was viewed by most as an extremely unlucky accident. The 1934 expedition, where ten people died, also involved bad luck with the weather, compounded by poor decision-making and a lack of attention to the safety of porters. If anything, the deaths of seven porters in an avalanche on Everest in 1922 was most directly attributable to recklessness from Mallory and Somervell; and it is sometimes forgotten that one porter and one Gurkha NCO died during the chaotic early weeks of the 1924 attempt. Paul Bauer took risks too, but tried to do extreme things in the safest way possible by careful planning, teamwork and when necessary tactical withdrawal.

Children of their time?

When Bauer died in 1990 in Munich, aged 93, the obituaries were generous. The *Alpine Journal* describing him as 'a great pioneer of the Himalaya and an outstanding man'.[48] Many prominent climbers visited Bauer's family home in his later life. As well as his expedition partners like Peter Aufschnaiter, Wilhelm Fendt and Eugen Allwein, there were Himalayan climbing greats like Tenzing Norgay and Reinhold Messner. Messner saw Bauer's lightweight expedition to Sikkim in 1936 as paving the way for the revolution that Messner led away from heavyweight expeditions in the 1970s. In the last thirty years other books have cast light on the less favourable episodes of Bauer's life. Bettina Hoerlin's book about her father Hermann calls Bauer his nemesis and describes how, 'in all too familiar Nazi fashion', he took 'every opportunity to intimidate and denigrate people'.[49] Peter Mierau's comprehensive account of National Socialist expedition politics explores in detail the history of this period.

Bauer can be criticized for using mountaineering to further nationalist objectives, but he was far from unique in doing this: the first ascents of Everest, Annapurna and K2 were all celebrated in highly nationalistic terms. Objectively, nationalism – the idea that we feel loyalty and affinity with people we have little in common with and will never meet, in what Benedict Anderson calls 'imagined communities' – is a strange but ubiquitous concept. Many people take the view that mild forms of patriotic nationalism are positive, encouraging social cohesion, shared culture and civic identity, and that it is only more extreme forms involving the exclusion of others, superiority and xenophobia that are negative: the twentieth century has provided plenty of examples of just how dangerous extreme nationalism can be. Others see nationalism as inherently bad, because it is divisive, foments xenophobia and can be a slippery slope towards war. The philosopher Bertrand Russell believed it was one of the main causes of war, writing in 1923 that 'the essence of nationalism is: the sense of rivalry between one's own nation and others. This brings with it a whole train of loyalties and friendly sentiments towards compatriots, with a correlative train of hatreds and pugnacities towards the members of rival nations.'[50] Russell was a friend of Francis Younghusband, which seems bizarre given Younghusband's imperialist views, but the First World War ended the friendship. Just after the Battle of the Somme, Younghusband wrote to a friend that 'the war is looking better now ... by this time next year we shall be by far the greatest and most powerful nation in the world.'[51] Russell was campaigning for peace and against conscription, which eventually led to him serving six months in Brixton Prison.

Even for those who view mild nationalism positively, its influence on mountaineering is often seen as unwelcome. This is perhaps because it is associated with a certain style of heavyweight expedition, trampling the country underfoot like a marauding army, involving siege-style climbing and risking the lives of large numbers of local porters, which feels completely alien to fundamental mountaineering values such as moving freely across wild places at one with nature. Accounts of expeditions up to the 1950s are littered with objectionable military vocabulary: Jim Perrin called the use of the word conquest 'loathsome in a mountain context'.[52]

Large national expeditions require strong leadership – the logistics of siege-style climbing can't work efficiently unless someone is directing the team – and this is also not to everyone's liking. Arlene Blum, who led one of the first women's expeditions to an 8,000-metre peak, found that her moderate and soothing character traits were 'not always compatible with effective leadership', and wrote that 'although I didn't yet sound like an authentic army general, I was moving in that direction.'[53] Julie Rak, who has researched climbing literature, points out that there is 'a liberal model of a good team structure ... composed of critically thinking individuals, with a strong yet consultative leader'.[54] Real life rarely conforms consistently to models. Between the wars there were both British and German heavy and lightweight expeditions, with the heaviest of all being the British on Everest, and the lightest some of Shipton and Tilman's. German expeditions had a more authoritarian leadership style, which worked well when there was a united and coherent team like Bauer's on Kangchenjunga and much less well when there were strong and independent characters who didn't trust the leader, like on Nanga Parbat in 1934. Hugh Ruttledge was seen as the archetypal weak and ineffective British leader, but the equally consultative Edward Norton earned respect by leading from the front in 1924.

Whilst nationalism tends to be frowned on in climbing, it is highly prevalent in sport, and is not usually viewed negatively. Despite their lofty ideals, the Olympic Games often lead to a fervour of patriotism, the watching public focusing on their national champions and television courage heavily slanted towards events where the local 'heroes' have a chance of winning. In 2021 ten Nepali climbers made the first winter ascent of K2, a renowned climb which had defeated very strong European climbers. They took the last steps to the summit together singing the Nepalese national anthem, and indeed Nepalese newspapers wrote of the climb being for the glory of Nepal, although internationally it was also viewed in a positive light. Perhaps it is more acceptable for a poor and sometimes downtrodden country to celebrate national triumphs than a powerful and oppressive one like the British Empire or Nazi Germany. Bertrand Russell pointed out that 'nationalism in the holders of power is called Imperialism; in oppressed nations it is called the principle of self-determination',[55] and nationalism is at its ugliest when it is associated with oppressive power.

Paul Bauer was unapologetically nationalistic, and his support for the Nazi Party should of course be condemned, but it is hard to judge fairly with hindsight. Supporters of Hitler's rise to power knew of the Nazis' antisemitism, lack of respect for democracy and militaristic foreign policy, but most of them could not have anticipated it would end in the Holocaust and the deadliest conflict in human history. Gary Lineker's 2023 tweet criticizing British right-wing politicians for talking about immigration in 'language ... not dissimilar to that used by Germany in the 30s'[56] was not hyperbolically comparing the UK government with the worst excesses of Nazi Germany, but warning that history tells us that dehumanizing language can lead down a very dangerous path. To avoid the repetition of such horrors it is important to understand why people espouse such ideas, as well as simply condemning them. Were people like Bauer to some extent 'children of their time', the outcome of the First World War and its aftermath leading them to succumb to what historian Richard Evans called 'a strongly right-wing atmosphere'[57] in every German university in the mid-to-late 1920s?

What is in no doubt is Bauer's enthusiasm for war. British climbers like Mallory, Norton and Somervell were also hugely impacted by the trauma of the trenches, and by what Wade Davis describes as a psychological rift which 'would haunt the nation for a generation, the impossible chasm between those who had been to war and those who remained at home to revel in its imagined glories'.[58] For the British the psychological scarring was deep, but at least they did not have the bitterness of defeat and what many Germans saw as the indignity of 'Versailles'. The fact that Bauer and many like him glorified war and felt nostalgia rather than revulsion for the First World War made it easier for them to join the *Freikorps*, accept the presence of the paramilitary organizations and support the Nazis' rise to power. Bauer had written that when the rifles were taken from his group in 1918, the orphaned hand reached out for the ice axe; in 1939 the hand was ready to take the rifle again.

Ultimately, we cannot know people's inner motivations with certainty, particularly not for something as ostensibly illogical as Himalayan mountaineering. Bauer's highly nationalistic and militaristic justifications for climbing might have been to some extent excuses for pursuing an activity he clearly also loved for more personal reasons. Many climbers ageed to go on nationalistic expeditions to the world's highest peaks, but often it was their only way to do so, since financing such trips was extremely difficult for all but those with private wealth. In *The Ascent of F6*, the fictional 1930s climber Michael Ransom is persuaded to undertake a climb for political motivations he doesn't approve of because he needs cash to pursue his hobby. Some undoubtedly believed they were winning glory for their countries, but the same climbers will have gone to lower and more local mountains many times without attracting public attention or being financed using nationalism. They would have faced all the things that go along with hard climbing – long exhausting days, separation from loved ones, cold bivouacs and personal risk – because they loved mountaineering, not because they were nationalists. George Mallory's own famous answer to the question 'Why climb Everest?' – 'Because it is there' – whether profound or evasive hints at the deeper spiritual motivations climbers have, but often struggle to express. Frank Smythe said the mountaineer had no answer to the question of why he climbed, but then gave the answer that 'to remember well is to have lived well. Mountaineering stores a fund of memories that will endure ... a lifetime.'[59]

Even if we struggle to understand the reasons why people took extreme risks to chase Mallory's dream, we are still left feeling those climbs have a spiritual depth and significance, rather than being a pointless struggle in the ice and snow. The period between the wars is the most fascinating in mountaineering history, despite its being, or maybe because it is, one of vain struggles and Shakespearean tragedies rather than glittering successes. Mallory made another attempt to explain climbing in an article written during the First World War:

> Have we vanquished an enemy? None but ourselves. Have we gained success? That word means nothing here. Have we won a kingdom? No ... and yes. We have achieved an ultimate satisfaction ... fulfilled a destiny.... To struggle and to understand ... with steps for children's feet.[60]

APPENDIX I

Main characters

Eugen Allwein (1900–1982) Munich-born climber and doctor who served in the First World War and was a member of the *Freikorps*. He was a leading member of the AAVM and made important alpine climbs with Willo Welzenbach and others. In 1928 he made the first ascent of 7,134-metre Peak Lenin with Wien and Schneider. He was part of the circle close to Paul Bauer and participated in the 1929 and 1931 Kangchenjunga expeditions, reaching the highest point both times.

Ang Tsering (1903–2002) Sherpa born in Thame near Everest. He worked as a high-altitude porter from 1924 until 1975. In 1933 he was part of the team which carried loads to set up Camp VI on Everest at 8,350 metres. He was the last man to get down from the terrible storm on Nanga Parbat in 1934. He later married the widow of Nima Dorje, the man whose body he had had to make difficult manoeuvres to pass on the ice slope of Rakhiot Peak. He adopted Nima Dorje's son and started a family of his own. He returned to work as a porter, first on lower treks and in the 1950s to high Himalayan peaks.

Peter Aschenbrenner (1902–1998) Austrian climber and mountain guide from Kufstein in the Tyrol. He was on Merkl's expeditions to Nanga Parbat in 1932 and 1934. In 1932 he made the first ascent of the 7,070-metre Rakhiot Peak with Kunigk. In 1934 he and Schneider got to the highest point reached and were the only Europeans to make it down from the terrible storm. According to a report from him in the files of the DAV, Aschenbrenner climbed the two rocky peaks either side of the Silver Saddle. They were exonerated by the court of honour demanded by Bauer but excluded from German expeditions prior to the Second World War.

In 1953 he was climbing leader of the team which made the first ascent of Nanga Parbat, when Hermann Buhl reached the summit alone.

Peter Aufschnaiter (1899–1973) Austrian mountaineer and cartographer. He participated in the 1929 and 1931 Kangchenjunga expeditions and led the 1939 Nanga Parbat reconnaissance. Interned in British India due to the outbreak of the Second World War, Aufschnaiter eventually escaped to Tibet with Heinrich Harrer. He spent many years in Tibet. When he was forced to leave, due to the Communist invasion, he settled in Nepal.

Paul Bauer (1896–1990) German mountaineer and notary. He led the 1929 and 1931 Kangchenjunga expeditions. From 1934 to 1938 he was head of the Hiking and Mountaineering Section of the Reich Commission for Physical Exercise. He led the rescue mission following the avalanche on Nanga Parbat in 1937 and the 1938 attempt.

Fritz Bechtold (1901–1961) German climber who was a boyhood friend of Merkl's. Bechtold went to Nanga Parbat four times in the 1930s. He was one of the founders of the Himalayan Foundation with Paul Bauer, with whom he was closely allied.

Charles Granville Bruce (1866–1939) British soldier and mountaineer. Bruce was a pioneer of Himalayan climbing, one of the originators of the idea of climbing Everest and a strong advocate and supporter of Gurkha soldiers. Bruce was involved in many of the first Himalayan mountaineering expeditions and led the 1922 and 1924 Everest attempts, although he had to withdraw from the second one through ill health.

Geoffrey Bruce (1896–1972) British army officer and cousin of Charles Granville Bruce, who participated in the 1922 and 1924 Everest expeditions. In 1922 he was a transport officer. Despite having no climbing experience, he reached a record altitude on the second summit attempt with Finch. He was considered as a possible leader in the 1930s, but was too busy with his career in the British Indian Army.

Günter Oskar Dyhrenfurth (1886–1975) German mountaineer and geologist who later took Swiss citizenship. Dyhrenfurth organized two pioneering international Himalayan expeditions in 1930 and 1934, which made several first ascents of 7,000-metre peaks.

Hettie Dyhrenfurth (1892–1972) German-born tennis player and mountaineer, wife of Günter Oskar. They went on two Himalayan expeditions together in 1930 and 1934. She set a female altitude record in 1934 on Sia Kangri. She later took Swiss citizenship and then emigrated to America to escape the persecution of the Jews.

Hans Ertl (1908–2000) Munich-born mountaineer who made important ascents in the Alps with the 'vagabond climbers' in the 1930s. He was on the 1934 Hidden Peak expedition, making the first ascent of 7,422-metre Sia Kangri. He was also a film-maker who worked with Leni Riefenstahl. Following the war he emigrated to Bolivia.

George Finch (1888–1970) Australian-born chemist and mountaineer. He studied in Paris and Switzerland and became one of the leading climbers in the Alps before the First World War. Excluded from the 1921 reconnaissance on medical grounds, he was a member of the 1922 team and reached a record height with Geoffrey Bruce. He was a strong advocate of using oxygen. He fell out with the Mount Everest Committee and was not invited on the 1924 expedition.

Heinrich Harrer (1912–2006) Austrian mountaineer who made the first ascent of the North Face of the Eiger in 1938 and participated in the 1939 Nanga Parbat reconnaissance. After this he was interned by the British before escaping to Tibet in 1945 with Aufschnaiter. He spent seven years in Tibet and wrote a bestselling book about his experience, but later his involvement with the Nazi Party, including SS membership, came to light.

Arthur Hinks (1873–1945) British astronomer and geographer. Hinks was not a climber but played an important role in the Everest expeditions through his role as joint secretary of the Mount Everest Committee, representing the Royal Geographical Society.

Hermann Hoerlin (1903–1983) German mountaineer and scientist, who was on the 1930 Kangchenjunga expedition, making the first ascent of the 7,462-metre Jongsong Peak. He also made the first ascent of Huascaran, Peru's highest mountain. An opponent of Paul Bauer in the DÖAV, he emigrated to the USA in 1938, where he had a distinguished scientific career.

Andrew 'Sandy' Irvine (1902–1924) The youngest member of the 1924 expedition – still an undergraduate at Merton College, Oxford, when he disappeared with Mallory. He had limited mountaineering experience, but had been on an exploratory expedition to Spitsbergen and was an excellent rower, in the winning Boat Race crew of 1923. Parts of his body were found in 2024.

Alexander Kellas (1868–1921) Scottish chemist and mountaineer, who made pioneering ascents in the Himalayas; first tested the use of artificial oxygen and was first to recognize the potential of Sherpas as high-altitude porters. He died from heart failure in Tibet during the 1921 Everest reconnaissance.

Jack Longland (1905–1993) Studied at Cambridge University. Became one of the leading British rock climbers of the 1930s. He was on the 1933 Everest expedition and guided eight porters down from Camp VI in a storm. He later had a distinguished career in education and broadcasting.

Tom Longstaff (1875–1964) English doctor and climber, who made pioneering ascents, including the first confirmed ascent of a 7,000-metre peak in 1907. He was a member of the 1922 Everest expedition.

George Mallory (1886–1924) British mountaineer who fought in the First World War and worked as a teacher. He was the only man on all of the 1921, 1922 and 1924 expeditions, breaking the altitude record in 1922. He disappeared when climbing towards the summit with Andrew Irvine in 1924. His body was found in 1999.

Kenneth Mason (1887–1976) British soldier, explorer and geographer. Mason was a candidate for a surveying role on the 1921 Everest reconnaissance. He was a founder member of the Himalayan Club and editor of the *Himalayan Journal* and provided valuable support to the two Bavarian Kangchenjunga expeditions. After leaving India, he was given a new professorial role in Geography at Oxford University. His papers are held in the Bodleian Library.

Willi Merkl (1900–1934) German climber who fought in the First World War and made many new routes in the Alps. He went to the Caucasus in 1929 and then led the German–American Nanga Parbat expedition in 1932. He also led the German expedition in 1934; his mistakes as leader contributed to nine deaths, including his own, in a storm.

Albert Mummery (1855–1895) Brilliant British climber who made important first ascents in the Alps and Caucasus and was the first person to attempt an 8,000-metre peak, Nanga Parbat, in 1895. He was lost during the expedition, presumed buried by an avalanche.

John Noel (1890–1989) British soldier, mountaineer and film-maker, who made a clandestine approach to Everest in 1913 and then participated in the 1922 and 1924 expeditions. He fell out with the Mount Everest Committee when the Tibetan government stopped giving permission to expeditions due to 'the affair of the dancing Lamas'.

Edward Norton (1884–1954) British Army officer and mountaineer. Norton was a grandson of Alfred Wills, a pioneer mountaineer and founding member of the Alpine Club. He was on the 1922 and 1924 Everest expeditions, taking over the leadership in 1924 after Bruce became ill. He twice broke the altitude record and in 1924 climbed alone to nearly 8,600 metres.

Nursang (1891–1942) One of the earliest Sherpas working with mountaineers when he portered for Alexander Kellas in Sikkim prior to the First World War. He served in a Gurkha regiment on the Western Front in the First World War and was then on many Himalayan expeditions during the 1920s and 1930s, including to Everest, Kangchenjunga and Nanga Parbat. In later expeditions he was usually working as Sirdar.

Noel Odell (1890–1987) British climber and geologist, who participated in the 1924 Everest expedition, when he was the last man to see Mallory and Irvine. He made the first ascent of Nanda Devi in 1936, with Tilman, and returned to Everest in 1938.

Hugh Ruttledge (1884–1961) British mountaineer and member of the Indian Civil Service. He carried out various exploratory expeditions in the Himalayas and led the 1933 and 1936 Everest expeditions. There was significant controversy about his appointment in 1936.

Erwin Schneider (1906–1987) Austrian mountaineer and cartographer, who made the first ascent of Peak Lenin in 1928, then participated in the 1930 Kangchenjunga expedition where he climbed two 7,000-metre peaks. He reached the highest point achieved on the 1934 Nanga Parbat expedition and escaped the deadly storm thanks to a quick descent with Peter Aschenbrenner, but this action created controversy and he was excluded from German expeditions in the 1930s. He was on a team which attempted Lhotse in 1955 and undertook mapping in Peru and Nepal.

Eric Shipton (1907–1977) British climber and explorer. After school he emigrated to Kenya to grow coffee, but by the 1930s he was a full-time mountain explorer. He made the first ascent of Kamet in 1931 and was on four Everest expeditions in the 1930s, reaching over 8,000 metres twice. He led the reconnaissance in 1951 but was pushed out of the leadership of the successful 1953 expedition.

Frank Smythe (1900–1949) British climber, photographer and writer. Smythe made his name with two important first ascents on Mont Blanc in the 1920s and was on Dyhrenfurth's 1930 Kangchenjunga expedition. He then led the 1931 Kamet expedition and was on the 1933, 1936 and 1938 Everest expeditions, reaching an altitude record in 1933.

Howard Somervell (1890–1975) British climber, doctor and painter. Somervell was on the 1922 and 1924 Everest expeditions, climbing twice to over 8,000 metres. He then dedicated his life to a mission hospital in Southern India.

Edward Strutt (1874–1938) British mountaineer and soldier. Fought in the Boer War and the First World War, where he rescued the Austrian Emperor Charles I from a revolutionary mob. He was deputy leader of the 1922 Everest expedition. Strutt was president of the Alpine Club and editor of the *Alpine Journal* for a number of years. He was an outspoken opponent of change and development in climbing.

Tenzing Norgay (1914–1986) Born either in Tengboche Nepal or Tibet, depending on accounts, Tenzing was on every Everest expedition from 1935 to 1953. He was the strongest porter in 1938, carrying to Camp VI at 8,300 metres. On the 1952 Swiss expedition, Tenzing broke Norton's altitude record together with Raymond Lambert. The following year he made the first ascent with Edmund Hillary.

Bill Tilman (1898–1977) British mountaineer and sailor. Tilman fought in the First World War and emigrated to Kenya to set up a plantation. He started Himalayan climbing with Shipton in 1934 and made the first ascent of Nanda Devi in 1936. He led the 1938 Everest expedition and reached over 8,000 metres. From 1954 he took up sailing; he was lost at sea in 1977 in the South Atlantic.

Lawrence Wager (1904–1965) British geologist and mountaineer, who started climbing at Cambridge University. Wager was part of the 1933 Everest expedition, reaching a record height of over 8,500 metres with Percy Wyn-Harris.

Willo Welzenbach (1899–1934) Munich-born climber, who was a key leader in standards of climbing, particularly on ice, in the 1920s. He was a member and chairman of the AAVM, where he was a rival of Paul Bauer's. He was deputy to Willi Merkl on the 1934 Nanga Parbat expedition, where he was killed by the terrible storm.

Uli Wieland (1902–1934) German climber, who was on the 1930 Kangchenjunga expedition and the1934 Nanga Parbat expedition, when he died in the storm which killed nine people.

Karl Wien (1906–1937) German climber, who was the son of Nobel prize-winning Wilhelm Wien. He made important ascents with Willo Welzenbach in the Alps and in 1928 climbed the highest mountain yet climbed, Peak Lenin. He was on the 1931 Kangchenjunga expedition, reaching the highest point achieved. A close associate of Paul Bauer, he led the 1937 Nanga Parbat expedition, where he was killed by an avalanche together with fifteen other climbers and Sherpas.

Fritz Wiessner (1900–1988) Born in Dresden, Germany, Wiessner started climbing on the sandstone towers of Saxony and was one of the first to climb Grade VI rock routes in the Eastern Alps. He emigrated to the USA in 1929 and became a naturalized US citizen. He participated in Merkl's 1932 Nanga Parbat expedition and in the 1939 American attempt on K2, where he reached 8,380 metres with Pasang Dawa Lama, before the tragedy which saw four people die.

Percy Wyn-Harris (1903–1979) British colonial administrator and mountaineer. He started climbing at Cambridge University and was a member of the 1933 and 1936 Everest expeditions, equally reaching the height record with Wager in 1933. He also found Irvine's ice axe high on Everest.

Francis Younghusband (1863–1942) British Army officer and explorer who was one of the originators and advocates for the plan to climb Everest. He carried out a number of bold exploratory expeditions in Asia and a military mission to Tibet in 1904. He was a founder member of the Mount Everest Committee. Later he promoted esoteric religious beliefs.

APPENDIX II

Abbreviations and glossary

ABBREVIATIONS

AAVM Munich Academic Alpine Club, the Akademischer Alpenverein München.

DAV German Alpine Club, the Deutscher Alpenverein.

DÖAV German and Austrian Alpine Club, the Deutscher und Österreichischer Alpenverein.
Note that following the *Anschluss* the DÖAV became the DAV and was incorporated within the National Socialist Reich Association for Physical Exercise (Nationalsozialistischen Reichsbund für Leibesübungen or NSRL). It was dissolved by the Allies in 1945 as part of the NSRL. A new DAV was refounded in 1950.

GLOSSARY OF MOUNTAINEERING TERMS

Abseil Technique for descending down a double-up rope, attached to a piton or rock spike. Also called **rappelling.**

Acclimatization The gradual process whereby the human body adapts to high altitudes by generating an additional quantity of red blood cells.

Altitude sickness Physiological problems caused by low amounts of oxygen at high altitude, particularly before the body has adapted through acclimatization. More severe forms include high-altitude pulmonary oedema and high-altitude cerebral oedema. These conditions were still poorly understood in the period covered by this book.

Arête A sharp rock or ice ridge.

Belay/Belaying Safeguarding a moving climber whilst attached to an anchor.

Bhotia People of Tibetan origin often used as high-altitude porters.

Bivouac A night in the open without a tent or snow cave.

Buttress A mass of rocks bulging out of a mountain slope.

Col A low point in a ridge between two peaks.

Cornice An overhanging snow structure at the side of a ridge or at the top of a gully.

Couloir A wide gully.

Crack A narrow fissure in a rock face.

Crampons Metal spikes strapped to the base of boots to dig into ice or hard snow, giving a more secure grip.

Crevasse Fissure in a glacier, which can be hundreds of metres deep. They are sometimes hidden due to snow cover.

Cutting steps Process of cutting footholds in an ice or snow face using an ice axe.

Fixed rope A rope left in place to safeguard a passage, typically attached by pitons.

Glacier A body of ice flowing down a mountain valley or mountain side under its own weight.

Gully Fissure in the mountainside, often filled with snow, but can be rocky.

Ice axe A tool for snow and ice mountaineering consisting of a stick (typically wooden in the period discussed in this book) with a head with a pick and an adze.

Icefall A steep and broken area of a glacier, the glacial equivalent of a waterfall in a river.

Moraine Banks of rocks and earth pushed to the side or middle of a glacier.

Overhang A section of mountainside which leans out more than vertically.

Pass A gap in a mountain range connecting two valleys.

Piton A metal spike which can be hammered into a fissure in rocks to attach ropes.

Rappel *see* **Abseil.**

Rib A small ridge on a mountain face.

Rockfall Rocks falling from a mountainside, can be a considerable hazard.

Saddle A ridge connecting two section of a mountain, often broad and 'saddle-shaped'.

Serac A block or pinnacle of ice, which can create an ice avalanche if it detaches from the glacier.

Sherpa People living in mountainous regions of Nepal and around Darjeeling. Often employed as high-altitude porters.

Sirdar The lead Sherpa porter of an expedition (comes from an Arabic word for an army rank).

Slab A flat sloping area of rock.

Snowblind Temporary blindness caused by the glare of mountain light reflected on snow or ice.

Spur A subsidiary ridge.

Traverse Roughly horizontal movement across a mountainside or along a ridge.

Windslab Type of avalanche in which a large sheet of snow compacted by wind can detach from a slope.

APPENDIX III

List of climbs

above and close to 8,000 metres before 1950

Climber	Nationality	Date	Height reached (m)	Mountain (bold if summit)	Comments
George Mallory	British	21/5/1922	8,120	Everest N Face	First ever climb above 8,000 m.
Howard Somervell	British	21/5/1922	8,120	Everest N Face	
Edward Norton	British	21/5/1922	8,120	Everest N Face	
George Finch	Australian-British	27/5/1922	8,380	Everest N Face	Attempt with oxygen. Height record. Tejbir Bura came to 7,925 m.
Geoffrey Bruce	British	27/5/1922	8,380	Everest N Face	
Narbu Yishe	Nepalese	03/6/1924	8,140	Everest Camp VI	First climb by porters above 8,000 m.
Llakpa Chede	Nepalese	03/6/1924	8,140	Everest Camp VI	
Semchumbi	Nepalese	03/6/1924	8,140	Everest Camp VI	
Howard Somervell	British	04/6/1924	8,530	Everest N Face	Stopped due to cough.
Edward Norton	British	04/6/1924	8,572	Everest N Face	New altitude record. Without oxygen

Climber	**Nationality**	**Date**	**Height reached** (m)	**Mountain** (bold if summit)	**Comments**
Amdo		07/6/1924	8,140	Everest Camp VI	Porters for Mallory and Irvine attempt. (either Nepalese or Tibetan).
Lobsang		07/6/1924	8,140	Everest Camp VI	
Nima		07/6/1924	8,140	Everest Camp VI	
Trawang		07/6/1924	8,140	Everest Camp VI	
George Mallory	British	08/6/1924	8,600	Everest NE Ridge	Disappeared on summit attempt. Doubt over where last seen.
Andrew Irvine	British	08/6/1924	8,600	Everest NE Ridge	
Noel Odell	British	08/6/1924	8,170	Everest Camp VI	Saw Mallory and Irvine.
Noel Odell	British	10/6/1924	8,200	Everest N Face	Went some way above Camp VI.
Frank Smythe	British	21/6/1931	7,756	**Kamet**	Highest peak ever climbed. Lewa suffered bad frostbite on descent.
Eric Shipton	British	21/6/1931	7,756	**Kamet**	
Romily Holdsworth	British	21/6/1931	7,756	**Kamet**	
Lewa	Nepalese	21/6/1931	7,756	**Kamet**	
Eugene Birnie	British	23/6/1931	7,756	**Kamet**	Second ascent.
Raymond Greene	British	23/6/1931	7,756	**Kamet**	
Kesar Singh	Indian	23/6/1931	7,756	**Kamet**	
Eugen Allwein	German	18/9/1931	7,940	Kangchenjunga	Top of Outpost Peak.
Karl Wien	German	18/9/1931	7,940	Kangchenjunga	Top of Outpost Peak.
Ang Tharkay	Nepalese	29/5/1933	8,350	Everest Camp VI	Sirdar on Annapurna in 1950.
Da Tsering	Nepalese	29/5/1933	8,350	Everest Camp VI	
Nima Dorje	Nepalese	29/5/1933	8,350	Everest Camp VI	Died on Nanga Parbat in 1934.
Ang Tsering	Nepalese	29/5/1933	8,350	Everest Camp VI	Survived on Nanga Parbat in 1934.

Climber	Nationality	Date	Height reached (m)	Mountain (bold if summit)	Comments
Kipa Lama	Nepalese	29/5/1933	8,350	Everest Camp VI	
Pasang	Indian/ Bhotia	29/5/1933	8,350	Everest Camp VI	
Tsering Tarke	Tibetan	29/5/1933	8,350	Everest Camp VI	
Rinzing	Indian/ Bhotia	29/5/1933	8,350	Everest Camp VI	
Jack Longland	British	29/5/1933	8,350	Everest Camp VI	Led porters in descent in storm.
Lawrence Wager	British	30/5/1933	8,572	Everest N Face	First summit attempt. Joint altitude record with Norton.
Percy Wyn Harris	British	30/5/1933	8,572	Everest N Face	
Frank Smythe	British	01/6/1933	8,572	Everest N Face	Second summit attempt. Smythe made joint altitude record.
Eric Shipton	British	01/6/1933	8,485	Everest N Face	
Erwin Schneider	Austrian	06/7/1934	7,895	Nanga Parbat	Halted due to orders from leader Willi Merkl.
Peter Aschenbrenner	Austrian	06/7/1934	7,895	Nanga Parbat	
Bill Tilman	British	29/8/1936	7,816	**Nanda Devi**	Highest peak ever climbed. Houston could not join due to illness.
Noel Odell	British	29/8/1936	7,816	**Nanda Devi**	
Rinzing	Indian/ Bhotia	08/6/1938	8,300	Everest Camp VI	Also carried to Camp VI in 1933.
Pasang	Indian/ Bhotia	08/6/1938	8,300	Everest Camp VI	Also carried to Camp VI in 1933.
Tenzing Norgay	Nepalese-Indian	08/6/1938	8,300	Everest Camp VI	Made first ascent of Everest in 1953.
Wangdi Nurbu	Nepalese	08/6/1938	8,300	Everest Camp VI	Fell in a crevasse on Kangchenjunga.
Lhakpa Tsering	Nepalese	08/6/1938	8,300	Everest Camp VI	

Climber	Nationality	Date	Height reached (m)	Mountain (bold if summit)	Comments
Da Tsering	Nepalese	08/6/1938	8,300	Everest Camp VI	
Lobsang	Nepalese	08/6/1938	8,300	Everest Camp VI	Not the Lobsang on 1924 expedition.
Frank Smythe	British	09/6/1938	8,335	Everest N Face	
Eric Shipton	British	09/6/1938	8,335	Everest N Face	
Bill Tilman	British	10/6/1938	8,335	Everest N Face	
Peter Lloyd	British	10/6/1938	8,335	Everest N Face	Used oxygen.
Charlie Houston	American	21/7/1938	7,925	K2 Abruzzi Ridge	
Paul Pezoldt	American	21/7/1938	7,925	K2 Abruzzi Ridge	
Fritz Wiessner	American	19/7/1939	8,380	K2 Abruzzi Ridge	German born.
Pasang Dawa Lama	Nepalese	19/7/1939	8,380	K2 Abruzzi Ridge	Made first ascent of Cho Oyu in 1954.

Notes

PREFACE

1. J. Longland, 'Everest, 1933', *Fell and Rock Club Journal*, vol. 9, no. 3, 1933, p. 329.
2. Frank Smythe, *Climbs and Ski Runs: Mountaineering and Ski-ing in the Alps, Great Britain and Corsica*, W. Blackwood & Sons, London, 1929.

ONE

1. Smythe, *Climbs and Ski Runs*, p. 138.
2. Lieutenant-Colonel E.F. Norton D.S.O. and Other Members of the Expedition, *The Fight for Everest: 1924*, Edward Arnold, London, 1925, p. 138.
3. Wade Davis, *Into the Silence: The Great War, Mallory and the Conquest of Everest,* Vintage, London, 2011, p. 234.
4. Ibid., p. 551.
5. Norton et al., *The Fight for Everest: 1924*, p. 145.
6. Francis Younghusband, *The Epic of Mount Everest*, Edward Arnold, London, 1926, p. 306.
7. Ibid., p. 307.
8. *The Smethick Telephone*, 19 July 1924.
9. Cecil Rawling, *The Great Plateau*, Edward Arnold, London, 1905, p. 212.
10. John Noel, 'A Journey to Tashirak in Southern Tibet, and the Eastern Approaches to Mount Everest', *Geographical Journal*, vol. 53, no. 5, 1919, pp. 289–303.
11. Robert Wainwright, *The Maverick Mountaineer: The Remarkable Life of George Ingle Finch: Climber, Scientist, Inventor*, Allen & Unwin, London, 2017, p. 129.
12. Walt Unsworth, *Everest: A Mountaineering History*, Oxford Illustrated Press, Yeovil, 1989, p. 23.
13. Charles Granville Bruce, *The Assault on Mount Everest, 1922*, Edward Arnold, London, 1923, p. 130.
14. Davis, *Into the Silence*, p. 21.
15. Tom Holzel and Audrey Salkeld, *First on Everest: The Mystery of Mallory and Irvine*, Jonathan Cape, London, 1986, p. 121.
16. John Morris, *Hired to Kill: Some Chapters of Autobiography*, Rupert Hart-Davis, London, 1960, p. 145.
17. Maurice Isserman and Stuart Weaver, *Fallen Giants: A History of Himalayan Mountaineering from the Age of Empire to the Age of Extremes*, Yale University Press, New Haven CT and London, 2008, p. 112.

18. Bruce, *The Assault on Mount Everest 1922*, p. 250.
19. Mallory to G.W. Young 11/6/22, Royal Geographical Society, Everest Expeditions Special Collection, EE/3/5/11.
20. Mallory account of accident, Royal Geographical Society, Everest Expeditions Special Collection, EE/3/5/12.
21. Mallory to G.W. Young 11/6/22.
22. Howard Somervell, *After Everest: The Experiences of a Mountaineer and Medical Missionary*, Hodder & Stoughton, London, 1936, p. 64.
23. Longstaff to Wollaston 19/8/22, Royal Geographical Society, Collection of letters addressed to Wollaston with notes and miscellaneous items.
24. *Leeds Mercury*, 15 July 1922.
25. There have been several recent ones – for example, S. Ortner, *Life and Death on Mt. Everest: Sherpas and Himalayan Mountaineering* (Princeton University Press, Princeton NJ, 2001); A. Adhikari and P. Bashyal, *Sherpa: Stories of Life and Death from the Forgotten Guardians of Everest* (Cassell, London, 2022); Nandini Purandare and Deepa Balsavar, *Headstrap: Legends and Lore from the Climbing Sherpas of Darjeeling* (Mountaineers Books, Seattle WA, 2024); B. McDonald, *Alpine Rising: Sherpas, Baltis, and the Triumph of Local Climbers in the Great Ranges* (Mountaineers Books, Seattle WA, 2024).
26. Smythe – Comments and Suggestions, Royal Geographical Society, Everest Expeditions Special Collection, EE44/7.
27. Lachlan Fleetwood, 'Himalayan Mountaineering, Imperial Masculinity and Altitude Records Before Everest', *Journal of Imperial and Commonwealth History*, vol. 52, no. 2, 2024, pp. 231–59.
28. Frank Smythe, *Kamet Conquered*, Victor Gollancz, London, 1933, p. 34.
29. Purandare and Balsavar, *Headstrap*.
30. Patrick French, *Younghusband: The Last Great Imperial Adventurer*, HarperCollins, London, 1994, p. 336.
31. Davis, *Into the Silence*, p. 489.
32. Unsworth, *Everest*, p. 96.
33. Sandy Irvine's Everest Expedition Journal, Sandy Irvine Archive, Merton College, Oxford.
34. Sandy Irvine, letter to his mother dated 26/5/1924, Sandy Irvine Archive, Merton College, Oxford.
35. Somervell, *After Everest*, p. 127.
36. Jochen Hemmleb, Larry A. Johnson and Eric R. Simonson, *Ghosts of Everest: The Authorised Story of the Search for Mallory & Irvine*, Macmillan, London, 1999, p. 7.
37. Sandy Irvine's Everest Expedition Journal, Sandy Irvine Archive, Merton College, Oxford.
38. Julie Summers, *Fearless on Everest: The Quest for Sandy Irvine*, Iffley Press, Oxford, 2000, p. 149.
39. Davis, *Into the Silence*, p. 479.
40. Summers, *Fearless on Everest*, p. 33.
41. Email from Julie Summers to the author, 10 March 2025.
42. Christopher Isherwood, *Lions and Shadows: An Education in the 1920s*, Hogarth Press, London, 1938, p. 11.
43. Email from Julie Summers to the author, 10 March 2025.
44. Summers, *Fearless on Everest*, p. 147
45. Davis, *Into the Silence*, p. 90.

TWO

1. Summers, *Fearless on Everest*, p. 229
2. Mindy Weisberger, 'Last Letters of Pioneering Climber Who Died on Everest Reveal Dark Side of Mountaineering', CNN, 17 April 2024, edition.cnn.com/2024/04/26/asia/george-mallory-digitized-letters-mount-everest-scn (accessed 24 October 2024).
3. Hinks to India Office 29/5/25, Royal Geographical Society, Everest Expeditions Special Collection, EE/27/6 India Office I. 1924–1927.
4. Hinks to Bruce 13/4/26, Royal Geographical Society, Everest Expeditions Special Collection, EE43/4/11.
5. Unsworth, *Everest*, p. 157.
6. Longland – Comments and Suggestions, Royal Geographical Society, Everest Expeditions Special Collection, EE44/7.
7. Hinks to Bormann 16/6/31, Royal Geographical Society, Everest Expeditions Special Collection, EE43/5/12.
8. Hinks to Bernard 24/3/26, Royal Geographical Society, Everest Expeditions Special Collection, EE/31/4.
9. Fleetwood, 'Himalayan Mountaineering, Imperial Masculinity and Altitude Records Before Everest'.
10. Rudolf Rother letter to MEC, Royal Geographical Society, Everest Expeditions Special Collection, EE/33/9.
11. Hinks to Howard Bury 3/11/21, Royal Geographical Society, Everest Expeditions Special Collection, EE/13/1 Correspondence with Lt. Col. C. Howard Bury.
12. Hinks to India Office 5/11/24, Royal Geographical Society, Everest Expeditions Special Collection, EE/27/6 India Office I. 1924–1927.
13. Hinks to *The Times* 2/12/24, Royal Geographical Society, Everest Expeditions Special Collection, EE34/8/41.
14. India Office to Mount Everest Committee 23/9/25, Royal Geographical Society, Everest Expeditions Special Collection, EE/27/6 India Office I. 1924–1927.
15. Hinks to Noel 31/7/25, Royal Geographical Society, Everest Expeditions Special Collection, EE/27/7/20 India Office II. 1925.
16. Hugh Norton, *Norton of Everest: The Biography of E.F. Norton, Soldier and Mountaineer of Everest*, Vertebrate, Sheffield, 2017, p. 38.
17. Somervell, *After Everest*, p. 75.
18. Percy Farrar, 'The Season of 1926 in the Mont Blanc Group', *Alpine Journal*, vol. 38, no. 233, 1926, pp. 270–76.
19. Adolphus Moore, 'Ascent of the Viecherhorn', *Alpine Journal*, vol. 1, no. 5, 1864, pp. 236–47.
20. Tait Keller, *Apostles of the Alps: Mountaineering and Nation Building in Germany and Austria, 1860–1939*, University of North Carolina Press, Chapel Hill NC, 2016, p. 23.
21. William Coolidge, *The Alps in Nature and History*, Methuen, London, 1908, p. 250.
22. Hermann Woolley, 'In Memoriam, Charles Pilkington', *Alpine Journal*, vol. 32, no. 219, 1919, pp. 346–53.
23. John Norman Collie, 'Climbing on the Nanga Parbat Range', *Alpine Journal*, vol. 18, no. 131, 1896, pp. 17–32.
24. Aleister Crowley, *The Confessions of Aleister Crowley*, Routledge & Kegan Paul, London, 1979, p. 135.
25. Ibid., p. 440.

26. 'The Disaster on Kangchenjunga', *Alpine Journal*, vol. 23, no. 171, 1906, pp. 51–4.
27. Paul Preuss, 'Künstliche Hilfsmittel auf Hochtouren', *Deutsche Alpenzeitung*, August 1911, pp. 242–4.
28. Geoffrey Winthrop Young, 'The Fatal Accident to Dr. Paul Preuss', *Alpine Journal*, vol. 27, no. 202, 1913, pp. 427–9.
29. Riccardo Cassin, 'Italian Climbing between the Wars', *Alpine Journal*, vol. 77, no. 321, 1972, pp. 149–56.
30. Gian Piero Motti, *La Storia del Alpinismo*, I Licheni Priuli & Verlucca, Scarmagno, 2016.
31. Francis Younghusband, *The Heart of Nature or The Quest for Natural Beauty*, John Murray, London, 1921, p. 213.
32. Wainwright, *The Maverick Mountaineer*, p. 89.
33. Unsworth, *Everest*, p. 43.
34. Harald Höbusch, *Mountain of Destiny: Nanga Parbat and Its Path into the German Imagination*, Camden House, London, 2016, p. 28.
35. India Office to Hinks 1/3/27, Royal Geographical Society, Everest Expeditions Special Collection, EE/27/6 India Office I. 1924–1927.
36. Hinks to Zoeller 1/6/27, Royal Geographical Society, Everest Expeditions Special Collection, EE/43/5/1.
37. Hinks to Stock 9/3/28, Royal Geographical Society, Everest Expeditions Special Collection, EE43/5/11.

THREE

1. Paul Bauer, *Himalayan Campaign: The German Attack on Kangchenjunga: The Second Highest Mountain in the World*, Basil Blackwell, Oxford, 1937, p. 95.
2. Ibid., p. 95.
3. Ibid., p. xv.
4. Paul Bauer, *Himalayan Quest: The German Expeditions to Siniolchum and Nanga Parbat*, Nicholson & Watson, London, 1938, p. 3.
5. Paul Fussell, *The Great War and Modern Memory*, Oxford University Press, Oxford, 1975, p. 29.
6. Bauer, *Himalayan Quest*, p. 3.
7. Erich-Maria Remarque, *All Quiet on the Western Front*, Vintage Classics, London, 2019, p. 14.
8. Bauer, *Himalayan Quest*, p. 3.
9. Helmuth Zebhauser, *Alpinismus im Hitlerstaat. Gedanken, Erinnerungen, Dokumente*, 1998, Bergverlag Rother, Oberhaching, 1998, p. 195.
10. Fussell, *The Great War and Modern Memory*, p. 90.
11. Der Akademische Alpenverein München in Kriege (1914–1918), *Jahresbericht AAVM*, vols 22–7, p. 86.
12. Nicholas Mailänder, *Im Zeichen des Edelweiss. Die Geschichte Münchens als Bergsteigerstadt*, AS Verlag, Zurich, 2011, p. 127.
13. Nicholas Mailänder, *Er ging voraus nach Lhasa: Peter Aufschnaiter. Die Biographie*, Tyrolia, Innsbruck, 2019, p. 34.
14. Ibid., p. 37.
15. Ibid.
16. Bauer, *Himalayan Campaign*, p. 1.
17. Ibid., p. 2.
18. Ibid., p. 3.
19. Mailänder, *Er ging voraus nach Lhasa*, p. 43.

20. Nicholas Mailänder, *Im Zeichen des Edelweiss: Die Geschichte Münchens als Bergsteigerstadt*, AS Verlag, Zurich, 2011, p. 174.
21. Peter Mierau, *Nationalsozialistische Expeditionspolitik: Deutsche Asien-Expeditionen 1933–1945*, Herbert Utz Verlag, Munich, 2005, p. 57.
22. Ibid., p. 52.

FOUR

1. Bauer, *Himalayan Campaign*, p. 11.
2. Charles G. Bruce, *Himalayan Wanderer*, A. Maclehose, London, 1934, p. 208.
3. See 'India and WWI: Piecing together the Impact of the Great War on the Subcontinent', South Asia@LSE, https://blogs.lse.ac.uk/southasia/2014/09/24/piecing-together-the-impact-of-the-great-war-on-india.
4. Ibid., p. 22.
5. 'Himalayan Notes', *Alpine Journal*, vol. 40, no. 237, 1928, pp. 410–13.
6. John Martyn, 'The Story of the Himalayan Club', *Himalayan Journal* 35, 1979, pp. 1–56.
7. Kenneth Mason, *Autobiography* (unpublished), Bodleian Library, MS. 6187/1 and MS. 6187/2, p. 437.
8. Isserman and Weaver, *Fallen Giants*, p. 225.
9. Mailänder, *Er ging voraus nach Lhasa*, p. 53.
10. Bauer, *Himalayan Campaign*, p. 28.
11. Ibid., p. 54.
12. Ibid., p. 61.
13. Norton, *The Fight for Everest 1924*, p. 49.
14. Paul Bauer War Record at Kriegsranglisten und -stammrollen des Königreichs Bayern, 1. Weltkrieg 1914–1918, Bayerisches Hauptstaatsarchiv.
15. Bauer, *Himalayan Campaign*, p. 73.
16. Ibid., p. 83.
17. 'Calcutta Local Dinners', *Himalayan Journal* 2, 1930, pp. 187–91.

FIVE

1. Andreas Nickel, *Dyhrenfurth: Zum Dritten Pol*, AS Verlag, Zurich 2011, p. 49.
2. Zebhauser, *Alpinismus im Hitlerstaat*, p. 70.
3. Ibid., p. 76.
4. Nickel, *Dyhrenfurth: Zum Dritten Pol*, p. 79.
5. Hinks to Boormann 16/6/31, Royal Geographical Society, Everest Expeditions Special Collection, EE43//5/12.
6. Tony Smythe, *My Father, Frank: The Forgotten Alpinist*, Baton Wicks, Sheffield, 2013, p. 46.
7. Kristian Mennen, '"Milksops" and "Bemedalled Old Men": War Veterans and the War Youth Generation in the Weimar Republic', *Fascism*, vol. 6, no. 1, 23 June 2017, pp. 13–41.
8. Graves and Hodge, *The Long Weekend*, p. 260.
9. Hugh Ruttledge, 'In Memoriam – Frank Smythe', *Himalayan Journal* 15, 1949, p. 102.
10. John Millar, 'Smythe's Himalayan Trails', *Himalayan Journal* 54, 1998.
11. Percy Farrar, 'In Memoriam – Mrs. Fanny Bullock Workman', *Alpine Journal,* vol. 37, no. 230, 1925, pp. 180–82.
12. Hettie Dyhrenfurth, *Memsahb im Himalaja*, Verlag Deutsche Buchwerkstätten, Leipzieg, 1931, p.15.

13. Nickel, *Dyhrenfurth: Zum Dritten Pol*, p. 88.
14. Frank Smythe, *The Kangchenjunga Adventure*, Victor Gollancz, London, 1930, p. 92.
15. Ibid., p. 94.
16. Douglas Freshfield, *Round Kangchenjunga: A Narrative of Mountain Travel and Exploration*, Edward Arnold, London, 1903, p. 172.
17. Smythe, *My Father Frank*, p. 220.
18. Tom Longstaff, 'In Memoriam – Chettan', *Himalayan Journal* 3, 1931, p. 116.
19. Smythe, *My Father Frank*, p. 132.
20. Smythe, *The Kangchenjunga Adventure*, p. 417.
21. Dyhrenfurth, *Memsahb in Himalaya*, p. 59.

SIX

1. Smythe, *My Father Frank*, p. 135.
2. Ibid.
3. Peter Foster, 'Edward Lisle Strutt A Portrait', *Alpine Journal*, vol. 123, no. 367, 2019, pp. 189–99.
4. Raymond Greene, *Moments of Being: The Random Recollections of Raymond Greene*, Heinemann, London, 1974, p. 95.
5. Shipton, *That Untravelled World*, p. 73.
6. Mierau, *Nationalsozialistische Expeditionspolitik*, p. 79.
7. Ibid., p. 55.
8. Bauer, *Himalayan Campaign*, p. 110.
9. Ernst Jünger, *Storm of Steel*, Penguin Books, London, 2004, p. 58.
10. Bauer, *Himalayan Campaign*, p. 110.
11. Ibid., p. 112.
12. Karl Wien, 'Willo Welzenbach', *Jahresbericht AAVM*, vol. 42, 1934, pp. 2–5.
13. Bauer, *Himalayan Campaign*, p. 122.
14. Ibid., p. 128.
15. Ibid., p. 141.
16. Davis, *Into the Silence*, p. 229.
17. Isserman, Weaver, *Fallen Giants*, p. 81.
18. Ibid. p. 149.
19. Robert Graves, *Good-bye to All That,* Jonathan Cape, London, 1929, p. 219.
20. Ibid., p. 160.
21. Bauer, *Himalayan Campaign*, p. 174.
22. Der 1. Weltkrieg 1916 – 'Zwischen La Bassée und Arras' [The 1st World War 1916 – 'Between La Bassée and Arras'], www.stahlgewitter.com.

SEVEN

1. Smythe, *Kamet Conquered*, pp. xv–xvi.
2. Elizabeth Knowlton, *The Naked Mountain*, G.P. Putnam's Sons, New York, 1933 p. 31.
3. Knowlton, *The Naked Mountain*, p. 303.
4. Edward Strutt, 'The English Mount Everest Expedition 1933', *Alpine Journal*, vol. 44, no. 245, 1932, pp. 262–3.
5. Ibid.
6. Ibid.
7. Strutt, *The English Mount Everest Expedition 1933*.
8. Alan Hankinson, *Geoffrey Winthrop Young: Poet, Educator, Mountaineer*, Hodder & Stoughton, London, 1995, p. 304.

9. Jack Longland, 'Between the Wars 1919–193', *Alpine Journal*, vol. 62, no. 295, 1957, pp. 83–98.
10. Edward Strutt, 'A Superiority Complex?', *Alpine Journal*, vol. 46, no. 249, 1934, pp. 374–7.
11. Ibid.
12. Robert Boyce, 'The Persistence of Anglo-Saxonism in Britain and the Origins of Britain's Appeasement Policy towards Germany', *Histoire Politique*, vol. 15, no. 3, 2011, pp. 110–29.
13. Paul Bauer, 'The Fight for Kangchenjunga, 1936', *Alpine Journal*, vol. 42, no. 240, 1930, pp. 185–202.
14. Edward Norton, 'The German Attack on Kangchenjunga (correspondence)', *Himalayan Journal* 2, 1930, pp. 180–81.
15. Edward Strutt, 'Reviews', *Alpine Journal*, vol. 43, no. 242, 1931, pp. 192–4.
16. Unsworth, *Everest*, p. 161.
17. Smythe, *My Father* Frank, p. 142.
18. Hugh Ruttledge, *Everest 1933*, Hodder & Stoughton, London, 1934, p. 29.
19. Peter Foster, 'Everest 1936: The Leadership Question Re-visited', *Alpine Journal*, vol. 124, no. 368, 2020, pp. 129–40.
20. Longstaff – Comments and suggestions, Royal Geographical Society, Everest Expeditions Special Collection, EE44/7.
21. Jane Hargreaves, *L.R. Wager A Life 1904–1965*, privately published, 1991, p. 24.
22. Ibid., p. 39.
23. Royal Geographical Society, Everest Expeditions Special Collection, EE42.
24. Greene – Comments and Suggestions, Royal Geographical Society, Everest Expeditions Special Collection, EE44/7.
25. Ibid.
26. Smythe, *My Father Frank*, p. 174.
27. Ruttledge, *Everest 1933*, p. 134
28. Ruttledge, Ibid., p. 144.
29. Frank Smythe, *Camp Six: An Account of the 1933 Mount Everest Expedition*, Victor Gollancz, London, 1937, p. 151.
30. Ruttledge, *Everest 1933*, p. 151.
31. Hargreaves, *L.R. Wager*, p. 42.
32. Eric Shipton, *Upon That Mountain*, Hodder & Stoughton, London, 1943, p. 140.
33. Jack Longland, 'Everest, 1933', *Fell and Rock Club Journal*, vol. 9, no. 3, 1933, pp. 327–43, p. 329.
34. Ibid., p. 335.

EIGHT

1. Nickel, *Dyhrenfurth: Zum Dritten Pol*, p. 112.
2. Walter Welsch, *Geschichte der Sektion Bayerland des Deutschen Alpenvereins e.V.: Die Zeit des Dritten Reiches 1933–1945*, DAV Bayerland, 2013, p. 257.
3. Ibid.
4. Ibid.
5. Bettina Hoerlin, *Steps of Courage: My Parents' Journey from Nazi Germany to America*, Author House, Bloomington IN, 2011 p. 79.
6. Ibid., p. 56.
7. Letter from Schneider to Hoerlin 6/9/33 Deutsche Alpinverein Alpinarchiv.
8. Ibid.
9. Nickel, *Dyhrenfurth: Zum Dritten Pol*, p. 119.

10. Hoerlin, *Steps of Courage*, p. 82.
11. Jonathan Neale, *Tigers of the Snow: How One Fateful Climb Made the Sherpas Mountaineering Legends*, Little, Brown, London, 2002, p. 136.
12. Ibid.
13. Bechtold, *Nanga Parbat Adventure*, p. 51.
14. Neale, *Tigers of the Snow*, p. 136.
15. Report on Court of Honour 21/2/35 DAV Alpinarchiv.
16. Eric Roberts, *Welzenbach's Climbs: A Biographical Study and the Collected Writings of Willo Welzenbach*, West Col Productions, Reading, 1981, p. 250.
17. Ibid., p. 250.
18. Bechtold, *Nanga Parbat Adventure*, p. 60.
19. Roberts, *Welzenbach's Climbs*, p. 248.
20. Ibid., p. 251.
21. Report on Court of Honour.
22. Bechtold, *Nanga Parbat Adventure*, p. 75.
23. Erwin Schneider, 'The Accident on Nanga Parbat', *Alpine Journal*, vol. 46, no. 249, 1934, pp. 423–7.
24. Bechtold, *Nanga Parbat Adventure*, p. 75.
25. Paul Bauer, *The Siege of Nanga Parbat: 1856–1953*, Rupert Hart-Davis, London, 1956, p. 162.

NINE

1. *NS-Kurier*, 25 September 1934.
2. Mierau, *Nationalsozialistische Expeditionspolitik*, p. 195.
3. Mennen, '"Milksops" and "Bemedalled Old Men"'.
4. Fritz Bechtold, *Nanga Parbat Adventure*, John Murray, London, 1935, p. 88.
5. Edward Strutt, 'Accidents in 1934', *Alpine Journal*, vol. 46, no. 249, 1934, pp. 414–27.
6. Ed Douglas, *Tenzing: Hero of Everest. A Biography of Tenzing Norgay*, National Geographic Society, Washington DC, 2003, p. 63.
7. Nickel, *Dyhrenfurth: Zum Dritten Pol*, p. 153.
8. Ibid.
9. Bauer letter to von Tschammer 10/12/34 DAV Alpinarchiv.
10. Richard Evans, *The Coming of the Third Reich: How the Nazis Destroyed Democracy and Seized Power in Germany*, Penguin Books, London, 2004, p. 84.
11. Bauer letter to von Tschammer 10/12/34 DAV Alpinarchiv.
12. Ruttledge – Comments and Suggestions, Royal Geographical Society, Everest Expeditions Special Collection, EE44/7.
13. Bauer letter to von Tschammer 10/12/34 DAV Alpinarchiv.
14. Hoerlin, *Step of Courage*, p. 95.
15. Political Officer in Sikkim to the Foreign Secretary to the Government of India 2/10/33, Royal Geographical Society, Everest Expeditions Special Collection, EE44/5.
16. Ibid.
17. Hargreaves, *L.R. Wager*, p. 44.
18. Eric Shipton, *Nanda Devi*, Hodder & Stoughton, London 1936, p. 19.
19. Shipton, *Upon That Mountain*, p. 296.
20. Eric Shipton, 'The Mount Everest Reconnaissance, 1936', *Alpine Journal*, vol. 48, no. 252, 1936, pp. 1–14.
21. Smythe, *My Father Frank*, p. 143.

22. Eric Shipton, *That Untravelled World*, Hodder & Stoughton, London, 1969, p. 99.
23. Mason, *Autobiography*, p. 451.
24. Ibid., p. 455.
25. Mierau, *Nationalsozialistische Expeditionspolitik*, p. 125.
26. Paul Bauer, 'The German Sikkim Expedition 1936', *Alpine Journal*, vol. 49, no. 254, 1937, pp. 41–8.
27. Unsworth, *Everest*, p. 186.
28. Brocklebank – Comments and Suggestions, Royal Geographical Society, Everest Expeditions Special Collection, EE44/7.
29. Foster, 'Everest 1936. The Leadership Question Re-visited', p. 131.
30. Ibid.
31. Ruttledge to GWY 22/4/35 Royal Geographical Society, Everest Expeditions Special Collection.
32. Unsworth, *Everest*, p. 208.
33. Ruttledge to GWY 22/4/35.
34. Smythe, *My Father Frank*, p. 212.
35. Hugh Ruttledge, *Everest: The Unfinished Adventure*, Hodder & Stoughton, London, 1937, p. 105.
36. Unsworth, *Everest*, p. 206.
37. Smythe, *My Father Frank*, p. 215.
38. Wainwright, *The Maverick Mountaineer*, p. 388.
39. Jim Perrin, *Shipton & Tilman: The Great Decade of Himalayan Exploration*, Hutchinson, London, 2013, p. 283.
40. Shipton, *Upon That Mountain*, p. 191.
41. W.H. Auden and Christopher Isherwood, *The Ascent of F6*, Faber & Faber, London, 1936, p. 61.
42. Deborah Baker, *The Last Englishmen: Love, War and the End of Empire*, Penguin Random House, London, 2018.
43. John Maynard Keynes, *The Collected Writings of John Maynard Keynes: The Economic Consequences of the Peace*, Macmillan, London, 1971, p. 143.
44. Gerald Lehner, *Zwischen Hitler und Himalaya. Die Gedächtnislücken des Heinrich Harrer*, Czernin, Vienna, 2016, p. 110.

TEN

1. Bauer, *Himalayan Quest*, p. 100.
2. Nickel, *Dyhrenfurth: Zum Dritten Pol*, p. 242.
3. Ibid., p. 167.
4. Mierau, *Nationalsozialistische Expeditionspolitik*, p. 147.
5. Bauer, *The Siege of Nanga Parbat*, p. 136.
6. Ibid., p. 137.
7. *The Times*, 21 June 1937.
8. *Statesman of Calcutta*, June 1937.
9. In 2015 this tent emerged from the lower Rakhiot Glacier. It contained the diary of Peter Müllritter with entries relating to both the 1934 and the 1937 expeditions.
10. Bauer, *The Siege of Nanga Parbat*, p. 138.
11. Hoerlin, *Steps of Courage*, p. 150.
12. Edward Strutt, 'Accidents in 1937', *Alpine Journal*, vol. 49, no. 255, 1937, pp. 282–7.
13. Bauer, *Himalayan Quest*, p. vii.
14. *The Yorkshire Post*, 22 June 1937.

15. Bauer, *Himalayan Quest*, p. xiv.
16. Bill Tilman, *Everest 1938*, University Press, Cambridge, 1948, p. 27.
17. Years later a porter's boot and Merkl's right boot were found at the foot of the Rupal Face, leading Karl Maria Herrligkoffer to suspect the bodies were thrown down the mountain, rather than buried, in 1938.
18. Harald Höbusch, 'In the Face of Tragedy – Nanga Parbat and National Socialist Radio', *International Journal of the History of Sport*, vol. 37, no. 8, 2020, pp. 633–50.
19. Unsworth, *Everest*, p. 210.
20. Bauer, *Himalayan Quest*, p. xiii.
21. Bill Tilman, 'Mount Everest, 1938', *Alpine Journal*, vol. 48, no. 51, 1939, pp. 3–17.
22. H.W. [Bill] Tilman, *Snow on the Equator*, in *The Seven Mountain Travel Books*, Diadem, London, 1983, p. 19.
23. Shipton, *That Untravelled World*, p. 85.
24. Smythe, *My Father Frank*, p. 234.
25. Royal Geographical Society, The Eric Shipton Collection, ESH-14: Correspondence 1938–1939.
26. Tilman, *Everest 1938*, p. 121.
27. Ibid., p. 79.
28. Ibid., p. 82.
29. Shipton, *Upon That Mountain*, p. 210.
30. Tilman, *Everest 1938*.

ELEVEN

1. Charles Houston, 'A Reconnaissance of K2, 1938', *Himalayan Journal* 11, 1939, pp. 114–27.
2. Andrew Kauffman and William L. Putnam, *K2: The 1939 Tragedy*, Mountaineers Books, Seattle WA, 1992, p. 189.
3. Ibid., p. 33.
4. Edward Strutt, 'Accidents in 1936', *Alpine Journal*, vol. 48, no. 252, 1936, pp. 365–75.
5. Ibid.
6. Ibid.
7. Heinrich Harrer, Anderl Heckmair, Fritz Kasparek and Ludwig Vörg, *Um die Eiger-Nordwand*, Zentralverlag der NSDAP, Munich, 1938, p. 96.
8. Mierau, *Nationalsozialistische Expeditionspolitik*, p. 172.
9. Anderl Heckmair, *My Life,* Mountaineers Books, Seattle WA, 2002, p. 161.
10. Roger Croston, 'Prisoners of the Raj', *Alpine Journal*, vol. 111, no. 355, 2006, pp. 213–24.
11. Ibid.
12. Frank Smythe, *Mountaineering Holiday*, Hodder, London, 1940.
13. Shipton, *That Untravelled World*, p. 118.

TWELVE

1. Albert Speer, *Inside the Third Reich*, Orion, London, 1969, p. 239.
2. Höbusch, *Mountain of Destiny*, p. 105.
3. Alexander Statiev, *At War's Summit: The Red Army and the Struggle for the Caucasus Mountains in World War II*, Cambridge University Press, Cambridge, 2018, p. 32.
4. *Weltkrieg Soldaten Nr. 37*, Erlebnisberichte, Feldwebel Alois Gugganig.
5. Oxford, Bodleian Library, MS. Eng. c. 8327.

6. Isserman and Weaver, *Fallen Giants*, p. 226.
7. George Rodway, 'Ulrich C. Luft and Physiology on Nanga Parbat: The Winds of War', *High Altitude Medicine & Biology*, vol. 10, no. 1, 2009, pp. 89–96.
8. Scott Ellsworth, *The World beneath Their Feet*, John Murray, London, 2020, p. 374.
9. Lehner, *Zwischen Hitler und Himalaya*, p. 310.
10. Ibid., p. 311.
11. Correspondence, *American Alpine Journal*, vol. 15, no. 2, 1944.
12. Félicité Herzog, *Un héros*, Grasset, Paris, 2012, p. 70.
13. Auden and Isherwood, *The Ascent of F6*, p. 40.
14. Isserman and Weaver, *Fallen Giants*, p. 252.
15. Gérard Herzog and Louis Lachenal, *Carnets du vertige*, Editions Guérin, Chamonix, 1996, p. 299.
16. Maurice Herzog, *Annapurna: Conquest of the First 8,000-metre Peak*, Jonathan Cape, London, 1952, p. 191.
17. David Roberts, *True Summit: What Really Happened on the Legendary Ascent of Annapurna*, Simon & Schuster, New York, 2000.
18. Shipton, *That Untravelled World*, p. 212.
19. Mick Conefrey, *Everest 1953: The Epic Story of the First Ascent*, Oneworld, London, 2013.
20. Ibid.
21. Peter Hansen, *The Summits of Modern Man*, Harvard University Press, Cambridge MA, 2013, p. 250.
22. Ibid., p. 246.
23. Isserman and Weaver, *Fallen Giants*, p. 204.
24. Bill Tilman, 'The Problem of Mount Everest', *Himalayan Journal* 13, 1946, p. 133.
25. John Anderson, *High Mountains and Cold Seas: A Biography of H.W. Tilman*, Gollancz, London, 1980, p. 282.
26. Stephen Goodwin, 'Lino Lacedelli: Mountaineer whose Ascent of K2 in 1954 Was Shrouded in Controversy', *Independent*, 24 November 2009.
27. Mick Conefrey, *Ghosts of K2: The Race for the Summit of World's Most Deadly Mountain*, Oneworld, London, 2016, p. 192.
28. Longland, *Between the Wars*, p. 96.
29. Isserman and Weaver, *Fallen Giants*, p. 326.
30. Conrad Anker and David Roberts, *The Lost Explorer: Finding Mallory on Mount Everest*, Robinson, London, 2000.
31. Mark Synnott, *The Third Pole: Mystery, Obsession, and Death on Mount Everest*, Penguin, London, 2022, p. 379.
32. Isserman and Weaver, *Fallen Giants*, p. 357.
33. Ruttledge – Comments and Suggestions, Royal Geographical Society, Everest Expeditions Special Collection, EE44/7.
34. Graves and Hodge, *The Long Weekend*, p. 73.
35. Longland, *Between the Wars*, p. 96.
36. Wilfred Noyce, *Scholar Mountaineers: Pioneers of Parnassus*, Dennis Dobson, London, 1950, p. 134.
37. Ibid., p. 135.
38. William Murray and Jeremiah Wright, *The Craft of Climbing*, N. Kaye, London, 1964.
39. Friedrich Nietzsche, *Thus Spoke Zarathustra,* Penguin, London, 1969, pp. 173–4.

40. Friedrich Nietzsche, *Untimely Meditations*, Cambridge University Press, Cambridge 1997, p. 129.
41. Leo Maduschka, *Junger Mensch in Gebirg*, Gesellschaft Alpiner Bücherfreunde, Munich, 1936, p. 168.
42. Jeff Connor, *Dougal Haston: The Philosophy of Risk*, Canongate, London, 2002, p. 61.
43. Longstaff to Wollaston 19/8/22.
44. Davis, *Into the Silence,* p. 456.
45. Anker and Roberts, *The Lost Explorer*, p. 165.
46. Stephen Venable, lecture to the Alpine Club, 18 November 2021, www.youtube.com/watch?v=m99O5wERBgI.
47. Graham Hoyland, *Last Hours on Everest*, William Collins, London, 2013, p. 128.
48. Erich Vanis, 'Paul Bauer In Memoriam', *Alpine Journal*, vol. 96, no. 340, 1991, pp. 297–9.
49. Hoerlin, *Steps of Courage*, p. 95.
50. Bertrand Russell, *The Prospects of Industrial Civilization*, George Allen & Unwin, London, 1923, p. 28.
51. French, *Younghusband*, p. 303.
52. Perrin, *Shipton & Tilman*, p. 14.
53. Arlene Blum, *Annapurna: A Woman's Place*, Sierra Club Books, San Francisco CA, 1980, p. 36.
54. Julie Rak, *False Summit: Gender in Mountaineering Nonfiction*, McGill–Queen's University Press, Montreal, 2021, p. 22.
55. Russell, *The Prospects of Industrial Civilization*, p. 27.
56. Gary Lineker on X, 7 March 2023, twitter.com/GaryLineker/status/1633111662352891908 (accessed 25 October 2023).
57. Richard Evans, *The Third Reich in Power, 1933–1939*, Penguin, London, 2005, p. 183.
58. Davis, *Into the Silence*, p. 89.
59. Smythe, *Climbs and Ski Runs.*
60. George Mallory, 'Mont Blanc from the Col du Géant by the Eastern Buttress of Mont Maudit', *Alpine Journal*, vol. 32, no. 218, 1918, pp. 148–62.

Bibliography

BOOKS

Adhikari, A., and P. Bashyal, *Sherpa: Stories of Life and Death from the Forgotten Guardians of Everest*, Cassell, London, 2022.

Amstädter, R., *Der Alpinismus: Kultur – Organization – Politik*, Facultas, Vienna, 1996.

Anderson, J.L.R., *High Mountains and Cold Seas A Biography of H.W. Tilman*, Gollancz, London, 1980.

Ang Tharkay, *Mémoires d'un Sherpa*, Amiot-Dumont, Paris, 1954.

Anker, C., and D. Roberts, *The Lost Explorer: Finding Mallory on Mount Everest*, Robinson, London, 2000.

Astill. T., *Mount Everest: The Reconnaissance 1935: The Forgotten Adventure*, Tony Astill, London, 2005.

Auden, W.H., and C. Isherwood, *The Ascent of F6*, Faber & Faber, London, 1936.

Baker, D., *The Last Englishmen: Love, War and the End of Empire*, Chatto & Windus, London, 2018.

Balke, B., and others, *Nanga Parbat, Berg der Kameraden*, Union, Berlin, 1943.

Band, G., *Summit: 150 years of the Alpine Club*, Collins, London, 2006.

Bates, R., et al., *Five Miles High: The Story of an Attack on the Second Highest Mountain in the World*, R. Hale, London, 1940.

Bauer, P., *Himalayan Campaign: The German Attack on Kangchenjunga, Second Highest Mountain in the World*, Basil Blackwell, Oxford, 1937.

Bauer, P., *Himalayan Quest: The German Expeditions to Siniolchum and Nanga Parbat*, Nicholson & Watson, London, 1938.

Bauer, P., *The Siege of Nanga Parbat: 1856–1953*, Rupert Hart-Davis, London, 1956.

Bauer, P., *Paul Bauer. Wegbereiter für die Gipfelsiege von heute*, Steiger Verlag, Berwang, 1987.

Bechtold, F., *Nanga Parbat Adventure*, John Murray, London, 1935.

Blum, A., *Annapurna: A Woman's Place*, Sierra Club Books, San Francisco CA, 1980.

Bruce, C.G., *The Assault on Mount Everest 1922*, Edward Arnold, London, 1923.

Bruce, C.G., *Himalayan Wanderer*, A. Maclehose, London, 1934.

Chicken, L., *Durchs Jahrhundert. Mein Leben als Arzt und Bergsteiger*, Edition Raetia Bolzano, 2004.

Conefrey, M., *Everest 1953: The Epic Story of the First Ascent*, Oneworld, London, 2013.
Conefrey, M., *Ghosts of K2: The Race for the Summit of World's Most Deadly Mountain*, Oneworld, London, 2016.
Conefrey, M., *Everest 1922*, Allen & Unwin, London, 2022.
Conefrey, M., *Fallen: George Mallory, the Man, the Myth and the 1924 Everest Tragedy*, Allen & Unwin, London, 2024.
Connor, J., *Dougal Haston: The Philosophy of Risk*, Canongate, London, 2002.
Coolidge, W.A.B, *The Alps in Nature and History*, Methuen, London, 1908.
Crowley, A., *The Confessions of Aleister Crowley*, Routledge & Kegan Paul, London, 1979.
Davis, W., *Into the Silence: The Great War, Mallory and the Conquest of Everest*, Vintage, London, 2012.
Douglas, E., *Tenzing: Hero of Everest, A Biography of Tenzing Norgay*, Washington DC, National Geographic Society, 2003.
Dyhrenfurth, H., *Memsahb im Himalaja*, Verlag Deutsche Buchwerkstätten, Leipzig, 1931.
Dyhrenfurth, G.O., *Dämon Himalaya. Bericht der Internationalen Karakoram-Expedition 1934*, Benno Schwabe, Basle, 1935.
Dyhrenfurth, G.O., *Himalaya-Fahrt. Unsere Expedition 1930*, Orell Füssli, Zurich, 1942.
Dyhrenfurth, G.O., *Das Buch vom Kantsch. Die Geschichte seiner Besteigung*, Nymphenburger Verlag, Munich, 1955.
Ellsworth, S., *The World beneath Their Feet*, John Murray, London, 2020.
Evans, R.J., *The Coming of the Third Reich*, Allen Unwin, London, 2003.
Evans, R.J., *The Third Reich in Power, 1933–1939: How the Nazis Won Over the Hearts and Minds of a Nation*, Penguin, London, 2005.
Finch, G.I., *The Making of a Mountaineer*, Arrowsmith, London, 1924.
Fleming, F., *Killing Dragons: The Conquest of the Alps*, Granta, London, 2001.
French, P., *Younghusband: The Last Great Imperial Adventurer*, HarperCollins, London, 1994.
Freshfield, D., *Round Kangchenjunga: A Narrative of Mountain Travel and Exploration*, Edward Arnold, London, 1903.
Fussell, P., *The Great War and Modern Memory*, Oxford University Press, Oxford, 1975.
Gerwarth, R., *War in Peace: Paramilitary Violence in Europe after the Great War*, Oxford University Press, Oxford, 2012.
Gerwarth, R., *The Vanquished: Why the First World War Failed to End, 1917–1923*, Penguin, London, 2017.
Graves, R., *Good-bye to All That*, Jonathan Cape, London, 1929.
Graves, R., and A. Hodge, *The Long Weekend: A Social History of Great Britain*, Faber & Faber, London, 1940.
Greene, R., *Moments of Being: The Random Recollections of Raymond Greene*, Heinemann, London, 1974.
Hansen, P., *The Summits of Modern Man*, Harvard University Press, Cambridge MA, 2013.
Hargreaves, J., *L.R. Wager: A Life, 1904–1965*, privately published, 1991.
Harrer, H., *Seven Years in Tibet*, Rupert Hart Davis, London, 1953.
Harrer, H., A. Heckmair, F. Kasparek and L. Vörg, *Um die Eiger-Nordwand*, Zentralverlag der NSDAP, Munich, 1938.

Hartmann, H., *Das Kantschtagebuch. mit Zeichnungen von Jürgen Klein*, Kösel & Pustet, Munich, 1934.
Hartmann, H., *Ziel Nanga Parbat Tagebuchblätter einer Himalaja Expedition*, Wilhelm Limpert Verlag, Berlin, 1942.
Heckmair, A., *My Life*, Mountaineers Books, Seattle WA, 2002.
Hemmleb, J., L.A. Johnson and E.R. Simonson, *Ghosts of Everest: The Authorised Story of the Search for Mallory & Irvine*, Macmillan, London, 1999.
Herzog, F., *Un héros*, Grasset, Paris, 2012.
Herzog, G., and L. Lachenal, *Carnets du vertige*, Editions Guérin, Chamonix, 1996.
Herzog, M., *Annapurna: Conquest of the First 8000-metre Peak*, Jonathan Cape, London, 1952.
Höbusch, H., *Mountain of Destiny: Nanga Parbat and its Path into the German Imagination*, Camden House, London, 2016.
Hoerlin, B., *Steps of Courage: My Parents' Journey from Nazi Germany to America*, AuthorHouse, Bloomington IN, 2011.
Holzel, T., and A. Salkeld, *First on Everest: The Mystery of Mallory and Irvine*, Jonathan Cape, London, 1986.
Howard-Bury, C.K., and other members of the Everest Expedition, *Mount Everest: The Reconnaissance, 1921*, Edward Arnold, London, 1922.
Hoyland, G., *Last Hours on Everest*, William Collins, London, 2013.
Isherwood C., *Lions and Shadows: An Education in the 1920s*, Hogarth Press, London, 1938.
Isserman, M., and S. Weaver, *Fallen Giants: A History of Himalayan Mountaineering from the Age of Empire to the Age of Extremes*, Yale University Press, London, 2008.
Jones, N., *A Brief History of the Birth of the Nazis: How the Freikorps Blazed a Trail for Hitler*, John Murray, London, 1987.
Jünger, E., *Storm of Steel*, Penguin, London, 2004.
Kauffman, A., and W.L. Putnam, *K2: The 1939 Tragedy: The Full Story of the Ill-fated Wiessner Expedition*, Mountaineers Books, Seattle WA, 1992.
Keller, T., *Apostles of the Alps: Mountaineering and Nation Building in Germany and Austria, 1860–1939*, University of North Carolina Press, Chapel Hill NC, 2016.
Keynes, J.M., *The Collected Writings of John Maynard Keynes: The Economic Consequences of the Peace*, Macmillan, London, 1971.
Knowlton, E., *The Naked Mountain*, G.P. Putnam's Sons, New York, 1933.
Lehner, G., *Zwischen Hitler und Himalaya. Die Gedächtnislücken des Heinrich Harrer*, Czernin, Vienna, 2016.
Longstaff, T., *This is My Voyage*, John Murray, London, 1950.
McDonald, B., *Alpine Rising: Sherpas, Baltis, and the Triumph of Local Climbers in the Great Ranges*, Mountaineers Books, Seattle WA, 2024.
Maduschka, L., *Junger Mensch in Gebirg*, Gesellschaft Alpiner Bücherfreunde, Munich, 1936.
Mailänder, N., *Im Zeichen des Edelweiss. Die Geschichte Münchens als Bergsteigerstadt*, AS Verlag, Zurich, 2011.
Mailänder, N., *Er ging voraus nach Lhasa. Peter Aufschnaiter. Die Biographie des großen Himalaya-Pioniers*, Tyrolia Verlagsanstalt Gm, Innsbruck, 2019.
Marcowitz, R., *Die Weimarer Republik 1929–1933*, Herder Verlag, Darmstadt, 2018.
Märtin, RP., *Nanga Parbat. Wahrheit und Wahn des Alpinismus*, Berlin Verlag, Berlin, 2002.

Mason, K., *Abode of Snow*, Rupert Hart Davis, London, 1955.
Mason, K., *Autobiography* (unpublished), Oxford, Bodleian Library, MS. 6187/1 and MS. 6187/2, 1966.
Merkl, W., F. Schmitt and K. Herrligkoffer, *Willy Merkl Ein Weg zum Nanga Parbat*, Bergverlag Rudolf Rother, Munich, 1936.
Messner, R., *Der Eispapst. Die Akte Welzenbach*, S. Fischer, Frankfurt am Main, 2019.
Mierau, P., *Himalaja-Stiftung (Dokumente des Alpinismus)*, Bergverlag Rudolf Rother, Munich, 1999.
Mierau, P., *Nationalsozialistische Expeditionspolitik. Deutsche Asien-Expeditionen 1933–1945*, Herbert Utz Verlag, Munich, 2005.
Mitchell, A., *Revolution in Bavaria, 1918–1919: The Eisner Regime and the Soviet Republic*, Princeton University Press, Princeton NJ, 1965.
Morris, J., *Hired to Kill: Some Chapters of Autobiography*, Rupert Hart-Davis, London, 1960.
Morshead, I., *The Life and Murder of Henry Morshead*, Oleander Press, Cambridge, 1982.
Motti, G.P., *La Storia del Alpinismo*, I Licheni Priuli & Verlucca, Scarmagno, 2016.
Murray, W.H., and J.E.B. Wright, *The Craft of Climbing*, N. Kaye, London, 1964.
Neale, J., *Tigers of the Snow: How One Fateful Climb Made the Sherpas Mountaineering Legends*, Little, Brown, London, 2002.
Nickel, A., *Dyhrenfurth: Zum Dritten Pol*, AS Verlag, Zurich, 2011.
Nietzsche, F., *Thus Spoke Zarathustra*, Penguin, Harmondsworth, 1969.
Nietzsche, F., *Untimely Meditations*, Cambridge University Press, Cambridge, 1997.
Norton, E.F., et al., *The Fight for Everest: 1924*, Edward Arnold, London, 1925.
Norton, H., *Norton of Everest*, Vertebrate, Sheffield, 2017.
Noyce, W., *Scholar Mountaineers: Pioneers of Parnassus*, Dennis Dobson, London, 1950.
Ortner, S., *Life and Death on Mt. Everest: Sherpas and Himalayan Mountaineering*, Princeton University Press, Princeton NJ, 2001.
Perrin, J., *Shipton & Tilman: The Great Decade of Himalayan Exploration*, Hutchinson, London, 2013.
Purandare, N., and D. Balsavar, *Headstrap: Legends and Lore from the Climbing Sherpas of Darjeeling*, Mountaineers Books, Seattle WA, 2024.
Rak, J, *False Summit: Gender in Mountaineering Nonfiction*, McGill Queen's University Press, Montreal, 2021.
Rawling, C., *The Great Plateau*, Edward Arnold, London, 1905.
Remarque, E.M., *The Way Back*, Vintage Classics, London, 2019.
Remarque, E.M., *All Quiet on the Western Front*, Vintage Classics, London, 2019.
Roberts, A., *The Forgotten Man of Everest: A Biography of Major General Geoffrey Bruce CB DSO MC*, Alistair Roberts, Cheltenham, 2019.
Roberts, D., *True Summit: What Really Happened on the Legendary Ascent of Annapurna*, Simon & Schuster, New York, 2000.
Roberts, E., *Welzenbach's Climbs: A Biographical Study and the Collected Writing of Willo Welzenbach*, West Col, Reading, 1981.
Roch, A., *Karakoram Himalaya: Sommets de 7000m*, Éditions Victor Attinger, Neuchâtel, 1945.
Russell, B., *The Prospects of Industrial Civilization*, George Allen & Unwin, London, 1923.
Ruttledge, H., *Everest 1933*, Hodder & Stoughton, London, 1934.
Ruttledge, H., *Everest: The Unfinished Adventure*, Hodder & Stoughton, London, 1937.

Schmidkunz, W., *Berg-Vagabunden. Ein Hans-Ertl-Buch*, Gebr. Richter Verlagsanstalt, Erfurt, 1937.
Scott, D., *Kangchenjunga: The Himalayan Giant*, Vertebrate, Sheffield, 2021.
Shipton, E., *Nanda Devi*, Hodder & Stoughton, London, 1936.
Shipton, E., *Upon That Mountain*, Hodder & Stoughton, London, 1943.
Shipton, E., *That Untravelled World*, Hodder & Stoughton, London, 1969.
Simon, F., *Felstürme und Eiswände. Vom Elbsandstein zum Eis des Nanga Parbat*, Brockhaus Verlag, Leipzig, 1958.
Smart, D., *Paul Preuss, Lord of the Abyss*, Rocky Mountain Books, Victoria BC, 2019.
Smythe, F.S., *Climbs and Ski Runs: Mountaineering and Skiing in the Alps, Great Britain and Corsica*, W. Blackwood & Sons, London, 1929.
Smythe, F.S., *The Kangchenjunga Adventure*, Victor Gollancz, London, 1930.
Smythe, F.S., *Kamet Conquered*, Victor Gollancz, London, 1932.
Smythe, F.S., *Camp Six: An Account of the 1933 Mount Everest Expedition*, Victor Gollancz, London, 1937.
Smythe, F.S., *Mountaineering Holiday*, Hodder & Stoughton, London, 1940.
Smythe, T., *My Father, Frank: Unresting Spirit of Everest*, Baton Wicks, Sheffield, 2013.
Somervell, T.H., *After Everest: The Experience of a Mountaineer and Medical Missionary*, Hodder & Stoughton, London, 1936.
Speer, A., *Inside the Third Reich*, Orion, London, 1969.
Statiev, A, *At War's Summit: The Red Army and the Struggle for the Caucasus Mountains in World War II*, Cambridge University Press, Cambridge, 2018.
Summers, J., *Fearless on Everest*, Iffley Press, Oxford, 2000.
Synnott, M., *The Third Pole: Mystery, Obsession, and Death on Mount Everest*, Penguin, London, 2022.
Taylor, A.J.P., *The Origins of the Second World War*, Hamish Hamilton, London, 1961.
Tilman, H.W., *The Ascent of Nanda Devi*, University Press, Cambridge, 1937.
Tilman, H.W., *Mount Everest 1938*, University Press, Cambridge, 1948.
Tilman, H.W., *Snow on the Equator*, in *The Seven Mountain Travel Books*, Diadem, London, 1983.
Unsworth, W., *Everest: A Mountaineering History*, Oxford Illustrated Press, Yeovil, 1989.
Wainwright, R., *The Maverick Mountaineer: The Remarkable Life of George Ingle Finch: Climber, Scientist, Inventor*, Allen & Unwin, London, 2016.
Wiessner, F., *K2, Tragödien und Sieg am zweithöchsten Berg der Erde*, Bergverlag Rother, Munich, 1955.
Younghusband, F., *The Heart of Nature or The Quest for Natural Beauty*, John Murray, London, 1921.
Younghusband, F., *The Epic of Mount Everest*, Edward Arnold, London, 1926.
Zebhauser, H., *Alpinismus im Hitlerstaat. Gedanken, Erinnerungen, Dokumente (Dokumente des Alpinismus)*, Bergverlag Rother, Oberhaching, 1998.

JOURNAL ARTICLES

Bauer, P., 'The Fight for Kangchenjunga, 1936', *Alpine Journal*, vol. 42, no. 240, 1930, pp. 185–202.
Bauer, P., 'The German Sikkim Expedition 1936', *Alpine Journal*, vol. 49, no. 254, 1937, pp. 41–8.

Bechtold, F., 'Nanga Parbat 1938', *Alpine Journal*, vol. 65, no. 258, 1939, pp. 70, 78.
Blakeney, T.S., 'Some Notes on A.F. Mummery', *Alpine Journal*, vol. 60, no. 190, 1955, pp. 118–31.
Blakeney, T.S., and D.F.O. Dangar, 'Oscar Eckenstein', *Alpine Journal*, vol. 65, no. 300, 1960, pp. 62–79.
Boyce, R., 'The Persistence of Anglo-Saxonism in Britain and the Origins of Britain's Appeasement Policy towards Germany', *Histoire@Politique* 2011/3, no. 15, pp. 110–29.
Cassin, R., 'Italian Climbing between the Wars', *Alpine Journal*, vol. 77, no. 321, 1972, pp. 149–56.
Chicken, L., 'Nanga Parbat – Reconnaissance 1939', *Himalayan Journal* 14, 1947, pp. 53–8.
Collie, J.N., 'Climbing on the Nanga Parbat Range, *Alpine Journal*, vol. 18, no. 131, 1896, pp. 17–32.
Croston, R., 'Prisoners of the Raj', *Alpine Journal*, vol. 111, no. 355, 2006, pp. 213–24.
Farrar, J.P., 'The Season of 1926 in the Mont Blanc Group', *Alpine Journal*, vol. 38, no. 233, 1926, pp. 270–76.
Foster, P., 'Edward Lisle Strutt A Portrait', *Alpine Journal*, vol. 123, no. 367, 2019, pp. 189–99.
Foster, P., 'Everest 1936: The Leadership Question Re-visited', *Alpine Journal*, vol. 124, no. 368, 2020, pp. 129–40.
German Bundesarchiv, *Vom V-Mann der SS zum Stasi-Spitzel*.
Höbusch, H., 'In the Face of Tragedy – Nanga Parbat and National Socialist Radio', *International Journal of the History of Sport*, vol. 37, no. 8, 2020, pp. 633–50.
Houston, C., 'A Reconnaissance of K2, 1938', *Himalayan Journal* 11, 1939, pp. 114–27.
Longland, J., 'Everest, 1933', *Fell and Rock Club Journal*, vol. 9, no. 3, 1933, pp. 327–43.
Longland, J., 'Between the Wars 1919–193', *Alpine Journal*, vol. 62, no. 295, 1957, pp. 83–98.
Longstaff, T.G., 'In Memoriam – Chettan', *Himalayan Journal* 3, 1931, p. 116.
Mallory, G.L., 'Mont Blanc from the Col du Géant by the Eastern Buttress of Mont Maudit', *Alpine Journal*, vol. 32, no. 218, 1918, pp. 148–62.
Martyn, J., 'The Story of the Himalayan Club', *Himalayan Journal* 35, 1979, pp. 1–56.
Mason, K. (ed.), 'Calcutta Local Dinners', *Himalayan Journal* 2, 1930, pp. 187–91.
Mennen, K., '"Milksops" and "Bemedalled Old Men": War Veterans and the War Youth Generation in the Weimar Republic', *Fascism*, vol. 6, no. 1, 23 June 2017, pp. 13–41.
Millar, J., 'Smythe's Himalayan Trails', *Himalayan Journal* 54, 1998.
Moore, A.W., 'Ascent of the Viecherhorn', *Alpine Journal*, vol. 1, no. 5, 1864, pp. 236–47.
Noel, J.B., 'A Journey to Tashirak in Southern Tibet, and the Eastern Approaches to Mount Everest', *Geographical Journal*, vol. 53, no. 5, 1919, pp. 289–303.
Norton, E.F., 'Everest Dispatches', *Alpine Journal*, vol. 36, no. 229, 1924, pp. 195–241.
Norton, E.F., 'The German Attack on Kangchenjunga (correspondence)', *Himalayan Journal* 2, 1930 pp. 180–81.
Preuss, P., 'Künstliche Hilfsmittel auf Hochtouren', *Deutsche Alpenzeitung*, August 1911, pp. 242–4.

Rodway, G.W., 'Ulrich C. Luft and Physiology on Nanga Parbat: The Winds of War', *High Altitude Medicine & Biology*, vol. 10, no, 1, 2009, pp. 89–96.
Schneider, E., 'The Accident on Nanga Parbat', *Alpine Journal*, vol. 46, no. 249, 1934, pp. 423–7.
Strutt, E.L. (ed.), 'Himalayan Notes', *Alpine Journal*, vol. 40, no. 237, 1928, pp. 410–13.
Strutt, E.L., 'Reviews', *Alpine Journal*, vol. 43, no. 242, 1931, pp. 192–4.
Strutt, E.L., 'The English Mount Everest Expedition 1933', *Alpine Journal*, vol. 44, no. 245, 1932, pp. 262–3.
Strutt, E.L., 'A Superiority Complex?', *Alpine Journal*, vol. 46, no. 249, 1934, pp. 374–7.
Strutt, E.L., 'Accidents in 1934', *Alpine Journal*, vol. 46, no. 249, 1934, pp. 414–27.
Shipton, E.L., 'The Mount Everest Reconnaissance, 1936', *Alpine Journal*, vol. 48, no. 252, 1936, pp. 1–14.
Strutt, E.L., 'Accidents in 1936', *Alpine Journal*, vol. 48, no. 252, 1936, pp. 365–75.
Strutt, E.L., 'Accidents in 1937', *Alpine Journal*, vol. 49, no. 255, 1937, pp. 282–7.
Tilman, W.H., 'Mount Everest, 1938', *Alpine Journal*, vol. 48, no. 51, 1939, pp. 3–17.
Tilman, W.H. 'The Problem of Mount Everest', *Himalayan Journal* 13, 1946, pp. 130–33.
Vanis, E., 'Paul Bauer In Memoriam', *Alpine Journal*, vol. 96, no. 340, 1991, pp. 297–9.
West, J.B., 'A.M. Kellas: Pioneer Himalayan Physiologist and Mountaineer', *Alpine Journal*, vol. 94, no. 338, 1989–90, pp. 207–13.
Wien, K., 'Willo Welzenbach', *Jahresbericht AAVM* 42, 1934, pp. 2–5.
Woolley, H., 'In Memoriam, Charles Pilkington', *Alpine Journal*, vol. 32, no. 219, 1919, pp. 346–53.
Yeld, G. (ed.), 'The Disaster on Kangchenjunga', *Alpine Journal*, vol. 23, no. 171, 1906, pp. 51–4.
Young, G.W., 'The Fatal Accident to Dr. Paul Preuss', *Alpine Journal*, vol. 27, no. 202, 1913, pp. 427–9.

Acknowledgements

I would like to thank all my family for their support and encouragement. My son Arthur has worked on the project from the beginning, helping with research and preparing the route diagrams. My wife Corinne and my children Hannah, Oliver, Charlotte and James have read drafts and provided suggestions. Charlotte and Johannes Lenschow played a key role in the interview with Michael Germann Bauer; Johannes also checked German translations and did the difficult job of deciphering Paul Bauer's First World War service record at the Bavarian State Archive. Michael Germann-Bauer, son of Paul, kindly invited us to his home in Bavaria and provided many insights into his father's life. Julie Summers provided valuable input on her great-uncle Sandy Irvine, Hugh Mason on his great-uncle Kenneth, and Alistair Roberts on his grandfather Geoffrey Bruce. I have received helpful input from many other people, including Peter Hansen, Rodolphe Popier, Nandini Purandare, Deepa Balsavar, Julie Rak, Jochen Hemmleb, Wade Davis and Sergey Boiko. Janet Phillips, Samuel Fanous and Leanda Shrimpton of Bodleian Library Publishing had faith in my idea for the book and have provided many useful suggestions to improve it. Peter Forbes of the City University helped develop my writing skills and encouraged me to seek a publisher. I have been patiently assisted by Katie Parker and others at the Royal Geographical Society in London, the librarians at the Bodleian Library in Oxford, and Verity Parkinson of Merton College Library. Finally, thanks to all my climbing partners and teammates for their companionship in the mountains over the last forty-five years.

Picture credits

page

9 Image from *The Fight for Everest* by E.F. Norton, 1924. Bodleian Library, 20648 d.35, opposite p. 124

15 Image from *The Assault on Mount Everest* by Brigadier-General Hon. C.G. Bruce, 1922. Bodleian Library, 20648 d.34, opposite p. 290

18 Diagram of Everest North Face route by Arthur Morgan

19 Everest map by Edward Morgan

20 Image from *The Assault on Mount Everest* by Brigadier-General Hon. C.G. Bruce, 1922. Bodleian Library, 20648 d.34, opposite p. 204

26 Courtesy of the Warden and Fellows of Merton College Oxford

29 Image from *The Fight for Everest* by E.F. Norton, 1924. Bodleian Library, 20648 d.35, opposite p. 190

31 Image from *The Fight for Everest* by E.F. Norton, 1924. Bodleian Library, 20648 d.35, opposite p. 324

33 Courtesy of the Warden and Fellows of Merton College Oxford/©The Warden and Fellows of Merton College Oxford

52 Alpine Club Photo Library, London. Photo by Geoffrey Winthrop-Young

61 Archiv des DAV, München

74 Archiv des DAV, München

86 Diagram of Kanchenjunga North-East Spur route by Arthur Morgan

87 Kanchenjunga map by Edward Morgan

91 Archiv des DAV, München

103 Image from *The Kangchenjunga Adventure* by F.S. Smythe, 1930. Bodleian Library, (OML) OML/Himalayas:SMY, opposite p. 192

106 Image from *The Kangchenjunga Adventure* by F.S. Smythe, 1930. Bodleian Library, (OML) OML/Himalayas:SMY, opposite p. 252

123 Image from *Um dem Kantsch*, by Paul Bauer, 1933, Abb. 45

125 Image from *Um dem Kantsch*, by Paul Bauer, 1933, Abb. 53 and 54

126 Image from *Um dem Kantsch*, by Paul Bauer, 1933, Abb. 55

128 Image from *Um dem Kantsch*, by Paul Bauer, 1933, Abb. 65

145 Image from *Camp Six: An Account of the 1933 Mount Everest Expedition* by F.S. Smythe, 1937. Bodleian Library, 20648 d.50, opposite p. 152

149 Royal Geographical Society, London

152 Image from *Everest 1933* by Hugh Ruttledge, 1934. Bodleian Library, (OML) OML/Himalayas:RUT, opposite p. 240

162 Diagram of Nanga Parbat Rakhiot Face route by Arthur Morgan
163 Nanga Parbat map by Edward Morgan
165 Photo by Peter Mullritter from *Nanga Parbat Adventure: A Himalayan Expedition*, by Fritz Bechtold, 1935. Bodleian Library, 20648 d.46, plate 39
169 Archiv des DAV, München
173 Archiv des DAV, München
179 Photo by Peter Mullritter from *Nanga Parbat Adventure: A Himalayan Expedition*, by Fritz Bechtold, 1935. Bodleian Library, 20648 d.46, plate 70
183 Photo by Peter Mullritter from *Nanga Parbat Adventure: A Himalayan Expedition*, by Fritz Bechtold, 1935. Bodleian Library, 20648 d.46, plate 71
195 Photo by Karl Wien from *Himalayan Quest: The German Expeditions to Siniolchum and Nanga Parbat*, edited by Paul Bauer, 1938. Bodleian Library, (OML) OML/Himalayas:HIM
202 Royal Geographical Society, London
210 Photograph by Adolf Goettner from *Himalayan Quest: The German Expeditions to Siniolchum and Nanga Parbat*, edited by Paul Bauer, 1938. Bodleian Library, (OML) OML/Himalayas:HIM
215 Archiv des DAV, München
224 Royal Geographical Society, London
227 Alpine Club Photo Library, London
230 Photo by Jack Durrance. Courtesy of American Alpine Club Library
241 Archiv des DAV, München
246 Archiv des DAV, München

Index